DEPRESSION

Basic Mechanisms, Diagnosis, and Treatment

DEPRESSION

Basic Mechanisms, Diagnosis, and Treatment

Edited by

A. John Rush and Kenneth Z. Altshuler
University of Texas Health Science Center, Dallas

The Guilford Press
New York London

A Division of Guilford Publications, Inc.
200 Park Avenue South, New York, N.Y. 10003

Printed in the United States of America

Library of Congress Cataloging in Publication Data
Main entry under title:
Depression—basic mechanisms, diagnosis, and treatment.
Includes index.
1. Affective disorders—Physiological aspects.
2. Depression, Mental—Physiological aspects.
3. Affective disorders—Chemotherapy. 4. Depression, Mental—Chemotherapy. I. Rush, A. John.
II. Altshuler, Kenneth Z. [DNLM: 1. Depression—diagnosis. 2. Depression—therapy. 3. Affective Disorders. WM 171 D4228]
RC537.D42754 1986 616.85'27 83-19318
ISBN 0-89862-646-3

Contributors

MONTE S. BUCHSBAUM, MD, Department of Psychiatry and International Institute on Brain and Behavior, Visual Imaging Center, University of California, Irvine, California

PAULA J. CLAYTON, MD, Department of Psychiatry, University of Minnesota, Minneapolis, Minnesota

JANICE CAMPBELL, MD, Department of Psychiatry, University of Kansas College of Medicine, Kansas City, Kansas

RAYMOND R. CROWE, MD, Department of Psychiatry, University of Iowa College of Medicine, Iowa City, Iowa

L. DELISI, MD, Laboratory of Psychology and Psychopathology, National Institute of Mental Health, Bethesda, Maryland

JOHN P. FEIGHNER, MD, Department of Psychiatry, University of California, San Diego, La Jolla, California, and Feighner Research Institute, La Mesa, California

DAVID L. GARVER, MD, Department of Psychiatry, Pharmacology and Cell Biophysics, University of Cincinnati College of Medicine, Cincinnati, Ohio

NANCY GOEKEN, PhD, Departments of Medicine and Pathology, University of Iowa College of Medicine, Iowa City, Iowa

H. H. HOLCOMB, MD, Laboratory of Psychology and Psychopathology, National Institute of Mental Health, Bethesda, Maryland

E. HAZLETT, MD, Department of Psychiatry and International Institute on Brain and Behavior, Visual Imaging Center, University of California, Irvine, California

DAVID S. JANOWSKY, MD, Departments of Psychiatry, Veterans Administration Medical Center, San Diego, and University of California, San Diego, La Jolla, California

DAVID J. KUPFER, MD, Department of Psychiatry, University of Pittsburgh School of Medicine and Western Psychiatric Institute and Clinic, Pittsburgh, Pennsylvania

JAMES W. MAAS, MD, Department of Psychiatry, University of Texas Health Science Center, San Antonio, Texas

DAVID PAULS, PhD, Department of Human Genetics, Yale University College of Medicine, New Haven, Connecticut

JAY W. PETTEGREW, MD, Department of Psychiatry, University of Pittsburgh School of Medicine and Western Psychiatric Institute and Clinic, Pittsburgh, Pennsylvania

BRUCE PFOHL, MD, Department of Psychiatry, University of Iowa College of Medicine, Iowa City, Iowa

S. Craig Risch, MD, Departments of Psychiatry, Veterans Administration Medical Center, San Diego, and University of California, San Diego, La Jolla, California

A. John Rush, MD, Department of Psychiatry, University of Texas Health Science Center, Dallas, Texas

Michael A. Schlesser, MD, Department of Psychiatry, University of Texas Health Science Center, Dallas, Texas

Frank P. Zemlan, PhD, Department of Psychiatry, Physiology and Biophysics, University of Cincinnati College of Medicine, Cincinnati, Ohio

Preface

This book is designed for practitioners of medicine and psychology who wish to learn more about recent advances in descriptive diagnostic methods, laboratory test procedures, and new pharmacological interventions. Further, the reader is introduced to recent research findings that are not yet of direct clinical relevance, but which are likely, we think, to have clinical value over the next 3–5 years (e.g., receptor studies, brain-imaging techniques, studies of cellular membrane properties, and sleep electroencephalographic findings).

Each chapter provides an overview of a particular arena of clinical research and attempts to highlight both areas of consensus and controversy. Each author is a nationally recognized expert in his or her particular field. Nearly every author is both a practitioner and a researcher. These scientists have distilled and summarized the critical scientific findings to date and have commented upon the practical clinical applications that may derive from these research data. Each chapter highlights empirically based conclusions without embroiling itself in confusing theoretical debate.

The many new and exciting findings in diagnostic, genetic, epidemiological, neuroendocrinological, neurotransmitter, neurophysiological, neuroanatomic, and molecular approaches to understanding the affective disorders are clearly presented. Due to the limitation of space, psychological and psychosocial findings are not reviewed. We hope the reader will share our feeling that we are standing on the edge of a dramatic explosion in our knowledge of these disorders and in the available methods to better diagnose and treat these patients.

A. John Rush
Kenneth Z. Altshuler

Contents

1

Diagnosis of Affective Disorders

A. JOHN RUSH

Purpose of Diagnosis

Sydenham in the 17th century pioneered the clinical, descriptive approach that has led to diagnostic classification by signs, symptoms, and clinical course. The term "syndrome" refers to a constellation of signs (what the examiner sees) and symptoms (what the patient reports) that recur regularly in clinical populations. Diagnosis of a syndrome implies neither a specific etiology nor a common response to treatment. Diagnosis of a disease entity or specific disorder replaces syndrome diagnosis when a distinct pathological process is known or suggested.

A diagnosis (to know through) is a hypothesis, the clinician's best judgment about the nature of an ailment. Many medical diagnoses include a hypothesis about *what* the phenomenon is and about *how* it might be explained. Thus, medical diagnoses often involve both a classification and an explanation. In psychiatry, our knowledge is still too limited to specify particular pathophysiologic processes. Therefore, psychiatrists render syndrome diagnoses with the knowledge that multiple causes are likely to be found for each syndrome.

One purpose in diagnosis is to improve the match of available treatments with the problems presented by the patient. A second purpose is prognostication, to help patients, relatives, and society with regard to the likely outcome of a particular medical problem. Prognosis derives from recognition of a particular syndrome or illness and from careful study of its ultimate course and response to treatments. Diagnoses serve other practical needs as well: (1) the need to simplify complex data; (2) the need to communicate succinctly between professionals; and (3) the need to refine clinical research.

A. JOHN RUSH. Department of Psychiatry, University of Texas Health Science Center, Dallas, Texas.

Historical Perspective

Depressions have been described since mankind has kept a written history. Deranged behaviors were typically considered curses from the gods by the Ancients or as a sign of moral or personal weakness. Hippocrates, the first clinician to describe depression carefully, argued that psychiatric problems originated from natural rather than from supernatural causes. He emphasized the critical role of the brain in the development of these disorders (Beck, Brady, & Quen, 1977).

Aretaeus of Cappadocia (A.D. 120–180) was the first to recognize organic (more recently called endogenous) and external (situational) depressions as two separate illnesses. He also described both manic and depressive episodes, noting that some disorders included only recurrent episodes of depression (now called *unipolar depressions*), whereas others involved episodes of both depression and mania (now called *bipolar depressions*).

During the Dark Ages, Western civilization returned to beliefs in possession and supernatural forces as explanations for psychiatric disorders. Not until the Renaissance was there a return to enlightened empiricism, observation, and reasoned thought. Johann Weyer (1515–1588), a 16th-century physician noted for his opposition to witchcraft, was one of the first to focus his studies on mental illness. He considered depression to be linked to somatic or bodily symptoms. Timothy Bright, a physician at London's St. Bartholomew's Hospital, was the first to recognize suicide as a manifestation of despair. In his *Anatomy of Melancholy* (1630), Robert Burton summarized the existing theories and depicted the range of depressions as extending from natural grief at death or separation to depressive disorders.

A wider recognition of specific psychiatric disorders, as well as a tendency toward humane and enlightened treatments, unfolded in the 18th and early 19th centuries. In the late 19th and early 20th centuries, European clinicians focused their attention on both descriptive diagnosis (diagnosis based on the recognition of specific signs and symptoms) and on unconscious factors.

Emil Kraepelin (1856–1926) distinguished *manic-depressive insanity*, an episodic nondeteriorating disorder, from *dementia praecox*—later called "schizophrenia"—a more progressive, deteriorating disorder. Eugen Bleuler (1857–1939), a Swiss neurologist, further differentiated the concept of manic-depressive insanity. He coined the term "affective disorders," in which he included manic-depressive insanity, psychoneurotic depressive reactions, and involutional melancholia. He was, however, unable to delineate clearly the specific subtypes of affective disorder, a problem of separation that persists even today.

Sigmund Freud (1856–1939) focused attention on individual and personality development. Early psychoanalytic writers viewed depression as an attempt at intrapsychic repair: The loss of a loved person resulted in a psychic injury that could only be overcome by self-punishment. Melancholia was seen as a period of self-torment during which the emotional representation of the lost person received the negative portion of ambivalent feelings. Thus, depression represented anger turned on the self.

Bibring, a 20th-century psychoanalyst, emphasized causes in addition to loss of a loved one by separation or death. Not unlike Freud, he too thought that failure to attain a desired goal or person produced a loss of self-esteem and subsequent depression. Thus, loss of self-esteem was the common denominator for all depressions. Sandor Rado (1890–1972) noted that depressions were encountered in patients with neuroses, schizophrenia, syphilis, and other physical illnesses, including drug dependencies. He hypothesized that a single causal explanation for all depressions was very unlikely.

Early psychoanalytic thinkers did not recognize different types of depressions and, often, did not distinguish between normal feelings of sadness and specific depressive disorders. Those who followed, however, began to recognize that these distinctions were critical to further understanding of depression. In other words, all depressions are not explained by "anger turned inward" nor by "loss of self-esteem." Perhaps certain depressions are more likely than others to be accounted for by one or more of these hypothetical mechanisms (Rush & Fulton, 1982).

Advances in treatment gave further impetus to the need for accurate diagnosis. In 1934 von Meduna, a Hungarian psychiatrist, tried to treat schizophrenia by inducing convulsions with inhaled camphor. In 1938 Cerletti and Bini, two Italian physicians, induced convulsions by passing an electric current between electrodes placed on the forehead. Electroconvulsive therapy (ECT) is now recognized as an effective treatment for severe unipolar or bipolar depressions.

An Australian psychiatrist, John Cade, reported lithium to be effective in the treatment of mania in 1949. In the 1950s the antidepressant quantities of monoamine oxidase inhibitors were discovered. In 1957, the so-called "tricyclic" antidepressants were found, and the 1970s witnessed the introduction of new classes of antidepressants (e.g., the tetracyclic compounds). As Chapter 10 will detail, several additional, chemically unique antidepressants are not or will shortly become available to American practitioners. The discovery of antidepressant medications has led to a host of investigations designed to elucidate the underlying neurophysiology and neurochemistry of depression.

The last decade also witnessed the development of short-term psychotherapeutic methods specifically designed for the treatment of depression. These newer psychotherapies may help in the treatment of some depressions that respond poorly to currently available medications. Recent research also aims at determining whether such treatments may have prophylactic effect by changing the particular psychological processes that are believed to make some persons vulnerable to chronic or recurrent depression (Rush, 1982; Rush & Fulton, 1982).

In summary, depression is a broad syndrome with multiple causes. Depressions therefore represent a heterogeneous group of disorders, probably including a number of distinct pathophysiologic conditions.

Treatment for the depressions has substantially improved as specific antidepressant medications and psychotherapies have been developed. Since these interventions are likely to differ in their effect on different depressive disorders, improved diagnostic approaches for the depressions are needed.

Accuracy of Diagnosis

As already noted, diagnosis should serve the purpose of treatment selection, prognostication, and communication. Clinicians, however, have somewhat different needs than researchers with regard to diagnosis (Andreasen, 1982).

For clinicians, diagnosis mainly serves the needs of patient care. A diagnosis should be a useful statement about the patient's problems. Since practitioners see a broad variety of patients, broad diagnostic classes to encompass these patients may be of value. On the other hand, as more specific treatments become available, and as more specific prognoses are demanded, more restrictive diagnostic groupings may be called for.

The researcher, on the other hand, often prefers more narrowly defined categories so that "pure" or more homogeneous groups can be identified for further biological or psychological studies. Furthermore, such narrow groupings also facilitate clear communication and replicability of investigation.

Recently, the development of specific criteria for different psychiatric syndromes has dramatically improved clinical diagnostic practice. The third edition of the *Diagnostic and Statistical Manual of Mental Disorders* (DSM-III) (APA, 1980) incorporates these more specific criteria. Further, it employs a multiaxial system so that personality (Axis II) is separated from syndrome (Axis I) and from psychosocial stressors (Axis IV). These changes have significantly improved the reliability of syndrome diagnosis.

Spitzer, Endicott, and Robins (1978) have identified several sources of variance that can reduce the reliability of diagnosis. *Subject variance* can result from specific patients having different diagnoses at different times, which leads observers to classify them differently. For instance, a schizophrenic patient with persecutory delusions may be diagnosed as paranoid; later, this patient's symptoms may have a strong affective component and lead to the diagnosis of schizoaffective disorder.

Occasion variance occurs when patients with the same underlying condition display different symptoms because they are interviewed on different occasions (Andreasen, 1982). For example, the alcohol-dependent patient may be acutely intoxicated on one occasion and in delirium tremens at another time. *Information variance* occurs when observers gather their information from two different sources or ask different questions of the same information source. For example, an angry wife may stress her husband's drinking habits and behavioral disturbances as primary problems, whereas the patient may emphasize his disturbed mood and insomnia. *Observation variance* occurs when two clinicians observe the same information or data differently. For example, one practitioner might weigh more heavily symptoms suggestive of a formal thought disorder, while another clinician might focus on symptoms of an affective disturbance. *Criterion variance* occurs when two clinicians gather the same data, but render different diagnoses because they use different criteria. For example, Americans may diagnose schizophrenia more frequently than their British counterparts because they have a different concept of schizophrenia (Andreasen, 1982).

What can the clinician do about these sources of variance? Information variance can be reduced by the use of structured interviews and by standardizing information sources; interviewing both the patient and a close relative is particularly helpful in improving the reliability of descriptive diagnosis. Observation variance may also be decreased by the use of structured interviews and by interviewing the patient on more than one occasion. Two diagnostic interviews separated by several days will help decrease occasion variance. Reliance on criteria that are widely agreed to and have definition of terms will reduce criterion variance.

The Present State Examination (PSE) (Wing, Cooper, & Sartorius, 1974) and the Schedule for Affective Disorders and Schizophrenia (SADS) (Endicott & Spitzer, 1978) are structured interviews, developed recently for research purposes. Each contains specific questions designed to elicit information about particular symptomatology, and each defines ambiguous terms such as "formal thought disorder." The PSE focuses exclusively on current symptomatology, while the SADS evaluates both current and past symptoms—allowing thereby for both current and lifetime diagnoses. Neither system, however, covers organic brain or personality disorders in detail (Andreasen, 1982).

As noted above, diagnostic nomenclature has moved from general narrative descriptions of diagnostic entities as in DSM-II (APA, 1968) to the use of specific criteria to operationalize the diagnostic process (APA, 1980). In addition to DSM-III, the "St. Louis Criteria" (Feighner *et al.*, 1972) and the Research Diagnostic Criteria (RDC) (Spitzer *et al.*, 1978) are widely used by clinical researchers. Any of these operationalized criteria will significantly improve the reliability of diagnosis. Reliability is assessed by either the degree of agreement between raters (*interrater reliability*) or by the degree of agreement on two occasions (*test–retest reliability*). Both observer variance and criterion variance affect interrater reliability, while test–retest reliability is also affected by occasion variance. Thus, test–retest reliability is likely to be lower than interrater reliability (Andreasen, 1982).

The fact that patients change significantly between evaluations also reduces test–retest reliability. This is particularly so if the evaluations are spaced several days or weeks apart, and if they are receiving treatment. Thus, test–retest reliability may reflect the inherent variability in clinical populations, as much as the reliability of the diagnostic system itself (Andreasen, 1982).

Recently computerized approaches to diagnosis have been proposed. Most computerized diagnostic systems, such as the CATEGO and DIAGNO, employ a logical decision-tree approach (Fleiss, Spitzer, Cohen, & Endicott, 1972; Spitzer & Endicott, 1968, 1969; Spitzer, Endicott, Cohen, & Fleiss, 1974; Wing & Nixon, 1975). Such an approach closely approximates what occurs in actual clinical practice, as it is based on a heirarchical conceptualization of diagnoses. Both DIAGNO and CATEGO have modest to good agreement with clinicians' judgments, limited by their inherent rigidity. Computers do not conceptualize, perceive novel or unexpected relationships, or modify and redesign the problem-solving process as unanticipated difficulties arise. Thus, computerized approaches to diagnosis are likely to have only limited applications and will not replace traditional clinical diagnostic methods even for research purposes (Andreasen, 1982).

Let us turn to the issue of validity. Reliability is easier to establish in a diagnostic system than is validity. Conventionally, there are four types of validity: *face validity, content validity, construct validity,* and *criterion validity. Face validity* refers to whether or not the diagnostic category makes sense clinically and appears to describe a clinical condition that actually occurs. *Content validity* is assessed by determining whether or not patients actually fit the various diagnostic categories and whether or not all patients can be classified by the system. *Construct validity* refers to whether or not the diagnostic system is consistent with an underlying theory or construct as, for example, the genetic theory of manic–depressive illness. *Criterion validity,* the most important type of validity for the clinician, refers to whether or not a particular diagnosis is useful in making predictions about some future behavior, such as response to treatment, clinical course, or prognosis (Andreasen & Spitzer, 1979). External aids such as laboratory tests may be valuable in validating diagnostic categories. Much clinical research is currently aimed at evaluating the extent to which various laboratory tests may assist in the diagnostic process (Rush, Giles, Roffwarg, & Parker, 1982). However, these laboratory investigations depend entirely on whether diagnosticians can delineate homogeneous and internally consistent diagnostic groupings for study.

In addition to laboratory tests, other clinical correlates, such as family history, response to treatment, and prognosis or course (Robins & Guze, 1970, 1972), have been used to validate various diagnostic categories. Only rarely have these clinical correlates provided clear-cut validation of new nosological entities.

DSM-III (APA, 1980) employs a multiaxial system in an attempt to gain from both *typological* and *dimensional* approaches to diagnosis. The typological approach is based on the medical model and perceives classification systems as consisting of more or less discrete and independent categories of disease. Clinicians working typologically tend to think in terms of placing the patient's signs and symptoms into a single diagnostic category, recognizing, of course, that some patients may present with multiple disorders (Andreasen, 1982).

The dimensional approach characterizes each patient in terms of scores on several dimensions or variables, so that each patient is assigned a unique place utilizing multiple dimensions. The typological approach has the virtue of simplicity, while the dimensional approach can be extremely complex. However, the latter offers maximum flexibility. Some investigations have shown that the dimensional approach can predict outcome when multiple regression and statistical methods are employed. The majority of research reports so far, however, find that the validity of a typological classification system is at least as good as or better than that based on the dimensional approach (Carney, Roth, & Garside, 1965; Kiloh, Andrews, Neilson, & Bianchi, 1972; Pokorny, Thorby, Kaplan, & Ball, 1976). The multiaxial system of DSM-III (Table 1-1) separates syndrome (Axis I) from personality (Axis II; the patient's usual behavioral pattern when the syndrome is present). Coexistent medical and surgical disorders are described on Axis III. Environmental stresses are construed as independent variables (Axis IV), which do not determine diagnosis. Thus the term "reactive depression," referring to depressed states precipitated by recent psychosocial stressors, is no longer used. The presence of psychosocial stresses on Axis IV does not contribute to the Axis I diagnosis of the syndrome of depression.

Basis for Diagnosis

Several bases for diagnosis have been proposed including etiology, symptomatology, course, pathogenesis, and response to various treatments. If a predictable relationship is found between the factors of etiology, clinical symptom picture, and course, then a nosological

TABLE 1-1. Multiaxial System

Axis I	Clinical syndrome
Axis II	Personality disorders (developmental disorders)
Axis III	Physical disorders
Axis IV	Psychosocial stressors (1–7)
Axis V	Highest adaptive function within last year (1–6)

entity has been established. Such a disorder is likely to take a particular course *and* to be caused by a particular etiological constellation. Such a nosological entity is a rarity, if not a fiction, in present day psychiatry (van Praag, 1982a, 1982b). In our current state of knowledge, psychiatric syndromes are nonspecific etiologically. Similar or dissimilar precipitants, stressors, or other "causes" may provoke the same or different pathological reactions. In affective disorder the field is replete with ideas, but no current model is specific enough for us to understand fully the etiology or pathogenetic mechanisms in any given case.

When diagnoses are based on signs and symptoms alone, one must take into account the fact that sex, age, and the patient's personality, as well as a host of other variables, may affect the presentation of a particular syndrome. When one turns to diagnosis based on course, naturalistic studies of depressed patients are scarce, and most are confounded by concurrent therapeutic interventions that may range from psychoanalysis or short-term psychotherapies to antidepressant medications or ECT. While diagnosis based on treatment response may be of particular value for researchers, it does not allow the physician to select treatment for an individual patient.

In light of these problems, DSM-III diagnoses are simply based on the apparent phenomenology (the particular signs and symptoms) and do not imply a specific etiology.

Diagnostic Criteria

It is not possible to describe in detail all the criteria employed for the diagnosis of nine different forms of affective disorders as listed in DSM-III (APA, 1980). However, Tables 1-2 to 1-5 list the criteria for major depression, dysthymia, mania, and hypomania, according to DSM-III. Patients with major depression who present with only recurrent depressive episodes are diagnosed as having unipolar depression, whereas those who present with both major depressive and manic episodes or with manic episodes alone are called bipolar depressives. Some patients show major depression and only hypomanic episodes. In these instances, a diagnosis of atypical bipolar disorder is made.

Patients having a simultaneous mixture of both manic and depressive symptomatology pose a significant diagnostic problem. Their symptoms are likely to be confused with those of schizoaffective disorder, schizophrenia, or psychotic depressions. Proper diagnosis as mixed-phase bipolar patients is important, since the treatment to be instituted often includes both antidepressant medications and lithium.

TABLE 1-2. Major Depressive Episode

A. Dysphoria or loss of interest/pleasure in all or almost all usual activities.
B. At least four present for 2 weeks:
   1. Appetite/weight loss or gain
   2. Sleep disturbance
   3. Psychomotor changes
   4. Loss of interest/pleasure or libido
   5. Loss of energy; fatigue
   6. Self-critical (guilt or self-blame)
   7. Decreased concentration, speed of thought, decision making
   8. Recurrent thought of death or suicide, or suicide attempt
C. Picture not dominated by:
   1. Mood-incongruent hallucinations/delusions, or
   2. Bizarre behavior
D. Not superimposed on schizophrenia, schizophreniform, or paranoid disorder.
E. Not due to organic mental disorder or bereavement.

Differential Diagnosis of Dysphoria

Table 1-6 shows a flow chart or decision tree that can be employed clinically in the differential diagnosis of patients complaining of dysphoria. Dysphoria may be described by the patient as sadness, anxiety, irritability, or a combination of these dysphoric affects. Most dysphoria encountered in everyday life is *not* tied to a psychiatric or medical diagnosis. These dysphorias are normal affective responses to daily life events. Such normal dysphorias are typically brief and lead

TABLE 1-3. Dysthymic Disorder

A. During last 2 years, symptoms of depressive episode mostly present but insufficient to meet criteria for major depressive episode.
B. Normal periods do *not* exceed a few months.
C. Sad mood and/or loss of interest/pleasure.
D. During depressive episode, at least three of the following:
   1. Sleep changes
   2. Energy low
   3. Self-esteem low
   4. Low productivity
   5. Poor concentration
   6. Social withdrawal
   7. Loss interest/pleasure
   8. Irritable, angry
   9. Unable to respond with pleasure to rewards
   10. Less talkative
   11. Pessimistic attitude
   12. Tearful
   13. Thoughts of death/suicide
E. No psychotic features.
F. Mood is different than usual (if superimposed or preexisting mental disorder).

TABLE 1-4. Manic Episode

A. Elevated, expansive, or irritable mood.

B. Three (elevated) or four (irritable) for at least 1 week:
   1. Increased activity
   2. Pressured speech
   3. Flight of ideas or racing thoughts
   4. Inflated self-esteem
   5. Decreased need to sleep
   6. Distractability
   7. Excessive involvement in activities without recognition of painful consequences

C. Picture *not* dominated by mood-incongruent delusions or hallucination.

D. Not superimposed on schizophrenia, schizophreniform, or paranoid disorder.

E. Not due to organic mental disorder or substance intoxication.

neither to functional impairment nor to seeking help from psychiatric or other medical professionals.)

On the other hand, symptoms of many medical disorders (see below) may be associated with dysphoria. In addition, grief or bereavement is typified by dysphoria, but grief is by definition a state that occurs in relation to the loss of a particularly important other person, and is time-limited. If the symptomatology of a grieving patient per-

TABLE 1-5. Chronic Hypomanic Disorder

A. Two years or more with partial manic disorder.

B. Never symptom-free for more than 2 months.

C. Elevated, expansive, or unstable mood.

D. Three or more:
   1. Decreased need to sleep
   2. Increased energy
   3. Inflated self-esteem
   4. Increased productivity
   5. Sharpened/creative thinking
   6. Uninhibited people seeking
   7. Hypersexuality
   8. Excessive indiscretion
   9. Restless
   10. Talkative
   11. Excessive optimism
   12. Inappropriate laughing, joking

E. Impaired function.

F. No hallucinations/delusions.

TABLE 1-6. Differential Diagnosis of Dysphoria

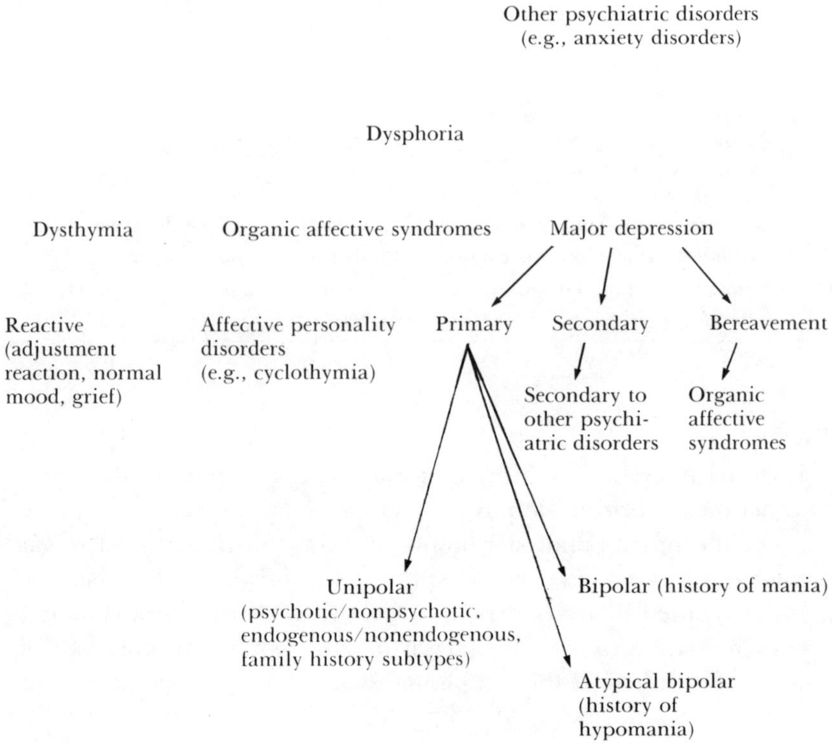

sists more than 6 months following a loss, and meets the criteria for major depression, a major depression is diagnosed.)

(Adjustment reactions may also be associated with dysphoria, but they do not meet the criteria for major depression or dysthymia. Organic affective disorders can also present as dysphoria, dysthymia, or major depression. Once organic affective disorders, grief or bereavement, adjustment reactions, and medical illnesses associated with dysphoria are eliminated, one is left with the psychiatric affective disorders. Thereafter, some argue that the subdivision of primary and secondary should be employed: Primary depression is diagnosed when no other major psychiatric syndrome precedes the onset of major depression; secondary depressions are those major depressions preceded by other major psychiatric syndromes such as alcoholism, schizophrenia, drug dependency, and so on. The primary depressions are subclassified variously into endogenous/nonendogenous, psychotic/nonpsychotic, and/or family history subgroups (see below).

Organic Affective Disorders

Organic affective disorders may present either as major depression or dysthymia. In addition, organic causes for both mania and hypomanic episodes are known. Table 1-7 enumerates many of the medical disorders that may be associated with depression. Table 1-8 lists medical causes for mania or hypomania, and Table 1-9 lists medications that may be associated with either major depression or dysthymia.

Our experience over the last 5 years in the Affective Disorders Unit at the University of Texas suggests that 10% to 20% of patients who meet descriptive criteria for major depression or dysthymia actually have an undiagnosed medical disorder or are taking medications that are causing the depression, in spite of the fact that most patients are referred by physicians. We speculate that, when a patient presents with dysphoria, the practitioner often interviews the patient to determine

TABLE 1-7. Medical Disorders Associated with Depression

Autoimmune disorders
Systemic lupus, rheumatoid disease, sarcoidosis

Cancers
Head, pancreas, gastrointestinal, lung, renal

Central nervous system diseases
Parkinson's disease, degenerative dementias, normal-pressure hydrocephalus, subarachnoid hemorrhages, Huntington's disease, reversible dementias, focal lesions (nondominant), temporal lobe epilepsy (?)

Disabling/deforming disorders
All types

Endocrinopathies/metabolic disorders
Hypo-, hyperthyroidism, Addison's disease, Cushing's disease, pituitary tumors, diabetes, hyperparathyroidism, hypoglycemia (?), porphyria

Intoxications
Lead, mercury, thallium, others (?)

Occult infections
Genitourinary tract, liver abscess, etc.

Viral infections
Influenza, viral pneumonias, mononucleosis, hepatitis, others

TABLE 1-8. Medical Disorders Associated with Mania or Hypomania

Central nervous system infections
Luetic, viral, parasitic

Central nervous system tumors
Especially cerebellar

Central nervous system degenerative disorders
For example, multiple sclerosis

Drugs
Steroids, amphetamines, methylphenidate, over-the-counter stimulants appetite suppressants (in vulnerable persons)

Endocrinopathies
Hyperthyroidism, Cushing's disease, hyperparathyroidism, etc.

Metabolic
Vitamin deficiencies, excess fat-soluble vitamins

Toxic
Inappropriate antidiuretic hormone secretion

whether the latter's life circumstances might account for the dysphoric response. If the judgment is positive, the patient is referred for psychiatric treatment, often without the thorough neurological, medical, historical, physical, and laboratory evaluation that would detect an iatrogenic or medical cause.

A word of caution is therefore in order: Most of us have a tendency, if not a proclivity, to explain our internal mood by external circumstances and the personal meaning we attribute to them. Patients, too, generalize from their usual day-to-day experience that dysphorias are explainable by life events. Moreover, major depres-

TABLE 1-9. Drugs Associated with Major Depression or Dysthymia

Anticancer
Vincristine, vinblastine

Antihypertensives
Reserpine, methyldopa, propanolol, guanethidine, hydralazine, clonidine

Antiinfectives
Cycloserine

Antiparkinson agents
Levodopa, amantadine, carbidopa

Corticosteroids

Hormones
Estrogens, progesterone

Psychotropics
Benzodiazepines (?), antipsychotics (?)

sions, dysthymias, or organic affective disorders are all likely to be associated with cognitive changes. What this means is that recall of recent and past events can be biased in a negative direction. As a result, patients are *very likely* to selectively recall one or more negative events in an attempt to explain their dysphoria. The events themselves may not have happened at all, not have happened at the recalled time, or not have been as negatively experienced then as now. Thus, patients—like the rest of us—can search their lives for significant current stresses to explain their affective or mood state. This is an incorrect attribution of cause. Neurochemical events are obviously beyond individual awareness.

Differential Diagnosis of Affective Disorders

Table 1-10 briefly outlines a number of other psychiatric syndromes that may confound the diagnostician in his or her evaluation of patients with depression or mania. Perhaps most common in this regard are symptoms of anxiety. Anxiety disorders have specific criteria, as enumerated in DSM-III. However, patients with major depression may also present with episodes of panic, with specific phobias, or even with agoraphobia. When major depression is present in association with these anxiety symptoms, major depression, and *not* the anxiety disorder, should be diagnosed and treated. This differential

TABLE 1-10. Other Psychiatric Syndromes That May Confound the Diagnosis of Depression

A. Anxiety disorders
   1. Panic disorder
   2. Phobic disorder (agoraphobia)
B. Obsessive-compulsive disorder
C. Sleep disorders
   1. Narcolepsy
   2. Sleep apnea
   3. Others
D. Schizophrenic disorders (especially schizoaffective disorder)
E. Anorexia nervosa; bulimia
F. Vague somatic complaints (? masked depression)
G. Dementia (pseudodementia)
H. Sexual dysfunctions

diagnosis is critical: Anxiolytic agents are correctly prescribed if the diagnosis of an anxiety disorder is made, but antidepressant medications are the appropriate choice in major depression, even though patients may report panic episodes or agoraphobia in association with the depressive episodes.

(It is also known that obsessive-compulsive personality or, for that matter, other personality styles may be magnified by the presence of an affective disorder. Thus, patients with major depression may present with a chief complaint of recurrent obsessions, or with compulsions. In such circumstances, again, treatment should generally be aimed primarily at the depressive disorder, rather than at the obsessive-compulsive symptomatology.) Should the latter symptomatology persist after clinical remission of the depression is obtained, further treatment should address the remaining symptoms.

(Disturbances in sleep and/or daytime drowsiness are found in various sleep disorders (e.g., narcolepsy or sleep apnea). Differentiating these disorders from depression is critical. Depressed patients often complain of difficulty in sleep and daytime *fatigue, but not of drowsiness.* And rarely, if ever, does a depressed patient report the acute, irresistible onset of sleep during the day. Other criteria for narcolepsy should be searched for, including cataplexy, and hypnogogic and hypnopompic hallucinations (Roffwarg, 1979). Sleep apnea can be detected by a history of snoring and profound daytime drowsiness, but without the profound disturbance in appetite, weight, and capacity for enjoyment seen in most patients with depression) In some instances, a sleep laboratory evaluation is useful to identify suspected sleep disorders.

(Patients may present with symptoms suggestive of an affective disorder in association with symptoms of formal thought disorder. The latter can include thought broadcasting, thought withdrawal, thought insertion, and similar disorders (see APA, 1980). In these cases, a diagnosis of schizoaffective disorder rather than schizophrenia is made.)Treatment typically includes but may not be limited to an antidepressant medication or electroconvulsive therapy.

(Some patients show profound disturbances in weight, appetite, and eating patterns. Anorexia nervosa, as well as bulimia, must then be considered in the differential diagnosis. We have seen a number of patients with major depression who also had symptoms of bulimia, a compulsion to eat plus a tendency to self-induced vomiting (Kumetz & Rush, 1983). In some cases, treatment aimed at the major depression will relieve both the bulimic and affective symptomatology.)

At times, the clinical presentation may be largely dominated by vague somatic complaints. Pain is particularly common in patients with major depression, with some 70% reporting headaches and 40% reporting abdominal or chest pain. Joint pains, muscle aches, and backaches are also common. Patients may attribute other symptomatology, such as sleep difficulties, poor appetite, and weight loss to the presence of the pain and its analgesic treatment. Regardless of whether these symptoms are attributed to the pain by the patient or by the clinician, they should be counted as present when determining whether the descriptive criteria for major depression are met. The same holds true when dysphoria is present, even if it is attributed by the patient to his pain or frustration in the pursuit of relief. Clinicians sometimes label these cases "masked depression" when patients deny dysphoria but do report sleep and appetite disturbances and other symptoms of the depressive syndrome. Treatment with antidepressant medication is often helpful here. Some therapists advocate the use of monoamine oxidase inhibitors alone or in combination with small doses of antipsychotic medication for these patients (Lesse, 1974).

Patients over the age of 50, and especially those over 65, may initially complain chiefly of troubles with concentration, decision making, or even short-term memory. A number of these patients, if carefully interviewed, will be found to meet the criteria for major depression. Some investigators suggest the term "pseudodementia" for patients who appear with prominent symptoms that suggest dementia, but who ultimately respond to antidepressant medications. The differential diagnosis of true dementia from pseudodementia is often difficult. Clinicians are best advised to supplement the patient's history with that obtained from important other persons who are familiar with his or her current and previous levels of functioning. Psychological or neuropsychological testing, as well as thorough neurologic evaluation, can also be helpful, but in some cases a trial of antidepressant medication may be the only definite method to differentiate pseudodementia from true dementia.

Finally, patients presenting with sexual complaints may attribute their dysphoria to these problems. Sleep disturbances, lack of interest, and self-criticism, as well as other symptoms of major or minor depression, may also be attributed to the sexual difficulty. When formerly orgasmic females become nonorgasmic, or males develop impotence or other difficulties in sexual performance, a careful interview for major depression or dysthymia is indicated. Treatment of the depression, if present, will often reverse the sexual complaints.

Difficulties in the Clinical Descriptive Diagnosis of Depression

(Table 1-11 lists various patient, medical, sociocultural, and iatrogenic factors that commonly confound the recognition and diagnosis of depression. With regard to patient factors, male patients may often deny many symptoms in an attempt to "look strong," and older patients are more likely than younger ones to manifest somatic or vegetative symptoms (such as disturbances in sleep, appetite, and weight). Socioeconomically disadvantaged patients may present with difficulties in impulse control or even trouble with the law, with their dysphoria only elicitable after careful interviewing. There is some suggestion that increased hostility and even paranoid thinking may characterize depression in members of the lower socioeconomic classes. In addition, lower-socioeconomic-class patients are more likely to present with complaints of chronic pain.)

(Unfortunately, clinicians too often rely on the patient as the sole

TABLE 1-11. Problems in Descriptive Diagnosis of Depression or Mania

Patient factors
1. Age/sex/racial background
2. Socioeconomic class
3. Negative cognitive bias/erroneous anamnesis
4. Memory/concentration problems

Medical factors
1. Taking psychotropics that modify symptom picture
2. Presence of other medical disorders or other drugs
3. Episodic nature of depression
4. Symptom picture leading to confusion between personality and syndrome

Sociocultural factors
1. Stigma, denial
2. Presence of life stresses that may be erroneously viewed as etiologic or explanatory by patient or physician
3. Presence of complications (consequences) of depression (e.g., alcoholism, truancy, drug dependency, legal problems, marital discord)
4. Patient-blaming social or religious systems that preclude seeking a diagnosis

Iatrogenic factors
1. Focus on one or two symptoms without eliciting the full syndrome (e.g., chronic pain, headaches, menstrual changes, gastrointestinal complaints)
2. Attribution of cause to life events, which may stop thorough descriptive psychiatric, medical, neurological evaluations
3. Premature symptomatic drug prescription (e.g., hypnotics) without sufficient history or observation
4. Failure to interview spouse/important other for diagnostic purposes
5. Overreliance on laboratory tests as opposed to historical and status data
6. Underutilization of psychiatric consultation
7. Failure to use criteria to characterize symptom picture

source of clinical diagnostic information. This practice is particularly problematic in depression, since depressed patients may negatively distort their recall of events (Rush & Giles, 1982), or confound history-taking by their profound problems with memory and concentration. To correct for such potential errors in anamnesis or recall, we routinely interview a family member or someone who knows the patient well, in addition to the patient himself or herself.

Next, a number of medical factors may present diagnostic problems. Patients already taking psychotropic medications commonly present themselves to the diagnostician. Since symptoms persist and motivate the patient to seek help, the presumably ineffective medications are notorious for confounding the clinical picture. Antipsychotic medications, for example, even in low doses may reduce insomnia or increase psychomotor retardation, and may blunt the intensity of dysphoria that is present. Anxiolytic medications can reduce the degree of dysphoria and partially help with insomnia, thereby making the recognition of the full depressive syndrome difficult, if not impossible. Whenever clinically possible, we stop all psychotropic medications for at least 7—and preferably 10–14 days—to unmask symptoms which, if present, allow an appropriate diagnosis to be made. Close telephone contact and additional appointments may be needed to assist patients through the drug-free period.

Other medications act not to obscure, but to cause the symptoms of depression. This is particularly the case with antihypertensive medications. A brief period off such medication, if this is possible, will often give a clear-cut answer if there is a question of whether the medication is playing a causal role.

Many patients will pressent with a concurrent significant medical illness that may not, in fact, be the cause for the depressive syndrome, but to which the clinician might erroneously attribute etiological importance. Consider the case of a 32-year-old nurse who suffered from multiple sclerosis that waxed and waned but did not prevent her from continuing her occupational activities. Over time, however, she developed a significant major depression. The natural tendency was to regard her depression as a response to her multiple sclerosis and to recommend supportive psychotherapy. However, further intensive evaluation finally revealed that the patient suffered from marked hypothyroidism which, when treated appropriatedly, led to complete remission of the depressive episode.

A further complication is that depressions are typically episodic in nature. Thus, patients may come to their doctor weeks after the real *nadir* of their depressive episode. Present symptoms may be less than the full-blown major depression—even with melancholic features—which may have existed before. And, finally, extensive interviewing is often required to separate the syndrome from the patient's usual personality. At times, this judgment is difficult, but by employing a second source of information (e.g., husband, wife, or close friend), this complicating factor can be reduced.

(Some patients and their families, unfortunately, still view psychiatric disorders as signs of weakness. This attitude may lead them to deny significant problems such as the presence of suicidal ideation or past episodes of major depression.) By having informational brochures available in patient waiting areas and by providing patients with educational information in the interview, one can often reduce the need for such denial and associated shame.

(Mention has already been made that life stresses may be erroneously viewed as etiological or fully explanatory by either the patient or physician. Even in bereavement, it is often difficult to determine whether the depressive symptomatology preceded substantially or followed the major loss. Normal grief reactions should not last longer than 6 months, although intermittent sadness over the loss may persist for a year or two.)

In addition, the complications or consequences of depression may confound the diagnostic impression. For example, juvenile delinquency, school truancy, alcohol dependency, marital problems, occupational conflicts, and the like are common sequelae of depression, but are often presented by the patients. Unless carefully interviewed for the signs and symptoms of major depression, these patients may be inappropriately shunted into treatment for a secondary problem (e.g., alcohol treatment programs when the alcoholism is an attempt to self-medicate depression or mania, or couples' therapy to treat the marital discord that ensues from major depression)—without appropriate focus on the underlying cause.

The fact that some social, religious, or family systems attribute cause for dysphoria solely to individual responsibility can lead some patients to refuse to seek needed attention and appropriate diagnosis for their disorder. Even when seeking help, such patients tend to focus on a single symptom, at times distracting the physician from other, more complex sides of the clinical picture. For example, tension headaches, gastrointestinal symptoms, abdominal pain, and even menstrual cycle changes are more common than not, in association with major depression. Premature focus on a single symptom and failure to recognize the full depressive syndrome may result in inappropriate treatment (e.g., anxiolytics) or expensive, unnecessarily complex evaluations.

Persons with complaints of pain pose a particular hazard in this regard. Expensive and time-consuming diagnostic evaluations by numerous specialists can be avoided when careful elicitation of signs and symptoms show the chronic pain to be part of the depressive episode. The analgesic medications often used in such cases may obscure or distort depressive symptoms. Discontinuation, if possible, is advisable during the diagnostic evaluation. In short, a high index of suspicion for depression is required throughout every initial evaluation, and an attempt should be made to elicit all its signs and symptoms.

On the clinician's side, the premature use of psychotropic medications for symptoms (rather than syndromes) is a common practice. It is erroneous to prescribe sedative–hypnotic medications for the insomnia associated with depression, especially if the full depressive syndrome goes unrecognized. Antidepressants are effective for the insomnia; it is rarely necessary to utilize more than a single psychotropic agent to treat most depressions. Multiple drugs can cloud the diagnostic picture, produce a partial response (with confusion about which drug is responsible), or cause complex drug interactions.

The new availability of laboratory tests for depression offers a final snare for the diagnostician. As criterion-based diagnosis is a recent development, most nonpsychiatric practitioners did not learn this system in medical school. Also, the dexamethasone suppression test, which has received considerable publicity, is easily ordered. These two developments tempt the practitioner toward an overreliance on laboratory findings as opposed to clinical information.

Subtypes of Depression

(Table 1-12 summarizes five currently employed methods to subdivide patients with unipolar major depressive episodes. In addition, DSM-III recognizes the subdivision of recurrent versus single episodes of major depression.) Much current clinical research is aimed at determining which of these subdivisions is valid, as well as evaluating the treatment implications of each. Let us briefly review the subdivisions and their clinical implications.

As noted, (primary depression is diagnosed when a major depressive episode is *not* preceded in time by another major psychiatric

TABLE 1-12. Proposed Subtypes of Unipolar Depression

Endogenous/nonendogenous	
Psychotic/nonpsychotic	
Primary/secondary	
Anxious-agitated/anergic-hypoactive	
Familial pure depression	Applies only to primary, unipolar depressions
Depressive spectrum	Applies only to primary, unipolar depressions
Sporadic depression	Applies only to primary, unipolar depressions

syndrome (e.g., schizophrenia, drug dependency, alcohol dependency, or the like). This subdivision was initially created for research purposes in order to develop a more "pure" group of depressions. The term "secondary" does not have etiological implications but, rather, has only chronological implications. The treatment implications for this dichotomy are unclear at this point, although secondary depressions as a group may be more difficult to treat (Clayton, 1983).

Some evidence suggests that primary depression is distinguishable from secondary depression by a higher incidence of dexamethasone nonsuppression and/or a more frequent or profound reduction in REM latency (see Chapter 8). These findings are tentative, however, as secondary depressions appear to be heterogeneous. Comparisons of primary and secondary depressions depend largely on constitution of the secondary group. Furthermore, there is controversy about which major psychiatric syndromes should be counted in determining whether a depression is secondary or not. Depressions secondary to medical disorders or drugs, however, are clearly classified as organic affective disorders and are not considered secondary.

A psychotic depression is one associated with depressive delusions (content: poverty, sin, deterioration of the body, and similar ideas) and/or hallucinations. If hallucinations or delusions are absent, the depression is classified as nonpsychotic. A number of studies suggest that psychotic depressions may not respond as well to tricyclic medications alone; a combination of antipsychotic and antidepressant medications or ECT may be required in more severe cases. ECT should also be considered when the psychotic depression responds only partially to medication.

Whether psychotic depressions are on a continuum with nonpsychotic depressions is unclear. It is also not clear whether patients who have one nonpsychotic episode will be nonpsychotic or psychotic in future recurrences.

The third subdivision, the endogenous/nonendogenous reactive (the nonendogenous group is called reactive in Europe, but not in the United States) dichotomy, is a classification that was initially based on an etiological presumption. Nonendogenous depressions were assumed to be responses to life problems, whereas endogenous depressions arose "from the inside." Recent data show that many patients with endogenous depression, if carefully interviewed, will also attribute cause to life events. Truly "endogenous" depression in the sense that it occurs without preexisting life stresses actually appears to be rare. Van Praag found that only 16% of 92 patients with endogenous (clinical) depressions did not report psychosocial (73%) or somatic (18%) stressors (van Praag, 1982a; van Praag, Uleman, & Spitz, 1965). Subsequent studies also found no correlation between the nature of the stressor and the nature of the depressive syndrome (Lloyd, 1980). Thus, stressors are not sufficient to cause depression, and a particular stressor does not provoke a particular type of depressive reaction (Paykel, 1978).

The term endogenous depression is still used, but no longer refers to the absence of life stresses. What then does endogenous mean? Endogenous now refers to a set of symptom features defined by Research Diagnostic Criteria (RDC) (Spitzer *et al.*, 1978) and codified with minor changes in the DSM-III, as "melancholic" symptom features. In order to be diagnosed as having endogenous symptom features by RDC, the patient must have a least one of the following four at the nadir or worst point in the depressive episode: unreactive mood, pervasive anhedonia, diurnal variation with mood worsening in the morning, and/or a distinct quality to the mood (i.e., the mood is qualitatively different from the mood associated with bereavement). In addition, other criteria include severe terminal insomnia, severe midnocturnal insomnia, a significant reduction in appetite, a significant weight loss (at least 2 lbs. per week or 10 lbs. per month), significant guilt, and/or significant psychomotor retardation or agitation. If a patient presents with at least one of the initial four symptoms and has a total altogether of six or more of the aforementioned ten items, a diagnosis of depression with definate "endogenous symptom features" or "endogenous depression" is made according to RDC.

Turning to DSM-III criteria for melancholic symptom features, *both* unreactive mood and pervasive anhedonia are required. In addition, at least three of the six following symptoms must be present: terminal insomnia, severe weight loss (greater than 2 lbs. a week), marked guilt, marked psychomotor changes, or diurnal mood variation (i.e., worse in the morning). Thus, nearly all depressions with melancholic symptom features will meet criteria for endogenous features, but the converse is not true. That is, endogenous depression, as defined by RDC, is a broader category than melancholic depression by DSM-III.

What are the clinical implications of the endogenous/nonendogenous dichotomy? Evidence both from the sleep laboratory and from neuroendocrine studies (to be amplified in subsequent chapters) suggests that endogenous depressions are more likely to be associated with a higher incidence of dexamethasone nonsuppression (i.e., abnormalities in the hypothalamic-pituitary-adrenal axis) and with shortened REM latencies, a reduction in Stage 4 sleep time, and other sleep EEG disturbances. Also, in the endogenous group, there may be a correlation between plasma levels of antidepressant medication and response to treatment. In general, depressions with endogenous symptom features appear to be more uniformly responsive to the antidepressant medications than the nonendogenous depressions.

A distinction held earlier—that endogenous depression appears in normal personalities and depression with nonendogenous features occurs in neurotic personalities—appears to be losing ground. A number of patients with endogenous depression may also suffer from disturbed, neurotic personality structure. Neurotic personality does not prevent endogenous depressions, and presence of a neurotic personality does not *de facto* imply that antidepressant medication will be ineffective (van Praag, 1982a).

Questions that remain about this dichotomy are: (1) Are these two entities etiologically distinct? (2) Does the history of depression in first-degree relatives differentiate endogenous from nonendogenous depressions? (3) Do patients who suffer one endogenous episode display endogenous symptoms features in all subsequent episodes? (4) Is the nonendogenous group more likely to benefit from the reeducative psychotherapies shown to be effective in patients with nonpsychotic, unipolar depression (Rush, 1983)? From the clinical perspective, patients with endogenous or melancholic symptom features should be given antidepressant medication. Should such a trial fail, the clinician should choose another antidepressant agent or ECT.

The fourth dichotomy, that of the anxious, agitated versus anergic, hypoactive depressions, leads clinicians sometimes to a differential prescription of anxiolytics and tricyclic antidepressants. Recent research suggests that this dichotomy does not have such clear-cut treatment implications. Endogenous symptom features may occur in the anergic or agitated. Patients with severe psychomotor agitation and marked *subjective* anxiety are often melancholic or endogenous and respond to tricyclics or electroconvulsive therapy. There are suggestions that some atypical depressions with marked anxiety *symtpoms*—especially panic or agoraphobia—may respond better to monoamine oxidase inhibitors than to standard tricyclic antidepressants (Klein, Gittelman, Quitkin, & Rifkin, 1980).

The final subdivision is limited to only unipolar primary depressions and comes from the work of Winokur and colleagues (van Valkenburg, Lowry, Winokur, & Cadoret, 1977). Three groups of patients are defined, based on which psychiatric illness is present in their first-degree relatives. Familial Pure Depressive Disease refers to patients with primary unipolar depression who have at least one first-degree relative with a history of major depression. Depressive Spectrum Disease is diagnosed if at least one first-degree relative has evidence of sociopathy and/or alcoholism. Sporadic Depression refers to patients with depression whose first-degree relatives have neither depression, alcoholism, nor sociopathy.

Neuroendocrine and other studies suggest that Familial Pure Depressive Disease is more likely to be associated with dexamethasone nonsuppression and reduced REM latency (Akiskal, 1982; Rush, Giles, Roffwarg, & Parker, 1982; Rush, Giles, Roffwarg, Schlesser, & Stone, 1982; Schlesser, Winokur, & Sherman, 1980), but treatment implications for this subdivision are yet to be elucidated.

Treatment Implications of Diagnosis

Tables 1-13 through 1-16 suggest guidelines as to when antidepressant medications, a psychiatric consultation, psychotherapy, and ECT should be used. These guidelines are derived from my own and others' personal clinical experience, and from available clinical research data.

With regard to the use of antidepressant medications: Most patients respond to a single drug, and do not require adjunctive sedative, hypnotic, or anxiolytic medication. Adjunctive drugs can also modify the plasma level of antidepressants and confound, reduce, or prevent a therapeutic response. Phenytoin, phenobarbital, and carbamazepine induce hepatic enzymes and thereby reduce the circulating level of most antidepressant drugs.

The most common cause for treatment failure is either incorrect diagnosis or failure to titrate dose with side effects and clinical re-

TABLE 1-13. Suggested Guidelines for Antidepressant Pharmacotherapy

1. Use one antidepressant at a time.
2. Beware of drug interactions.
3. Do not use sedatives/hypnotics.
4. Rarely use anxiolytics.
5. See patient weekly.
6. Titrate dose versus side effects versus response.
7. Measure treatment effect.
8. Treat to obtain complete symptom remission.

sponse. The latter difficulty can be reduced by regularly employing a clinician-completed or self-report of symptom severity (e.g., the Beck Depression Inventory [BDI]) (Beck & Beamesderfer, 1974; Beck, Ward, Mendelson, Mock, & Erbaugh, 1961). Too often the clinical effects of antidepressant treatment are measured only roughly. Without specific measures, both doctor and patient may be satisfied with a partial response. Experience suggests that if complete symptom remission is not obtained, either (1) the diagnosis is incorrect; (2) the patient is in need of alternative medication or increased dosage, or (3) medication should be supplemented by psychotherapy. A precise determination treatment effect allows the clinician to proceed appropriately.

A psychiatric consultation is indicated when the diagnosis is unclear; when psychotic or bipolar illness is present or suspected; when psychotherapy is a consideration; and/or when response to one or, at most, two adequate trials of antidepressant medication is poor, or only partial. It is also advisable whenever the clinician is uncertain about using a particular medication or choosing from the range of antidepressants. Since some depressions run in families, consultation may be wise if this history is present. Evaluation of first-degree relatives may be particularly useful for children and adolescents, where the

TABLE 1-14. Suggested Guidelines for Psychiatric Consultation

1. Diagnosis is unclear.
2. Treatment response after one good antidepressant trial is poor or partial.
3. Patient is psychotic.
4. Bipolar disorder is suspected or present.
5. Patient appears to require psychotherapy with or without medication.
6. Positive family history of depression (?).

depressive syndrome may be more difficult to detect and may be more easily accepted at the time the depressed patient is first seen. Obviously, most clinicians provide general information and support to patients and their family members. This ensures compliance with medication treatment, and educates and informs all involved so that countertherapeutic attitudes can be reduced. Suggestions about how to modify the consequences of the depression are also valuable.

But when should the nonpsychiatrist consider referral for psychotherapy in cases of depression? That certain psychotherapies are effective for some depressions is strongly suggested by available research data. Unfortunately, our capacity to identify which depressions will respond is still limited (Rush, 1982). The data are strongest with regard to cognitive (see Rush, 1982, for a review) and interpersonal therapies (Klerman & Weissman, 1982), where suggested indications include: (1) chronic course—especially with demoralization or despair, (2) nonendogenous symptom picture, (3) modest interepisode recovery, (4) clear presence of personality difficulties, and/or (5) a clear-cut pattern of psychological response to environmental events at the onset of each depressive episode.

Some of these indications are exemplified by a patient seen recently who, between the ages of 22 and 30, had had three major depressive episodes, each nonendogenous, and lasting 6–8 months. Each episode was associated with reemphasis of his failure to achieve occupational goals, and one with actually being fired. In intervals of recovery he still had lingering, consistent feelings of low self-esteem and a pessimistic outlook. He also remained highly critical of himself and others when the depressive syndrome was in remission. While all

TABLE 1-15. Suggested Guidelines for Psychotherapy of Depression

1. Refer to reeducative or reconstructive psychotherapy if:
   a. Chronic course
   b. Nonendogenous symptom picture at nadir
   c. Poor interepisode recovery
   d. Axis II diagnosis
   e. Demoralization present
   f. Clear pattern to precipitating events (e.g., rejection by lovers; occupational failures)
2. Provide support and information if:
   a. Compliance to treatment is poor
   b. Social system is countertherapeutic
   c. Consequences (e.g., unemployment) are interfering with recovery

TABLE 1-16. Indications for Electroconvulsive Therapy

1. Unipolar or bipolar major depression with melancholic features with one or more of the following:
   a. Time urgency
   b. Failure on one adequate antidepressant drug trial
   c. Psychotic (especially mood-incongruent) features
   d. Factors that increase risk for antidepressant drugs are present (e.g., old age, cardiac disease, pregnancy, drug allergies)
2. Schizoaffective disorder.
3. Selected treatment-resistant, nonmelancholic depressions.
4. Partial response to antidepressant medication and psychotherapy.
5. Manic delirium.
6. Persistent dexamethasone nonsuppression in clinically improved endogenous/melancholic major depressions (?).

depressions do not require psychotherapy, neither do all depressions require medication. It is important to consider the utilization of both modalities in selected cases.

A final consideration bears on the use of ECT. This treatment is highly effective and has very few side effects if used in appropriately diagnosed patients. Both unipolar and bipolar major depressions with melancholic features respond well to this treatment. Treatment-resistant nonmelancholic or nonendogenous depressions are additional, possible indications. A partial response to adequate antidepressant medication, with or without psychotherapy, should lead the clinician to ECT, especially if endogenous or melancholic symptom features were present at the nadir of clinical course. Some clinical studies also suggest that ECT should be used in schizoaffective disorder. Persistent dexamethasone nonsuppression, even in clinically improved patients, may constitute a new indication for ECT, if—as it now appears—it augurs for poor prognosis.

In conclusion, the last decade has witnessed four major advances in our ability to diagnose and treat depressions: criterion-based diagnosis (DSM-III), development of apparently effective and specific short-term psychotherapies for depression, development of new and different antidepressant medications, and the discovery of measurable biological derangements that may ultimately assist us in diagnosis and treatment selection for some patients. With these advances, it becomes the clinician's responsibility to more accurately diagnose and to creatively treat these patients. With them also comes the promise of more effective, shorter, safer, and less expensive treatment modes for our patients.

ACKNOWLEDGMENTS

The author wishes to express his appreciation to Marie Marks and David Savage for their secretarial support, and to Kenneth Z. Altshuler, MD, Professor and Chairman, Department of Psychiatry, University of Texas Health Science Center, Dallas, for his administrative support. Some of the author's studies referenced were supported in part by grants from the National Institute of Mental Health (MH-35370).

REFERENCES

Akiskal, H. S. (1982). Utility of the REM latency test in psychiatric diagnosis: A study of 81 depressed outpatients. *Psychiatry Research, 7*, 101–110.

American Psychiatric Association (APA). (1968). *Diagnostic and statistical manual of mental disorders* (2nd ed.), (DSM-II). Washington, DC: Author.

American Psychiatric Association (APA). (1980). *Diagnostic and statistical manual of mental disorders* (3rd ed.), (DSM-III). Washington, DC: Author.

Andreasen, N. C. (1982). Concepts, diagnosis and classification. In E. S. Paykel (Ed.), *Handbook of affective disorders.* New York: Guilford Press.

Andreasen, N. C., & Spitzer, R. L. (1979). Classification of psychiatric disorders. In H. M. van Praag, M. Lader, O. J. Rafaelsen, & E. J. Sachar (Eds.) *Handbook of biological psychiatry* (Vol. 1). New York: Marcel Dekker.

Beck, A. T., & Beamesderfer, A. (1974). Assessment of depression: The depression inventory. In P. Pichot (Ed.), *Modern problems in pharmacopsychiatry* (Vol. 7). Basel, Switzerland: Karger.

Beck, A. T., Brady, J. P., & Quen, J. M. (1977). *The history of depression.* New York: Insight Communications.

Beck, A.T., Ward, C. H., Mendelson, M., Mock, J. E., & Erbaugh, J. K. (1961). An inventory for measuring depression. *Archives of General Psychiatry, 4*, 561–571.

Carney, M. W. P., Roth, M., & Garside, R. F. (1965). The diagnosis of depressive syndromes and the prediction of ECT response. *British Journal of Psychiatry, 111*, 659–674.

Clayton, P. J. (1983). A further look at secondary depression. In P. J. Clayton & J. E. Barrett (Eds.), *Treatment of depression: Old controversies and new approaches.* New York: Raven Press.

Endicott, J., & Spitzer, R. L. (1978). A diagnostic interview: The schedule for affective disorders and schizophrenia. *Archives of General Psychiatry, 35*, 837–844.

Feighner, J. P., Robins, E., Guze, S. B., Woodruff, R. W., Winokur, G., & Muñoz, R. (1972). Diagnostic criteria for use in psychiatric research. *Archives of General Psychiatry, 26*, 57–63.

Fleiss, J. L., Spitzer, R. L., Cohen, J., & Endicott, J. (1972). Three computer diagnosis methods compared. *Archives of General Psychiatry, 27*, 643–649.

Kiloh, L. G., Andrews, G., Neilson, M., & Bianchi, C. N. (1972). The relationship of the syndromes called endogenous and neurotic depression. *British Journal of Psychiatry, 121*, 183–196.

Klein, D. F., Gittleman, R., Quitkin, F., & Rifkin, A. (1980). *Diagnosis and drug treatment of psychiatric disorders: Adults and children* (2nd ed.). Baltimore: Williams & Wilkins.

Klerman, G. L., & Weissman, M. M. (1982). Interpersonal psychotherapy: Theory and research. In A. J. Rush (Ed.), *Short-term psychotherapies for depression.* New York: Guilford Press.

Kumetz, N., & Rush, A. J. (1983). *The relationship between bulimia and depression.* Unpublished manuscript.

Lesse, S. (1974). *Masked depression.* New York: Jason Aronson.

Lloyd, C. (1980). Life events and depressive disorders reviewed. *Archives of General Psychiatry, 37,* 541–548.

Paykel, E. S. (1978). Contribution of life events to causation of psychiatric illness. *Psychological Medicine, 8,* 245–253.

Porkorny, A. P., Thornby, J., Kaplan, H. B., & Ball, D. (1976). Prediction of chronicity in psychiatric patients. *Archives of General Psychiatry, 33,* 932–937.

Robins, E., & Guze, S. B. (1970). Establishment of diagnostic validity in psychiatric illness: Its application to schizophrenia. *American Journal of Psychiatry, 126,* 983–987.

Robins, E., & Guze, S. B. (1972). Classification of affective disorders: The primary-secondary, the endogenous-reactive, and the neurotic-psychotic concepts. In T. A. Williams, M. M. Katz, & J. A. Shield (Eds.), *Recent advances in the psychobiology of depressive illnesses.* Washington, DC: U.S. Government Printing Office.

Roffwarg, H. P. (Chairman) (1979). Association for Sleep Disorders Centers. Diagnostic clarification of sleep and arousal disorder. Prepared by Sleep Disorders Classification Committee. *Sleep, 2,* 1–137.

Rush, A. J. (Ed.). (1982). *Short-term psychotherapies for depression,* New York: Guilford Press.

Rush, A. J. (1983). Cognitive therapy for depression. In M. R. Zales (Ed.), *Affective and schizophrenic disorders: New approaches to diagnosis.* New York: Brunner Mazel.

Rush, A. J., & Fulton, C. (1982). Affective disorders. In R. J. Gatchel, A. Baum, & J. E. Singer (Eds.), *Handbook of medical psychology.* New York: Springer.

Rush, A. J., & Giles, D. E. (1982). Cognitive therapy: Theory and research. In A. J. Rush (Ed.), *Short-term psychotherapies for depression.* New York: Guilford Press.

Rush, A. J., Giles, D. E., Roffwarg, H. P., & Parker, C. R. (1982). Sleep EEG and dexamethasone suppression test findings in outpatients with unipolar major depressive disorders. *Biological Psychiatry, 17,* 327–341.

Rush, A. J., Giles, D. E., Roffwarg, H. P., Schlesser, M. A., & Stone, L. (1982, May). *Cognitive and biologic characteristics of acute versus chronic depressions.* Paper presented at the meeting of the American Psychiatric Association, Toronto, Ontario, Canada.

Rush, A. J., Schlesser, M. A., Fulton, C., & Allen, M. A. (1983). Biologic basis of psychiatric disorders. In R. Rosenberg (Ed.), *Clinical neurosciences.* London: Churchill Livingstone.

Schlesser, M. A., Winokur, G., & Sherman, B. M. (1980). Hypothalmic-pituitary-adrenal axis activity in depressive illness: Its relationship to classification. *Archives of General Psychiatry, 37,* 737–743.

Spitzer, R. L., & Endicott, J. (1968). DIAGNO: A computer program for psychiatric diagnosis utilizing the differential diagnostic procedure. *Archives of General Psychiatry, 18,* 746–756.

Spitzer, R. L., & Endicott, J. (1969). DIAGNO II: Further developments in a computer program for psychiatric diagnosis. *American Journal of Psychiatry, 125,* 12–21.

Spitzer, R. L., Endicott, J., Cohen, J., & Fleiss, J. L. (1974). Constraints on the validity of computer diagnosis. *Archives of General Psychiatry, 31,* 197–203.

Spitzer, R. L., Endicott, J., & Robins, E. (1978). Research diagnostic criteria: Rationale and reliability. *Archives of General Psychiatry, 35,* 773–782.

van Praag, H. M. (1982a). A transatlantic view of the diagnosis of depressions according to the DSM III: I. Controversies and misunderstandings in depression diagnosis. *Comprehensive Psychiatry, 23,* 315–329.

van Praag, H. M. (1982b). A transatlantic view of the diagnosis of depressions according to the DSM III: II. Did the DSM III solve the problem of depression diagnosis? *Comprehensive Psychiatry, 23,* 330–338.

van Praag, H. M., Uleman, A. M., & Spitz, J. C. (1965). The vital syndrome interview: A structured standard interview for the recognition and registration of the vital depressive syndrome complex. *Psychiatria, Neurologia, Neurochirurgia, 68,* 329–346.

van Valkenburg, C., Lowry, M., Winokur, G., & Cadoret, R. (1977). Depressive spectrum disease versus pure depressive disease: Clinical, personality and course differences. *Journal of Nervous and Mental Disease, 165,* 341–347.

Wing, J. K., Cooper, J. E., & Sartorius, W. (1974). *The measurement and classification of psychiatric symptoms.* London: Oxford University Press.

Wing, J., & Nixon, J. (1975). Discriminating symptoms in schizophrenia: A report from the international pilot study of schizophrenia. *Archives of General Psychiatry, 32,* 853–859.

2

Prevalence and Course of Affective Disorders

PAULA J. CLAYTON

The affective disorders are disorders of mood. In the past, numerous names have been used to characterize these disorders. Such designations include reactive depression, neurotic depression, psychotic depression, endogenous depression, exogenous depression, agitated and retarded depression, depressive spectrum disorders, primary and secondary depression, manic-depressive disease, and involutional melancholia. DSM-III adopted the term "affective disorders" for all of the foregoing. The only remaining separate categories of affective disorders are—and these are perhaps tentative—major depressive disorder (comparable to unipolar affective disorder) and bipolar affective disorder.

Unipolar affective disorder (monopolar affective disorder) refers to patients who have depression only. Bipolar affective disorder refers to patients who have both episodes of mania and depression, or episodes of mania only. To date, there is no data to suggest that unipolar mania differs from bipolar disorder. Originally, mania alone was felt to be rare and to comprise only 2% to 5% of all patients who have episodes of mania. Nurnberger, Roose, Dunner, and Fieve (1982), however, recently reported that 16% of a group of bipolar I patients had never been hospitalized or treated for depression. Abrams, Taylor, Hayman, and Krishna (1979) also reported that 18% of patients hospitalized for affective disorder (not necessarily bipolar) were unipolar manics.

The DSM-III also includes a category of less severe but more chronic affective disorders. This group includes cyclothymic disorder and dysthymic disorder. Atypical affective disorders can also be coded.

PAULA J. CLAYTON. Department of Psychiatry, University of Minnesota, Minneapolis, Minnesota.

There is no depressive neurosis in the new categorization. Axis I classification codes the major psychiatric illness. On the other personality disorders, physical illness, stressors, and level of funct ing can be coded.

Because there are clinical, genetic, and perhaps treatment differences between the two major affective disorders (major depressive disorder and bipolar disorder), it is reasonable to review them separately. In the future, however, these disorders may again be considered as one, as Kraepelin (1921) did long ago. Major depressive disorder tends to begin later, to be more heavily female, to be less frequent, to necessitate less frequent hospitalizations, to be more likely to be chronic, to be less familial, and rarely to include a family history of mania.

Major Depressive Disorder

Epidemiology

The true prevalence of this disorder is unknown. In the population studies that have been done throughout the world, there is a marked difference in case definitions and case ascertainment. Weissman and Myers (1978) found that the lifetime prevalence in the United States population for a definite major depressive disorder was 18%. This means that over a liftime, 12% of men and 26% of women can be expected to develop a major depression. In a recent review, Boyd and Weissman (1981) similarly reported that in the two studies in the United States using treated and untreated community subjects studied with structured interviews and consistent criteria, the lifetime prevalence was between 8% and 12% for men and 20% and 26% for women. The range of prevalence in studies from all over the world, however, was more varied, from 2% to 12% for men and 5 to 26% for women. All studies show that unipolar depression is twice as common in women as in men (Clayton, 1983a). This is so whether the population studied is in the community, in a general practitioner's office, in a private psychiatrist's office, in a general psychiatric clinic, or in an inpatient setting. The age of onset is broad, ranging from 15 to 70, with the average age of onset being in the early 40s. Childhood depression and depression in later life are popular concepts but remain rare.

Unipolar affective disorder is a recurring illness. Earlier studies of hospital populations suggested almost half of the patients had single episodes. In these early studies, however, it was not clear how many people died by suicide or other causes after the first episode, in how many the onset was so late in life as to preclude a second episode, and in how many cases a single episode became chronic. More recent and carefully done follow-up studies of hospital populations (Angst, 1980; Angst *et al.*, 1973; Angst, Felder, & Frey, 1979; Grof, Angst, & Haines, 1973) show that only 5% to 15% of such cases have a single episode. An outpatient study of patients on maintenance therapy (Weissman, 1978) indicated that in these less severely ill patients, only 20% had a single episode. Recurrence is thus an important aspect of unipolar affective disorder, and the issue is not only treatment of the presenting episode but consideration of which patients require prophylactic treatment, and under what circumstances.

The duration reported for an episode of depression varies from one study to another. Between 4 and 8 months have been considered average (Winokur, 1978), but recent reports suggest that most depressions now last even longer.

The usual course reported is one of recurrent solitary depressions, separated by intervals of several symptom-free years; some people, however, have annual depressions often during a specific season of the year. Recent studies show that far more patients are intermittently symptomatic than had been thought previously.

The mean number of episodes in unipolar depression is five to six (Angst, 1980; Angst *et al.*, 1973, 1979; Grof *et al.*, 1973), and the best predictor of recurrence is previous course. If a patient has had three episodes in the past 2 years, for example, it is likely that she or he will follow a comparable course after the current episode. There is some indication that perhaps the relapse rate is higher and more frequent with increasing age, particularly in women.

Somewhere between 10% and 20% (Murphy, Woodruff, Herjanic, & Super, 1974; Robins & Guze, 1972) of all patients diagnosed with unipolar depression will have a chronic course. Higher frequency of chronicity may be more likely in those with older ages of onset. In one outpatient treatment study, 25% of the patients were chronically symptomatic for 1 year (Kovacs, Rush, Beck, & Hollon, 1981) even though they were under treatment. The average age was 33 years in this study, but older age and previous episodes were found to be related to symptomatic status. Another outpatient treatment study reported similar results, with about 21% of the subjects being mostly or chronically depressed (Weissman, Klerman, Prusoff, Sholomskas, & Padian, 1981). Thus, even in outpatient depressive illness (or perhaps in outpatient illness specifically), outcome is not as favorable as had been previously thought.

Genetics

Studies have shown that about 25% of patients with unipolar affective disorder have a parent or other first-degree relative with an affective disorder (Winokur, 1978). When families are studied by direct interview rather than history alone, almost one-third of patients are shown to have families in which two generations suffer from an affective disorder. Twin studies and adoption studies suggest that the increased family prevalence may be in large part genetic. Mania is relatively rare in families with unipolar affective disorder, as is schizophrenia. Alcoholism is common, especially in those cultures where heavy drinking is common. The question of assortative mating is controversial.

Life Events

Research has focused on life events and social factors as possible etiologic agents in depression, in addition to genetic and biological factors. Early losses through death or separation, recent life events, or chronic stressors (medical or social) have all been considered, with recent life events having received the most attention (Guze & Robins, 1970; Paykel, 1982).

Confirming an association between recent life events and the onset of depression is so difficult methodologically that some introductory discussion is required.

One difficulty for both researchers and subject is that of assessing life events. The depressed patient is prone, of course, to the ordinary inaccuracies of recall, but the distorted cognitions typical of the illness may cause a further or graver distortion. The solutions researchers use to address to this possibility are (1) to interview the patient rather than use a questionaire, (2) to use a second informant, and (3) to limit the duration of time under question to 6 months or a year preceding either the onset of the depression or the time the patient is seen.

A second fact to be considered is that depression in patients creates life events. The depressed patient may perform poorly at work or school, lose his job or fail, may be irritable at home or lose interest in friends and sex, can turn to drink, and can develop marital problems secondary to any of these. All of the events can be created by the depression rather than the reverse. Since dating the onset of depression is difficult, it is often impossible to decide whether life events precede or follow the development of symptoms. The best solution here seems to be to score only losses that seem to be "independent events" and thereby exclude job losses, marital discord, or other events that would derive from the depression itself.

A third consideration has to do with the definition of depressive disorder which varies across studies (Clayton, 1983b). One of the major research groups concerned with the impact of life events, for example, is Brown and Harris (1982) from England. Dealing for the most part with community samples of women, their research showed a relationship between the onset of depression and recent uncontrolled events, such as loss. Our own studies of recent bereavement on this side of the Atlantic, however, reported that 35% of recent widows and widowers met the criteria for depression at 1 month, 25% at 4 months, and 17% at 1 year. Despite these high rates, few of the subjects regarded themselves as abnormally depressed, and even fewer sought psychiatric care. Thus, a syndrome that meets criteria for depression appears to be the normal response to loss. Is that what Brown and Harris are measuring? If so, is their definition of a "case" reliable?

Confirming the impression that adversity in life causes unhappiness is the recent work comparing cases of depression in the community with that in outpatients. An increased rate of major life events occurred during the 3 months prior to onset for both groups but was most marked for the community cases. The conclusion was that the "cases" identified in the community had lesser disorders, persons reacting similarly to those normal but depressed individuals in the bereavement studies.

Our data from the collaborative study of depression also did not show a difference between inpatients and outpatients in the number or kinds of life events that the depressed patients experienced, although in most categories outpatients had higher scores (more events). One solution to the problem of case definition may be to refine criteria beyond those necessary to identify solely "a depressive episode." One might, for example, look specifically at the endogenous subtype of depression, or also use a rating that includes incapacity or the requirement of treatment. Another solution might be the use of a second validator such as family history or a biological marker.

A final question to be resolved in studies of life events is the matter of specificity. Are these life events that specifically precipitate depression, or do the same events occur with equal frequency in normals, or preceding schizophrenia or medical illness? Review of the data suggests that normals and schizophrenics have fewer or less specific life events than depressed patients. Most studies, however, do not show differences between the number of life events preceding a depressive disorder or the onset of a medical illness. Also, persons who have attempted suicide and patients with "secondary" depression report the highest number of recent life events (Clayton, 1983b). For the question of specificity to be resolved, clearly, every study of life events in relation to psychiatric disorder requires other controls, including the medically ill.

While all of these caveats limit the implications, the fact is that the majority of researchers have found an association between recent life events and depression. The importance of the association remains uncertain. Many people experience serious life events and don't develop depression, and many depressives report significant life events before one episode but not before another episode. Paykel (1982) estimated that 10% of exit events were followed by clinical depression. The current hypothesis for the association between life events and the onset of depression is that certain people carry a vulnerability for depression that can sometimes be precipitated by a life event.

Personality

Again, this is an area that is confounded by methodological difficulties. The major problem is that the assessment of a patient's personality made during an episode of depression is significantly different from his or her own assessment after recovery. Another problem is how the researchers define the patients. The patient's assessment of his or her own personality traits and attributes, moreover, is sometimes markedly different from what a close relative may report. Some researchers report similarities in personality patterns between unipolars and bipolars (Bech *et al.*, 1980) with both usually being within the normal range of scores. Others feel that the unipolar depressives report more introversion, obsessionality, shyness, and sensitivity (Hirschfeld & Cross, 1982; von Zerssen, 1982). Neuroticism is a trait of secondary depression and probably is not typical of the recurrent unipolar depressed patient (Clayton, 1983b).

Treatment

Tricyclic antidepressants have been found to be superior to placebos in treating depression (Biggs & Ziegler, 1977; Davis, 1976). Newer data indicate that cognitive-behavior therapy and interpersonal psychotherapy (IPT) are as good as pharmacotherapy in the treatment of depressed outpatients (Kovacs *et al.*, 1981; Rush, Beck, Kovacs, & Hollon, 1977; Weissman *et al.*, 1981). The exciting and yet to be tested question about these therapies is whether they could be prophylactic; that is, can the patient learn techniques for dealing with depression that would either prevent a recurrence or—failing prevention—that he could use to interrupt the course? In addition, electroconvulsive therapy (ECT) is an effective treatment for depression (Fink, 1978). In some studies, ECT has been shown to be more effective than antidepressants, particularly with the psychotically depressed patient, and no study has shown it to be less effective. In addition, it may reduce mortality, both from suicide and other causes in patients with affective disorder (Avery & Winokur, 1977).

Antidepressants are as good as lithium, if not better, in the prophylactic treatment of recurrent depressive disorder (Prien, 1983).

Complications

Increased mortality is associated with affective disorders. In large part this is due to the increase in suicide rate, but it stems also from other causes. A summary of the relationship between suicide and primary affective disorders with patients not divided by polarity, showed suicide risk in patients with these disorders to be over 30 times greater than that of the general population (Guze & Robins, 1970). Approximately 15% of all deaths of patients with affective disorder were due to suicide. Suicide is more common in men, although the disease itself is more common in women. The risk of suicide as compared with other causes of death is increased early in the course of the illness (Guze & Robins, 1970; Tsuang, 1978).

Suicide attempts are increasing in all countries. Suicide rates vary from country to country. In the United States, the suicide rate is increasing in the young and may continue to rise in this group as it gets older (Murphy & Wetzel, 1980).

Bipolar Affective Disorder

Epidemiology

Weissman and Myers (1978) reported a lifetime prevalence of bipolar I and II affective disorder to be 1.2%. While it is far less frequent than unipolar affective disorder, it is as common as schizophrenia. Boyd and Weissman (1981), looking at lifetime risk of bipolar I disorder, found the rate to be between 0.2% and 0.9%. Using a completely different way of estimating prevalence one based on the use of lithium carbonate, Eastwood, Stiasny, and Tice (1981) found the rate of bipolar affective disorder to be 1 to 2 per 1000 of the population, an estimate quite similar to those previously reported.

Follow-up studies of depressed inpatients have shown that about 13% to 15% develop a mania (Clayton, 1981). Even in the Perris study (1966), in which patients entering were required to have had three previous episodes of depression, 13% became bipolar. In most studies from inpatient settings, the ratio of unipolar to bipolar patients is reported to be 10:1; however, Krauthammer and Klerman (1979) estimated the ratio to be more like 4:1, with certain depressives excluded. Even this figure may change as psychiatrists become more astute in diagnosing more subtle cases of bipolar affective disorder. Akiskal, Bitar, Puzantian, Rosenthal, and Walker (1978), in a 4-year follow-up of neurotic depressive in- and outpatients, found that 22% were unipolar and 18% were bipolar. Egeland and Hostetter (1983), reviewing a total population of Amish, found the unipolar to bipolar ratio to be almost 1:1.

In bipolar illness, the ratio of women to men approaches 1:1. There is one report that in the early age group, the sex of the patient is more likely to be male if the disease starts as mania and female if the disease starts as depression. If this were correct, it would increase the percent of men identified as bipolar in small series with younger patients, since women would not as yet have manifested their bipolarity. The finding of Dunner and Hall (1980), that 80% of bipolars start with mania, is probably due to selection factors with population studied (patients in a lithium clinic). European researchers find that more than half of women start with depression, while approximately half of men do.

Bipolar illness is a disease of much earlier onset and much more limited risk than unipolar disease. The onset is usually from the *teens* through the 50s, with the average age of onset being 30. Numerous studies have indicated that in the teenage years there are more cases of bipolar affective disorder than schizophrenia. Because of the younger age of onset in bipolar illness, it is wise to consider all positively diagnosed teenage depressives as potential bipolars. In three studies, 91%, 90%, and 89% of the bipolar patients were ill by the time they were 50 (Clayton, 1981). There is some indication that manic illness with onset after the age of 50 is more deleterious and has a more chronic course. The literature on late onset bipolar illness is confusing, because many of the patients discussed had episodes of depression prior to age 50 but did not become manic until after that age. The age of onset of the entire illness, however, would be considered before 50.

Bipolar illness is definitely recurrent. In one hospitalized series of 393 patients, virtually every patient had a recurrence (Angst *et al.*, 1973; Grof *et al.*, 1973). In a second, only 7% were without recurrence (Bratfos & Haug, 1968). In a third series, there were, again, no patients without relapse (Murphy *et al.*, 1974). Until now, there has been no comparable series from an outpatient clinic; since recent data indicates that such patients can escape hospitalization (Boyd & Weissman, 1981), an outpatient study is indicated.

Bipolar patients have more episodes than unipolar, the median being around eight (Angst, 1980; Angst *et al.*, 1973, 1979; Grof *et al.*, 1973). The mean duration of the episode of bipolar affective disorder is shorter, usually about 4 months, with the episode of depression being longer than the episode of mania. As with unipolar affective disorder, the duration of episodes does not change remarkably with increasing number of episodes. Initially, the interval between episodes decreases, but it seems to bottom out in a set pattern with a cycle every 6 to 9 months. As with unipolar illness, the best way to predict a patient's course is by his previous course. In bipolar illness, too, there is a hint that there may be extinction of the repetitive pattern with a certain number of episodes. This possibility needs further investigation, but it may mean that despite a malignant short-term course, the long-term outlook may be better.

Chronicity in bipolar affective disorder remains unclear because of difficulties in defining chronicity. If chronicity is defined as the presence of symptoms, social decline, or both, estimates are that about one-third of bipolar patients have a chronic course (Clayton, 1981). Chronic mania, however, is rare. Given the prevalence, early onset, and likelihood of chronicity in bipolar illness, many patients previously thought to be schizophrenic should probably be rediagnosable as bipolar.

Genetics

Affective disorder is more common in the relatives of bipolar affective disorder than in unipolar. The affective disorder may be mania or depression. About half of the patients with bipolar affective disorder have a parent with affective disorder; about half also have two generations of illness (Winokur, 1978). Twin and adoption studies support the notion of a genetic component. Between 4% and 10% of bipolar patients had a relative with mania. Genetic markers have been proposed; but, to date, no firm statement can be made about the association between bipolar illness and X chromosome transmission or between bipolar illness and the HLA (human leukocyte antigen) (Nurnberger & Gershon, 1982; Weitkamp, Stancer, Persad, Flood, & Guttormsen, 1981); here, too, the question of assortative mating is controversial.

Life Events

Life events that precede a manic episode are far less well studied than in relation to depression (Dunner, Fleiss, & Fieve, 1976). Patients in a lithium clinic were found to have no excess of events prior to an affective episode. However, it's quite possible that lithium protected or buffered them from the effects of such life events. Other reports suggest more independent events preceding an episode of mania than in comparison to controls (Paykel, 1982). This is an area that clearly needs study.

Personality

Studies of patients stabilized on lithium show no differences in personality traits between bipolars and controls (von Zerssen, 1982). Some (Bech *et al.*, 1980) suggest that lithium mutes the cyclothymia of the bipolars and causes them to test more like unipolars. Others find that in remission manics evaluate themselves in a positive way (Jamison,

Gerner, Hammen, & Padesky, 1980). It would be valuable to have personality assessment prior to illness.

Treatment

The treatment of bipolar affective disorder is similar to the treatment of unipolar affective disorder. Depression is treated in exactly the same way. Mania can be treated with lithium, phenothiazines, lithium and phenothiazines in combination, perhaps by carbamazepine, and by ECT (Clayton, 1981; Juhl, Tsuang, & Perry, 1977). The efficacy of lithium in the treatment and prophylaxis of acute mania is now well accepted. It should be remembered, however, that only about 50% of bipolar patients in all studies remain free of relapse for 3 years (Clayton, 1981).

Complications

The risk of suicide in bipolar affective disorder is also high. Suicide may be as common in women as in men with the disorder. It appears that there is a trend, even in bipolars, for suicide to occur less frequently later than in the earlier stages of the disease (Tsuang, 1978). Studies are controversial with regard to whether marital disruptions, school interruptions, and job loss are more likely after the onset of bipolar illness than in the ordinary course of events. The occurrence of complications may depend on whether or not adequate stabilization of the disease is achieved. There may be a decrease in fertility in this illness (Baron, Risch, & Mendlewicz, 1982). Alcohol abuse is a possible complication (Reich, 1974).

ACKNOWLEDGMENT

The preparation of this chapter was supported, in part, by USPHS Grant MH-25430.

REFERENCES

Abrams, R., Taylor, M., Hayman, M., & Krishna, N. (1979). Unipolar mania revisited. *Journal of Affective Disorders, 1*, 59–68.

Akiskal, H., Bitar, A., Puzantian, V., Rosenthal, T., & Walker, P. (1978). The nosological status of neurotic depression. *Archives of General Psychiatry, 35*, 756–766.

Angst, J. (1980). Course of unipolar depressive, bipolar manic-depressive, and schizoaffective disorders: Results of a prospective logitudinal study. *Fortschritte der Neurologie-Psychiatrie, 48,* 3–30.

Angst, J., Baastrup, P., Grof, P., Hippius, H., Poldinger, W., & Weis, P. (1973). The course of monopolar depression and bipolar psychoses. *Neurologia, Neurochirugia i Psychiatria Polska, 76,* 489–500.

Angst, J., Felder, W., & Frey, R. (1979). The course of unipolar and bipolar affective disorders. In M. Schou & E. Stromgren (Eds.), *Origin, prevention and treatment of affective disorders.* New York: Academic Press.

Avery, D., & Winokur, G. (1977). The efficacy of electroconvulsive therapy and antidepressants in depression. *Biological Psychiatry, 12,* 507–523.

Baron, M., Risch, N., & Mendlewicz, J. (1982). Differential fertility in bipolar affective illness. *Journal of Affective Disorders, 4,* 103–112.

Bech, P., Shapiro, R., Sihm, F., Nielsen, B., Sorensen, B., & Rafaelsen, O. (1980). Personality in unipolar and bipolar manic-melancholic patients. *Acta Psychiatrica Scandinavica, 65,* 245–257.

Biggs, J., & Ziegler, V. (1977). Tricyclic antidepressants in outpatient therapy. In J. H. Masserman (Ed.), *Current psychiatric therapies* (Vol. 17). New York: Grune & Stratton.

Boyd, J., & Weissman, M. (1981). Epidemiology of affective disorders. *Archives of General Psychiatry, 38,* 1039–1046.

Bratfos, O., & Haug, J. (1968). The course of manic-depressive psychosis. *Acta Psychiatrica Scandinavica, 44,* 89–112.

Brown, G.W., & Harris, T. (1982). Disease, distress, and depression. *Journal of Affective Disorders, 4,* 1–8.

Clayton, P. (1981). The epidemiology of bipolar affective disorder. *Comprehensive Psychiatry, 22,* 31–43.

Clayton, P. (1983a). Gender and depression. In J. Angst (Ed.), *The origins of depression: Current concepts and approaches.* Berlin: Springer-Verlag.

Clayton, P. (1983b). A further look at secondary depression. In P. J. Clayton & J. E. Barrett (Eds.), *Treatment of depression: Old controversies and new approaches.* New York: Raven Press.

Davis, J. (1976). Overview: Maintenance therapy in psychiatry: II. Affective disorders. *American Journal of Psychiatry, 133,* 1–13.

Dunner, D., & Hall, K. (1980). Social adjustment and psychological precipitants in mania. In R.H. Belmaker & H.M. van Praag (Eds.), *Mania: An evolving concept.* New York: Spectrum.

Dunner, D., Fleiss, J., & Fieve, R. (1976). The course of development of mania in patients with recurrent depression. *American Journal of Psychiatry, 133,* 905–908.

Eastwood, R., Stiasny, S., & Tice, S. (1981). Estimates of the prevalence of bipolar affective disorder: Methods based on treatment with lithium. *Acta Psychiatrica Scandinavica, 63,* 83f–90.

Egeland, J.A., & Hostetter, A.M. (1983). Amish study, I: Affective disorders among the Amish, 1976–1980. *American Journal of Psychiatry, 140,* 56–61.

Fink, M. (1978). Efficacy and safety of induced seizures (EST) in man. *Comprehensive Psychiatry, 19,* 1–18.

Grof, P., Angst, J., & Haines, T. (1973). The clinical course of depression: Practical issues. In J. Angst (Ed.) *Classification and prediction of outcome depression.* New York: F. K. Schattauer Verlag.

Guze, S., & Robins, E. (1970). Suicide and primary affective disorders. *British Journal of Psychiatry, 117,* 437–438.

Hirschfeld, R., & Cross, C. (1982). Epidemiology of affective disorders, psycho-social risk factors, *Archives of General Psychiatry, 39,* 35–46.

Jamison, K., Gerner, R., Hammen, C., & Padesky, C. (1980). Clouds and silver linings:

Positive experiences associated with primary affective disorders. *American Journal of Psychiatry, 137,* 198–202.

Juhl, R., Tsuang, M., & Perry, P. (1977). Concomitant administration of haloperidol and lithium carbonate in acute mania. *Diseases of the Nervous Systems, 38,* 675–676.

Kovacs, M., Rush, A., Beck, A. & Hollon, S. (1981). Depressed outpatients treated with cognitive therapy or pharmacotherapy. *Archives of General Psychiatry, 38,* 33–39.

Kraepelin, E. (1921). *Manic-depressive insanity and paranoia.* Edinburgh: E & S Livingstone.

Krauthammer, C., & Klerman, G. (1979). The epidemiology of mania. In B. Shopsin (Ed.), *Manic illness.* New York: Raven Press.

Murphy, G., & Wetzel, R. (1980). Suicide risk by birth cohort in the United States, 1949–1974. *Archives of General Psychiatry, 37,* 519–523.

Murphy, G., Woodruff, R., Jr., Herjanic, M., & Super, G. (1974). Variability of the clinical course of primary affective disorder. *Archives of General Psychiatry, 30,* 757–761.

Nurnberger, J., Jr., Roose, S., Dunner, D., & Fieve, R. (1979). Unipolar mania: A distinct clinical entity? *American Journal of Psychiatry, 136,* 1420–1423.

Nurnberger, J., & Gershon, E. (1982) Genetics. In E. S. Paykel (Ed.), *Handbook of affective disorders.* New York: Guilford Press.

Paykel, E. S. (1982). Life events and early environment. In E. S. Paykel (Ed.), *Handbook of affective disorders.* New York: Guilford Press.

Perris, C. (1966). A study of bipolar (manic-depressive) and unipolar recurrent depressive psychoses. *Acta Psychiatrica Scandinavica, 42* (Suppl. 194).

Prien, R. (1983). Lithium and the long-term maintenance treatment of recurrent depression: A continuing controversy. In P. J. Clayton & J. Barrett (Eds.), *Treatment of depression: Old controversies and new approaches.* New York: Raven Press.

Reich, L., Davies, R., & Himmelhoch, J. (1974). Excessive alcohol use in manic-depressive illness. *American Journal of Psychiatry, 131,* 83–86.

Robins, E., & Guze, S. (1972). Classification of affective disorders: The primary-secondary, the endogenous-reactive, and the neurotic-psychotic concepts. In T. A. Williams, M. M. Katz, & J. A. Shield, Jr. (Eds.), *Recent advances in the psychobiology of the depressive illnesses: Proceedings of a workshop sponsored by the NIMH.* Washington, DC: U.S. Government Printing Office.

Rush, A., Beck, A., Kovacs, M., & Hollon, S. (1977). Comparative efficacy of cognitive therapy and pharmacotherapy in the treatment of depressed outpatients. *Cognitive Therapy Review, 1,* 17–37.

Tsuang, M. (1978). Suicide in schizophrenics, manics, depressives, and surgical controls. *Archives of General Psychiatry, 35,* 153–155.

von Zerssen, D. (1982). Personality and affective disorders. In E. S. Paykel (Ed.), *Handbook of affective disorders.* New York: Guilford Press.

Weissman, M., Klerman, G., Prusoff, B., Sholomskas, M., & Padian, M. (1981). Depressed outpatients: Results one year after treatment with drugs and/or interpersonal psychotherapy. *Archives of General Psychiatry, 38,* 51–55.

Weissman, M., & Myers, J. (1978). Affective disorders in a United States urban community: The use of research diagnostic criteria in an epidemiological survey. *Archives of General Psychiatry, 35,* 1304–1311.

Weissman, M. (1978). Personal communication.

Weitkamp, M., Stancer, H., Persad, E., Flood, C., & Guttormsen, S. (1981). Depressive disorders and HLA: A gene on chromosome 6 that can affect behavior. *New England Journal of Medicine, 305,* 1301–1306.

Winokur, G. (1978). Mania, depression: Family studies, genetics, and relation to treatment. In M. A. Lipton, A. DiMascio, & K. Killam (Eds.), *Psychopharmacology: A generation of progress.* New York: Raven Press.

3

Neuroendocrine Abnormalities in Affective Disorders

MICHAEL A. SCHLESSER

Physicians have noted an association between endocrinopathies and affective disorders for several decades. In 1835, Graves noted an association between affective symptoms and hyperthyroidism. Depressive symptomatology is not uncommon in Cushing's and Addison's disease, as well as in hyper- and hypothyroidism, and panhypopituitarism (Rose & Sachar, 1981).

Manic symptoms have also been reported in both Cushing's disease and hyperthyroidism. However, these associations were poorly understood in the absence of a coherent framework for the study of brain–endocrine interactions. In the last 15 years, several major advances in neuroendocrinology have enhanced this understanding.

Five major discoveries include: (1) the central nervous system, and in particular the limbic system, regulates pituitary function and programs the secretion of pituitary hormones; (2) feedback loops for circulating hormones extend above the pituitary level to include areas of the central nervous system; (3) the hypothalamus and the limbic system play critical roles in the integration of three major homeostatic systems of the body: behavioral, endocrine, and autonomic regulation; (4) the limbic system influence on hypothalamic neuroendocrine nuclei is effected by synaptic connections through neurotransmission; and (5) technical developments in hormone assay methodology and the development of perturbation tests to evaluate dynamic endocrine regulation. All of these developments have allowed more sophisticated studies of these endocrine systems and contributed to the advancement of neuroendocrinology (Carroll, 1978).

Clinical researchers have exploited these basic developments vigorously by adopting a neuroendocrine strategy as a means to assess

MICHAEL A. SCHLESSER. Department of Psychiatry, University of Texas Health Science Center, Dallas, Texas.

limbic system function in patients with affective disorders. Two major neuroendocrine abnormalities have been identified: abnormalities in the hypothalamic-pituitary-adrenal (HPA) axis and in the hypothalamic-pituitary-thyroid (HPT) axis.

The Hypothalamic-Pituitary-Adrenal Axis

Figure 3-1 provides a schematic diagram of the HPA axis. Putative neurotransmitters exert control on the hypophysiotropic neurons of the hypothalamus. Data from animal studies and in part from human

FIG. 3-1. HPA axis. From "Neuroendocrinology" by S. Reichlin, in R. H. Williams (Ed.), *Textbook of Endocrinology*, Philadelphia: Saunders, 1981, p. 615. Reprinted by permission.

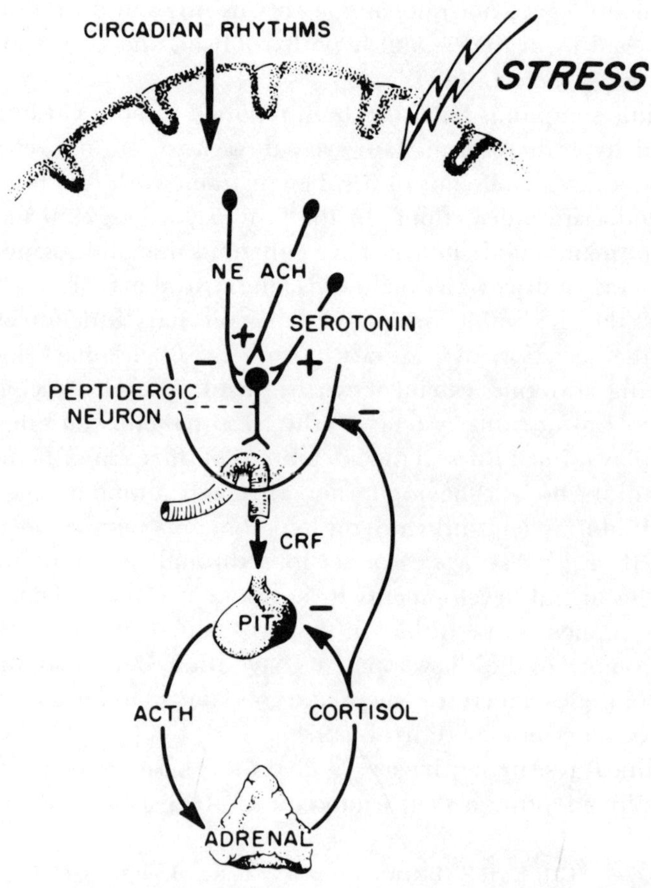

studies suggest that norepinephrine (NE) is inhibitory on this axis, while acetylcholine (ACh) and serotonin (5-HT) are excitatory (Carroll *et al.*, 1980; Reichlin, 1981). The hypophysiotropic neurons have their cell bodies in the median eminence of the hypothalamus. These neurons elaborate corticotropin-releasing factor (CRF), a low-molecular-weight neuropeptide. CRF is secreted by these neurons into the portal venous system of the pituitary. CRF stimulates certain cells in the anterior pituitary gland to secrete adrenocorticotropic hormone (ACTH), a high-molecular-weight polypeptide. ACTH enters the peripheral circulation and stimulates the adrenal cortex to synthesize and secrete cortisol, the main glucocorticoid produced by humans. The major endocrine effects of cortisol are on energy metabolism.

A negative-feedback servomechanism, which is dependent on plasma cortisol concentration, operates at the level of the anterior pituitary and hypothalamus. In a typical 24-hour period, the average adult produces approximately 20 mg of cortisol and 3 mg of corticosterone—the major glucocorticoids in man. For the most part, cortisol is protein bound; 77% is bound to transcortin, an alpha-globulin, and 15% is bound to albumin. The remaining 8% is not protein bound and is responsible for cortisol's tissue effects, as well as for controlling the feedback mechanisms operative in the hypothalamus and pituitary. Neural input from the limbic system also controls HPA axis function. A portion of this input mediates stress activation of the HPA axis. The adrenostat, another neural control, is the central nervous system (CNS) setpoint at which feedback inhibition occurs at the level of the hypothalamus. A third neuronal input into the HPA axis controls the circadian rhythm of cortisol and ACTH secretion (Carroll & Mendels, 1978).

Corticotropin-releasing factor (CRF) was the first hypothalamic hypophysiotropic hormone to be recognized and named, although its synthesis in the laboratory was only recently accomplished. CRF was isolated and purified from ovine hypothalamic extract, and recently CRF was characterized, sequenced, synthesized, and found to stimulate ACTH and β-endorphin release (Vale, Spiess, C. Rivier, & J. Rivier, 1981). Ovine CRF injected into normal humans promptly stimulates release of ACTH with a peak at 15 to 30 minutes. Cortisol secretion is also stimulated with peak levels at 60 minutes. There is a 30–45 minute lag period between ACTH and cortisol release (Grossman *et al.*, 1982). Since ovine CRF fails to stimulate release of several other hormones, it is possible that it or a related peptide is a CRF in man (Grossman *et al.*, 1982).

(In humans there is a definite circadian rhythm of cortisol secretion. Cortisol is secreted episodically with four to six major secretory episodes in a 24-hour period, the majority of which occur in the morning (Figure 3-2). After this morning burst of cortisol secretory activity, the system becomes increasingly quiescent, particularly late in the day) In fact, cortisol levels reach their nadir between midnight and 2 a.m. Approximately at 4 a.m. cortisol secretory activity commences again, with major secretory episodes occurring between the hours of 4 a.m. and 10 a.m., during which about 70% of the 24-hour cortisol secretion occurs. The remaining 30% is secreted between 10 a.m. and the next cycle.(It is thought that a CNS program controls this circadian release of the hormone. During most of the day the brain exerts an inhibitory influence on the HPA axis in the normal state. It is thought that this inhibitory influence is relaxed chiefly in the morning hours during the peak of cortisol secretory activity. It is hypothesized that this inhibitory brain influence on the HPA axis is reduced or absent in some depressed patients) (Carroll & Mendels, 1978).

(Table 3-1 summarizes those findings that support the observation of increased HPA axis activity in depression. First, elevated basal plasma and serum cortisol levels, with the greatest elevations occurring at night, have been found (Carroll, Curtis, & Mendels, 1976a; Sachar *et al.*, 1973). Second, increased plasma free and cortisol levels are found in depressed patients (Carroll & Mendels, 1978), as is increased 24-hour urinary free cortisol excretion (Carroll, Curtis, & Mendels, 1976b).

FIG. 3-2. Circadian profile of plasma cortisol in a normal subject before (day 1) and after dexamethasone (day 2). From "Neuroendocrine Regulation in Depression: I. Limbic System Adrenocortical Dysfunction" by B. J. Carroll, G. C. Curtis, & J. Mendels, in *Archives of General Psychiatry*, 1976, *33*, 1040. Copyright 1976, American Medical Association. Reprinted by permission.

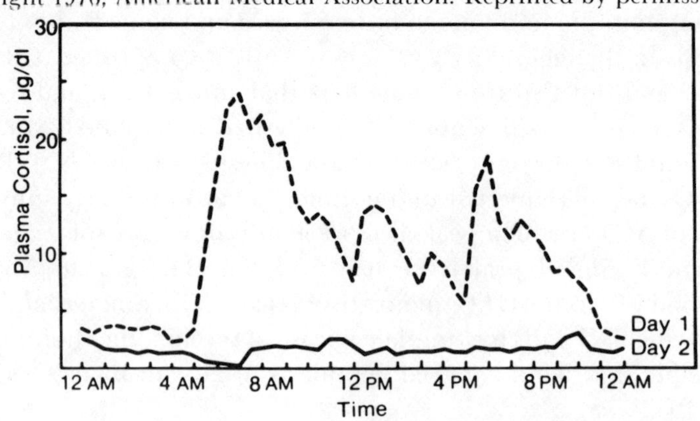

TABLE 3-1. Evidence for Increased HPA Axis Activity in Depression

1. Elevated basal plasma and serum cortisol (greatest elevations at night or 11:30 P.M.).
2. Increased plasma free and CSF cortisol.
3. Increased basal 24-hour urinary free cortisol (UFC) excretion.
4. Increased frequency, total number, and magnitude of secretory episodes.
5. Increased cortisol secretion in a 24-hour cycle.
6. Disturbance of the normal circadian profile of cortisol secretion.
7. Resistance to suppression of cortisol secretion and excretion to dexamethasone.
8. Increased plasma ACTH levels.

Depressed patients show an increased frequency, total number, and magnitude of cortisol secretory episodes (Sachar *et al.*, 1973). As many as 10 to 12 major secretory episodes have been found in depressed patients. Thus, the 24-hour cumulative cortisol secretion is increased (Sachar *et al.*, 1973). In some patients with a more severe abnormality, there is an actual disturbance of the normal circadian profile of cortisol secretion that renders these patients indistinguishable from those with diencephalic Cushing's disease (Carroll *et al.*, 1976a; Sachar *et al.*, 1973). Many depressed patients fail to suppress cortisol secretion, and hence serum or plasma cortisol concentrations remain elevated following dexamethasone, a synthetic glucocorticoid (Carroll *et al.*, 1976b, 1981; Rush, Giles, Roffwarg, & Parker, 1982; Rush *et al.*, submitted for publication; Schlesser, Winokur, & Sherman, 1979, 1980), and most reports indicate that there are increased plasma ACTH levels in depressed patients compared to normals (Carroll & Mendels, 1978).

Figure 3-3 shows a 19-year-old bipolar depressed male, who was studied in the depressed state. A catheter was inserted into the patient's forearm, through which serum samples were obtained for cortisol determination every 20 minutes for a 24-hour period. Note that this patient hypersecretes cortisol and, thus, the absolute levels of cortisol are elevated throughout the 24-hour period. In addition, there are 12 major secretory episodes in this patient compared to the normally expected 6–8 episodes. Finally, cortisol secretion occurs in the late afternoon, evening, and early morning hours when the system is normally inhibited and quiescent.

Another way to evaluate increased HPA axis activity is to perturb the system by attempting to suppress it with dexamethasone, commonly known as the dexamethasone suppression test (DST). Dexamethasone is a synthetic glucocorticoid that is 30 times more potent

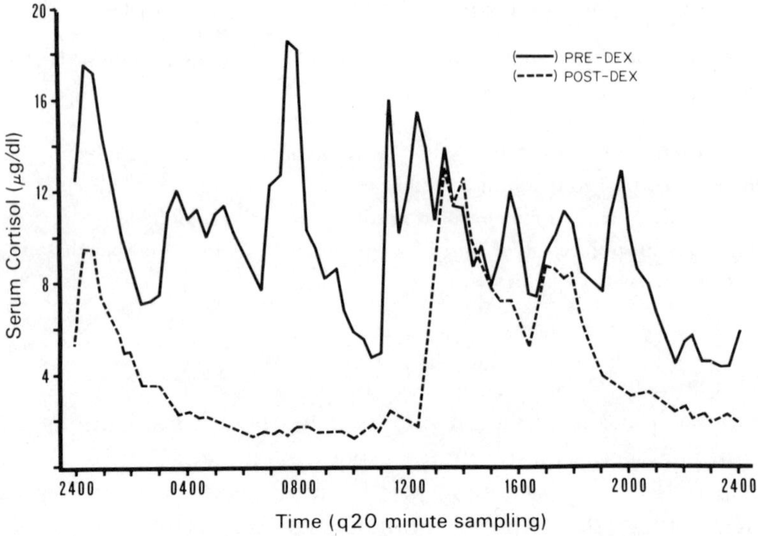

FIG. 3-3. Pre- and postdexamethasone serum cortisols in a bipolar depressed male.

than cortisol. One milligram of dexamethasone is approximately equal to the amount of glucocorticoid secreted by a normal adult in an entire day. Dexamethasone is absorbed in the gut and reaches a sufficient blood level to maximally activate the negative-feedback servomechanism at the hypothalamus and pituitary, to completely suppress cortisol secretory activity for 24 hours in the healthy normal adult. However, many depressed patients given dexamethasone fail to completely suppress cortisol secretion; hence blood cortisol concentrations remain elevated (Carroll *et al.*, 1976b, 1981; Rush *et al.*, 1981, submitted for publication; Schlesser *et al.*, 1979, 1980).

Figure 3-3 shows the same bipolar depressed male previously mentioned. Following dexamethasone at midnight, cortisol levels obtained by catheter at 20-minute intervals reveal that he rapidly suppressed HPA axis activity following dexamethasone. However, he had an early escape from dexamethasone suppression in the middle of the day. Carroll and colleagues (1976a, 1976b, 1981) have shown that most depressed subjects have an early, rather than absolute, escape from dexamethasone suppression.

While in normal people cortisol levels remain below 4–5 μg/dl for the 24-hour period following dexamethasone, many depressed patients exhibit early escape (Carroll *et al.*, 1976a, 1976b, 1981). However, when clinical remission ensues, complete suppression of cortisol following dexamethasone (i.e., a normal response) typically occurs, suggesting that the neuroendocrine fault is state-dependent (Albala, Greden, Tarika, & Carroll, 1981; Carroll *et al.*, 1976a; Greden *et al.*, 1980, 1983; Holsboer, Liebl, & Hofschuster, 1982; Papakostas, Fink, Lee, Irwin, & Johnson, 1981; Schlesser & Rush, 1981).

These phenomena have given rise to the DST for use in psychiatry, the standardized methodology having largely been developed by Carroll and co-workers (1981). One milligram of dexamethasone is given orally or intramuscularly at 11 p.m., and serum or plasma cortisol levels are obtained at 8 a.m., 4 p.m., and 11 p.m. on the following day. Serum cortisol is determined by radioimmunoassay (RIA) at most medical centers. The serum cortisol criterion or threshold is 4.0 μg/dl at our center. That is, nonsuppression is declared if one or more of these three postdexamethasone cortisol levels exceeds 4.0 μg/dl. This test will detect 50% to 70% of endogenously depressed inpatients (Carroll, 1982; Carroll *et al.*, 1981; Rush *et al.*, submitted for publication). The abnormality is relatively specific to endogenous or primary depression (Carroll *et al.*, 1976b, 1981; Rush, Giles *et al.*, 1982, submitted for publication; Schlesser *et al.*, 1979, 1980). In our normal control study, only one of the 23 normals had a postdexamethasone cortisol level greater than 4.0 μg/dl (Rush, Schlesser, *et al.*, 1982). Hence, the false-positive rate is 4%, and a theoretical psecificity of 96% can be expected.

The cortisol criterion used varies from 4 to 6 μg/dl at various centers and is dependent on the assay employed. It is critical that at each center a cortisol criterion is established on normal control subjects so that a sensitive and a reliable cortisol assay is established in the range of cortisol concentrations that are of interest (4–6 μg/dl), and that a longitudinally reliable cortisol assay with systematic quality control is in place. However, a number of conditions and situations may confound the DST results (see Table 3-2). Attention to these medical exclusion criteria is essential to interpretation of the DST results.

Of what value is the DST? Carroll and co-workers (1981) have demonstrated that 67% of inpatients symptomatic with endogenous or melancholic depression have a positive or nonsuppressed DST, whereas only 4% of normal and psychiatrically ill controls are positive. This finding has largely been confirmed by others (Carroll, 1982; Carroll *et al.*, 1976b, 1981; Rush *et al.*, submitted for publication) Carroll and colleagues (Carroll, 1982; Carroll *et al.*, 1981) have advo-

TABLE 3-2. DST Medical Exclusion Criteria

False-positive DST
Cushing's disease or syndrome
Pseudo-Cushing's syndrome of alcoholism
Hyperthyroidism or thyroid storm
Pregnancy
High-dose estrogens
Uncontrolled brittle diabetes mellitus
Significant fever, infection, allergy, trauma, etc.
Anorexia nervosa
Starvation
Hepatic-enzyme-inducing drugs (phenytoin, carbamazepine, alcohol, barbiturates, meprobamate, glutethimide)
Acute withdrawal from sedative-hypnotics such as alcohol, barbiturates, benzodiazepines, and possibly narcotic withdrawal
Reserpine (possible)
Narcotics, alcohol, and other sedatives (possible)

False-negative DST
Addison's disease
Panhypopituitarism
Hypothyroidism
Exogenous corticosteroids
High-dose benzodiazepines (possible)
Cyproheptadine (possible)

cated the use of the DST as a confirmatory diagnostic test for endogenous depression. However, the sensitivity in endogenously depressed outpatients is substantially lower, from 30% to 45% (Carroll *et al.*, 1981; Giles & Rush, 1982; Rush, Giles, *et al.*, 1982). Some but not all studies suggest that bipolar depressions are associated with a somewhat higher incidence of nonsuppression than are unipolars (Schlesser *et al.*, 1980). At any rate, the DST certainly cannot distinguish the two.

Bipolar patients in the mixed phase also have a high rate of DST nonsuppression (Carroll, 1979), although our data suggests that manic phase bipolar patients are not likely to show DST nonsuppression, unless they are about to enter a mixed or depressed phase (Schlesser, Rush, Orsulak, & Crowley, 1983). Nearly all schizophrenic patients have a normal DST response, as do patients with a variety of other psychiatric conditions, including dysthymic disorder, minor depression, panic disorder, alcohol and drug dependency (when studied drug-free), and uncomplicated personality disorders (Carroll, 1982; Carroll *et al.*, 1981; Rush *et al.*, submitted for publication). Figure 3-4 shows the highest postdexamethasone cortisol levels for each of 90 inpatients with primary depression (bipolar or unipolar) at our center.

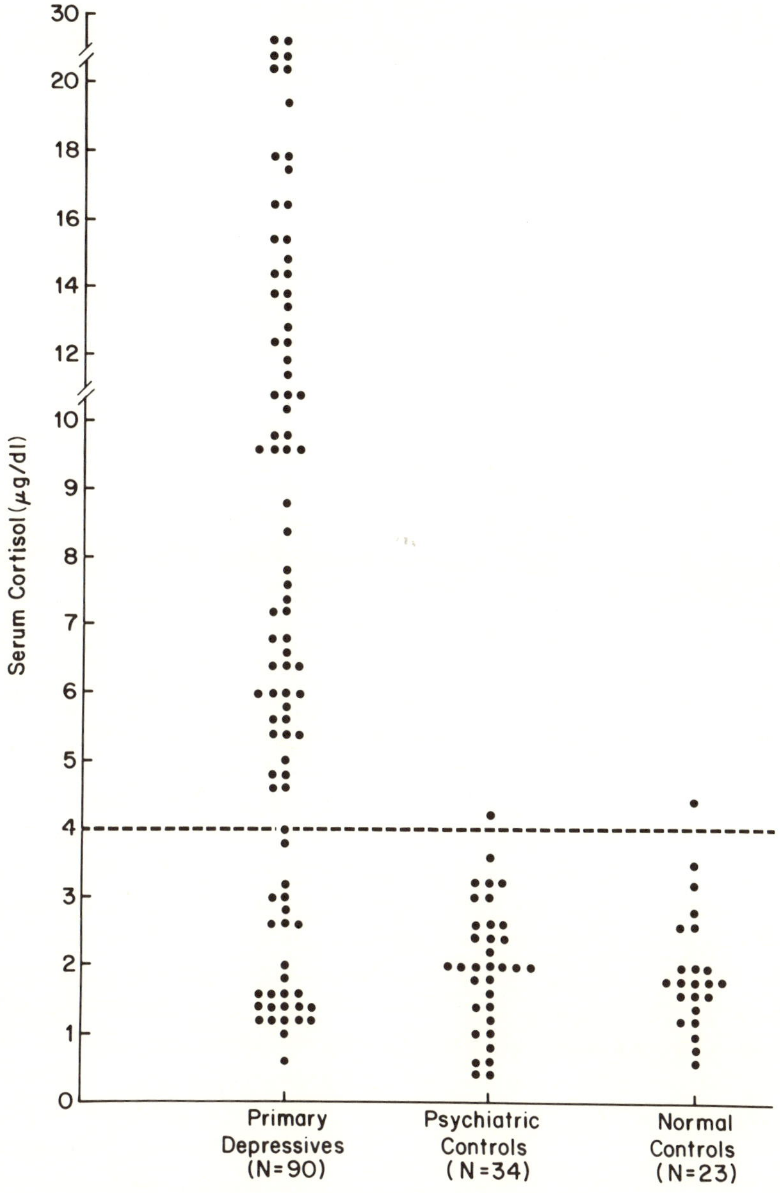

FIG. 3-4. Highest postdexamethasone cortisols in patients with primary depression (unipolar and bipolar), psychiatric controls, and normal controls.

Over 70% of this inpatient cohort (bipolar and unipolar depressed patients) were DST nonsuppressors using the 4.0 μg/dl threshold value, compared with a 4% nonsuppression rate in normal controls and in other subjects with psychiatric disorders (excluding anorexia nervosa, schizoaffective disorders, and dementia).

An abnormal DST has been described as being associated with various nosological subtypes of depression: endogenous but not nonendogenous; primary but not secondary; familial pure depressive disease but not depressive spectrum disease. Confirmatory and contradictory reports exist in each instance (Carroll, 1982; Gwirtsman, Gerner, & Sternbach, 1982). At this time, the finding of DST nonsuppression in endogenous but not nonendogenous depressives and in primary but not secondary depressives are the most widely replicated.

DST nonsuppression is also found in bipolar patients in the depressed and mixed phases but not in the manic phase (Carroll *et al.*, 1976a; Greden *et al.*, 1982; Schlesser *et al.*, 1980; Schlesser, Rush, Orsulak, & Crowley, 1983), schizoaffective depressives (Schlesser, Winokur, & Rush, 1981), depressed patients with pseudodementia (Carroll *et al.*, 1981), depressed patients with severe personality disorder, catatonic patients with affective disorder (Carroll, 1982), depressed children and adolescents (Carroll *et al.*, 1981), and patients with "masked" depression (Carroll *et al.*, 1981).

The DST has potential as a confirmatory diagnostic test in several clinical situations when the presentation is atypical or uncertain. It is critical to keep in mind that a positive DST may confirm a diagnosis of endogenous or primary depression, but that a negative DST is of no significance in that it certainly does not rule out a diagnosis of endogenous or primary depression. Similarly, a positive DST (nonsuppression) does not always mean that the patient is depressed, as many clinical conditions may cause nonsuppression. Thus, the DST may be a useful adjunct in the differential diagnostic process in selected clinical situations. Recent reports that the DST may be positive in dementia and other psychiatric disorders (Gwirtsman *et al.*, 1982) challenges the specificity of the DST and, if replicated, will narrow the range of clinical situations in which the DST will have a role as a diagnostic adjunct.

How does DST nonsuppression relate to treatment response? Figures 3-5 and 3-6 summarize data from our study of 12 patients (8 unipolars and 4 bipolars) studied through a course of electroconvulsive therapy (ECT). The 17-item Hamilton Rating Scale for Depression (HRS-D), a measure of severity of depressive symptoms, was

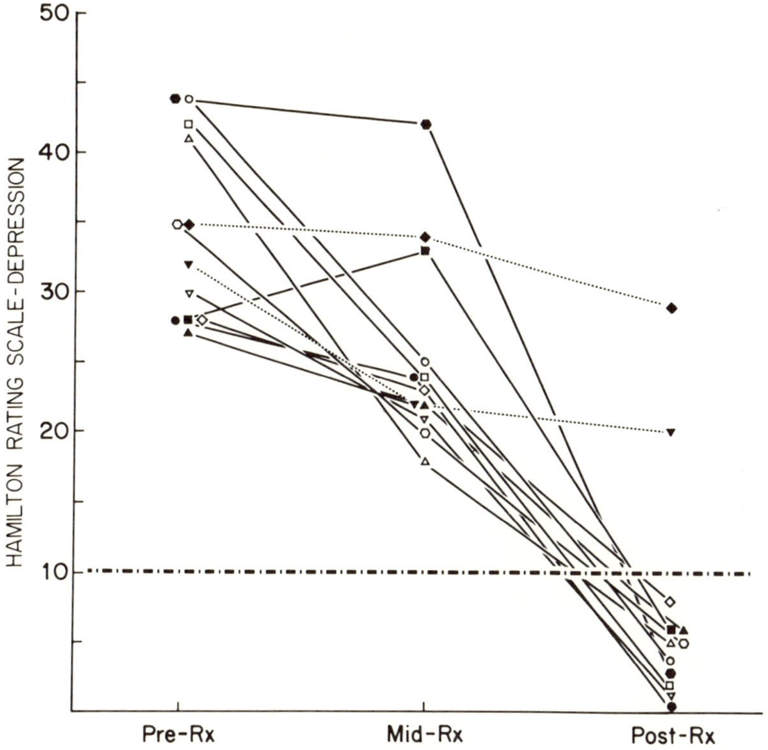

FIG. 3-5. Serial measurement of HRS-D in depressed subjects pre-, mid-, and post-ECT treatment ($n = 12$).

obtained before treatment, in the middle of treatment, and at the end of treatment. An HRS-D score below 10 is considered recovered. These patients were severely depressed, and most had psychotic depression. They showed some improvement by the middle of treatment, and by the end of treatment 10 of the 12 were recovered.

A DST was conducted before treatment, in the middle, and at the end of treatment. Figure 3-6 shows the highest postdexamethasone cortisol for each individual at each time point. All 12 patients were DST nonsuppressors before treatment. Note that 10 of the 12 patients converted their DST to normal by the end of treatment, but two did not. The two patients who failed to convert their DST were the same two patients who failed to respond clinically to the treatment.

Secondly, note that progressive improvement in the DST through treatment. Half of the patients who responded converted their DST to normal by the midpoint of treatment, yet all of these patients were still

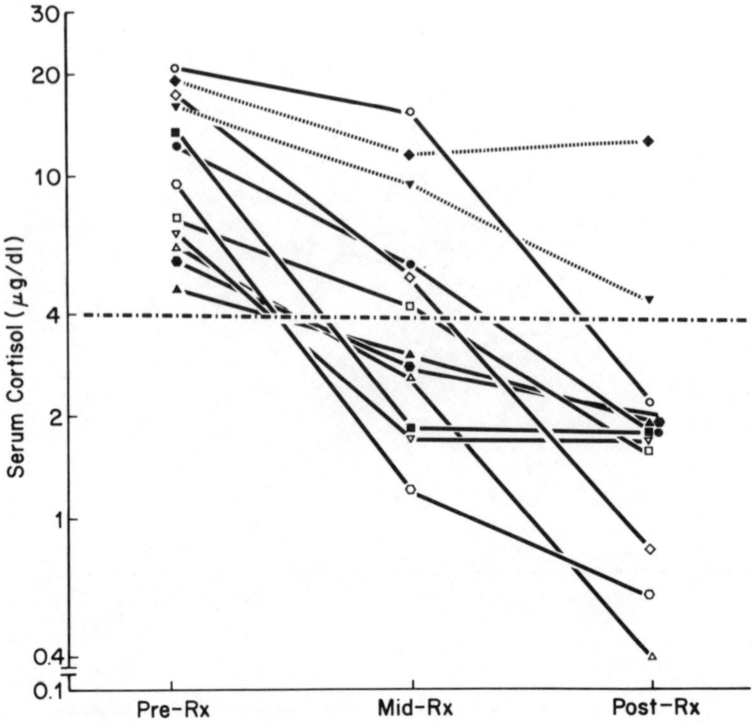

FIG. 3-6. Serial measurement of DST in depressed subjects pre-, mid-, and post-ECT treatment ($n = 12$).

significantly depressed by midtreatment. Thus, the DST reverts to normal when patients are euthymic, and perhaps in half, this conversion precedes substantial clinical change. These findings have been found in depressed patients treated with ECT (Albala *et al.*, 1981; Schlesser & Rush, 1981) and with antidepressant medications (Greden *et al.*, 1983; Holsboer *et al.*, 1982). In fact, Greden and colleagues (1980) found that those few patients who have a favorable response to antidepressant treatment but who fail to convert their DST to normal do poorly in follow-up, with return of depressive symptoms, rehospitalization, or suicide. Furthermore, Coryell and Schlesser (1981) and Carroll, Greden, and Feinberg (1981) report an association between a positive DST and completed suicide. The neuroendocrine fault of DST nonsuppression appears to be state-dependent, that is, present in the depressed state but not the euthymic or recovered state. The DST may be a useful laboratory monitor of clinical improvement, often normalizing somewhat prior to or at the time of complete clinical remission. Patients who remain DST-positive in the face of clinical remission warrant careful clinical follow-up.

Does the DST have prognostic value? Figure 3-7 shows the relationship between the HRS-D and DST in a male with unipolar major depression, who was studied and treated in the hospital and then followed as an outpatient. A DST was conducted weekly.

At first he was euthymic, and his DSTs remained normal over a period of several months. Then, this patient converted his DST to abnormal at week 2 (Figure 3-7). Two weeks later, the patient appeared clinically depressed. In other words, the DST became abnormal fully 2 weeks before the patient evidenced measurable depressive symptoms. He was then started on up to 250 mg per day of desipramine (DMI) at week 5. Note that his DST shows progressive normalization as the patient improves. Notably, his DST normalizes at week 8, but not until week 10 was the HRS-D below 10 (i.e., clinical recovery had occurred). Thus, there appears to be a lag time of about 2 weeks between DST normalization and subsequent clinical recovery in this patient. Of particular interest is the observation that the DST became abnormal 2 weeks prior to the onset of the episode of depression.

As noted above, the DST is often abnormal in the depressed and mixed phases of bipolar disorder, but is often normal in mania (Carroll, 1979; Carroll *et al.*, 1976a; Greden *et al.*, 1982; Schlesser *et al.*, 1980; Schlesser, Rush, Orsulak, & Crowley, 1983), although not all

FIG. 3-7. Serial DST and HRS-D in a unipolar depressive.

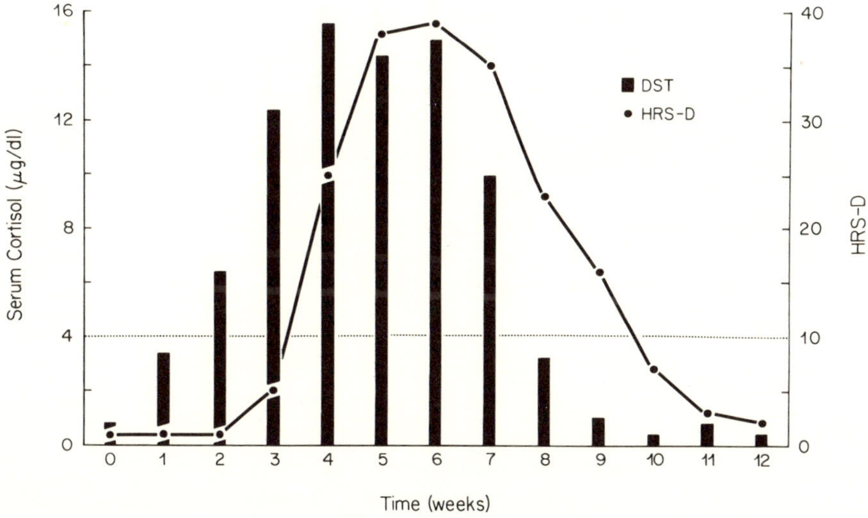

authors find this (Graham *et al.*, 1982). Figure 3-8 shows the DST, Mania Rating Scale (MRS), and HRS-D results in a bipolar patient followed at weekly intervals. This patient had a period of euthymia and normal DSTs.

During the initial part of the manic episode the DST was normal (weeks 1–4). At week 5 the DST became abnormal while the patient was still hypomanic. Two weeks later, the patient presented with significant depressive symptoms, and the DST remained abnormal during the depression. When antidepressant treatment was started, his depression improved and the DST normalized. The DST became normal at week 9, 2 weeks *before* complete clinical recovery.

Others have also described this phenomenon, suggesting that the DST may predict incipient depression in both unipolars (Holsboer, Steiger, & Maier, 1983) and bipolars (Carroll, 1982; Greden *et al.*, 1982; Holsboer *et al.*, 1983; Schlesser, Rush, Orsulak, & Crowley, 1983). They also report that the DST may become abnormal from 2 days to 3 weeks before the onset of a clinical episode of depression.

Whether the DST predicts response to somatic treatments (antidepressant medications or ECT) remains unclear. Some studies suggest

FIG. 3-8. Serial DSTs in a bipolar switching from mania to depression.

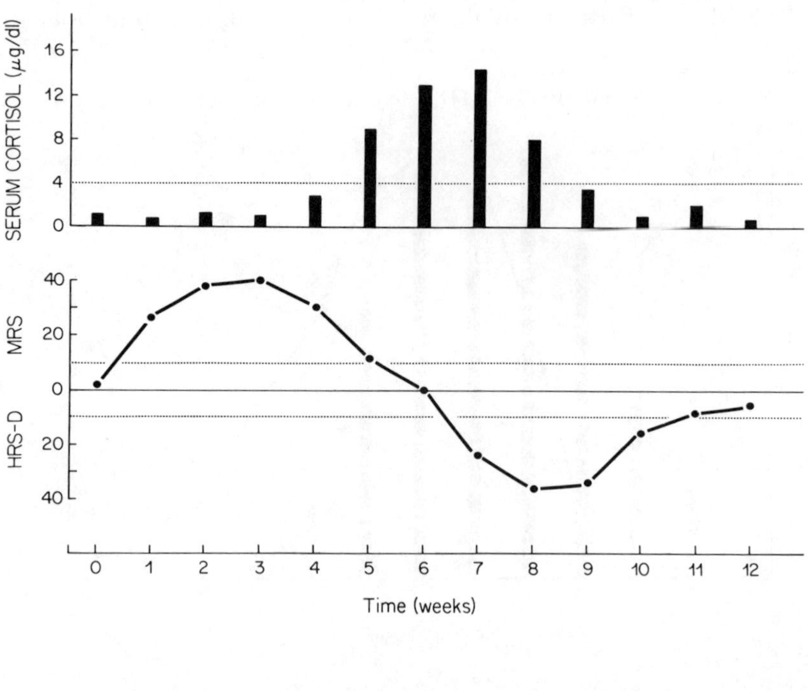

that a positive DST predicts a good response to somatic treatment, while other studies do not support this conclusion (Carroll, 1982; Gwirtsman *et al.*, 1982).

Whether DST status has any implications for the selection of a specific antidepressant is also yet unclear. In a recent study, we evaluated treatment response to DMI in a group of inpatients with endogenous, unipolar major depression. Thirty-six of the 43 DST nonsuppressors had a complete response (final HRS-D of 9 or less), whereas only 9 of 18 DST suppressors responded. This difference in response rate was statistically significant and was not accounted for by other factors (e.g., medication dose, length of treatment, or the like) (Schlesser & Rush, 1982). However, the ultimate role of the DST in treatment selection remains to be clarified, as other studies do not find that the DST predicts which drug will be the most efficacious (Carroll, 1982; Greden *et al.*, 1981; Gwirtsman *et al.*, 1982).

When the DST is used in outpatients, only the 4 p.m. postdexamethasone cortisol is typically sampled. This single sample detects only 65% to 80% of those detected with the three-sample inpatient method (Carroll *et al.*, 1981; Rush *et al.*, submitted for publication). This fact may in part account for the lower sensitivity of the DST in outpatients. Most studies suggest that the DST has a 50% to 70% sensitivity for inpatients with endogenous or primary depressions (Carroll *et al.*, 1981; Rush *et al.*, submitted for publication; Schlesser *et al.*, 1980), and a 30% to 40% sensitivity in outpatients (Carroll *et al.*, 1981; Giles & Rush, 1982; Rush, Giles, *et al.*, 1982). The specificity is usually over 90% to 95%. That is, the false-positive rate is usually less than 5% to 10%. These figures compare very favorably with other laboratory tests used in internal medicine (Carroll, 1982).

Does the DST have application in clinical practice? The DST appears to have utility as a confirmatory diagnostic test for endogenous or primary depression. It may confirm the clinical descriptive diagnosis of major depression in typical cases. It may be helpful in identifying endogenous depression in the atypical or unusual presentations such as psychotic depression, schizoaffective depression, depression with a concomitant personality disorder, catatonic depression, masked depression, depression with panic attacks, and depression in children and adolescents. Althought the DST may be positive in patients with depression and pseudodementia, it may also be positive in nondepressed demented patients; hence, it may not differentiate the two. Only further research will answer this question. Nonetheless, the DST appears to be reasonably specific and sensitive for the diagnosis of endogenous or primary depression in both inpatients and outpatients.

Table 3-3 summarizes the recommended DST procedure for inpatients and outpatients. The DST has many features of a useful laboratory test, including reasonable sensitivity and specificity and a definite range of abnormal results. The cortisol assay is available in most clinical laboratories and has been standardized in large populations. Since the DST requires few special test conditions, has no known side effects, and is highly acceptable to patients, it is practical to do in routine settings.

It is important to bear in mind that the DST is simply a confirmatory diagnostic test. A positive DST will confirm a diagnosis of endogenous or primary depression when the signs and symptoms are present (see Chapter 1). A negative DST is of no particular significance; that is, it does not rule out a diagnosis of depression. This conclusion follows from the less-than-perfect sensitivity and the substantial minority of false-negative tests.

The DST should be used when a diagnosis of endogenous depression is within the differential diagnosis being considered. It should not be used as a general screening test for all psychiatric patients. It is of critical importance that the medical exclusion criteria in Table 3-2 be strictly applied to avoid false positives and negatives. It is of equal importance to discuss the cortisol assay with your pathologist and tell him or her what you need with particular emphasis on the assay method, setting the standards in the critical range of cortisol concentrations (4–6 μg/dl), establishment of a cortisol criterion based on normals, and establishment of longitudinal assay quality control.

The DST appears to have further clinical utility as a laboratory index of recovery from depression. As noted earlier, in depressed pa-

TABLE 3-3. Recommended DST Procedure

Dexamethasone 1.0 mg p.o. or i.m. at 11 P.M.
Serum or plasma cortisol at 8 A.M., 4 P.M., and 11 P.M. the following day for inpatients and 4 P.M. hours for outpatients.
Serum or plasma cortisol criterion: 1. Competitive protein binding assay: 5.0 μg/dl 2. Radioimmunoassay: 4.0 μg/dl
An elevated serum or plasma cortisol in any blood sample is abnormal or nonsuppression.

tients with an initially positive DST treated with ECT or thymoleptic drugs, the DST shows progressive normalization as the depressive syndrome remits and it becomes normal at or just prior to complete clinical remission in most patients. Those few patients who remain DST-positive but appear to be in clinical remission have a poor short-term prognosis, with the likelihood of return of depressive symptoms, rehospitalization, or suicide during follow-up period. The suggestion is that the underlying depressive physiology is not completely treated. These findings have led some authors to suggest the DST is superior to clinician's judgment in deciding if the patient is in full remission—an interesting possibility.

While serial DSTs may be useful to monitor the efficacy of the somatic intervention and to determine when the patient is in full remission, serial DSTs should not be done more often than every 5–7 days to avoid the cumulative effects of dexamethasone. Greden and colleagues (1983) have shown that serial DSTs have no utility in monitoring treatment response in patients with an initially negative test, although they have found that patients withdrawn from antidepressant medications may convert a negative DST to positive in the drug-free state, perhaps due to partially remitted patients becoming more symptomatic. Whether the DST predicts response to somatic treatment in general or to a specific antidepressant drug remains to be clarified by further studies.

Other potentially useful applications of the DST include the prediction of relapse, the prediction of a new depressive episode, and the prediction of a phase shift (mania to depression or depression to mania) in bipolar patients. Further research is needed to explore these possibilities.

What is the theoretical significance of DST nonsuppression? DST nonsuppression reflects a neuroendocrine abnormality that is hypothesized to be a failure of the normal brain inhibitory mechanisms on the HPA axis (Carroll & Mendels, 1978; Sachar *et al.*, 1973). In other words, in depression there is a disinhibition of the HPA axis. Carroll *et al.* (1981) have shown that this is not just a nospecific stress response, since it is not present in other hospitalized psychiatric patients suffering from schizophrenia, nonendogenous depression, or a number of other stress-associated psychiatric illnesses.

This neuroendocrine abnormality is temporally associated with and relatively specific to episodes of endogenous depression. The limbic system exerts neural influence on the HPA axis and other physiological systems that are disturbed in endogenous depression, such as mood, sleep, appetite, pain, volition, pleasure, and psychomotor activity. This suggests that the neuroendocrine disturbance may be an indirect indicator of limbic system dysfunction in depression. The observation that the neuroendocrine fault may precede the development of the endogenous depressive syndrome further suggests that it may have greater pathophysiological or etiological significance.

Investigations into the neurotransmitter control of the HPA axis done largely in nonhuman subjects suggest that NE is inhibitory and 5-HT and ACh are excitatory (Carroll *et al.*, 1980; Reichlin, 1981). Carroll *et al.* (1980) have shown that physostigmine, a reversible acetylcholinesterase inhibitor, caused normal subjects to escape from dexamethasone suppression. Physostigmine induces an incomplete depressive syndrome in normal subjects, worsens symptoms in depressed subjects, and reduces manic symptomatology (Janowsky, El Yousef, & Davis, 1972). Taken together these data raise the possibility that a common neurotransmitter mechanism, cholinergic hyperactivity, may be responsible for both the neuroendocrine fault and the depressive syndrome. These findings are sure to be the subject of future research.

The Hypothalamic–Pituitary–Thyroid Axis

The hypothalamic–pituitary–thyroid (HPT) axis has many parallels to the HPA axis (see Figure 3-9). Thyrotropin-releasing hormone is the hypothalamic hormone that is produced by the hypophysiotropic neurons in the median eminence of the hypothalamus. TRH is secreted into the portal venous system of the pituitary. It stimulates the synthesis and release of thyroid-stimulating hormone (TSH). TSH stimulates the thyroid gland to produce and secrete thyroid hormones (T_3 and T_4). There is a negative-feedback servomechanism operative at both the pituitary and the hypothalamic level (Reichlin, 1981).

Thyroid function tests in patients with affective disorders have generally been found to be within the normal range. T_4, T_3, and T_3 resin uptake, as well as baseline TSH levels, are almost uniformly in the normal range in patients with depression and mania (Loosen & Prange, 1982). Some reports have noted a slight elevation of T_4 and the free thyroid index (FTI) in the early part of the depressive episode or mania, but these "elevations" are typically within the normal range (Loosen & Prange, 1982).

Another abnormality has been described in 24-hour catheter studies of TSH levels. A normal circadian rhythm for TSH secretion

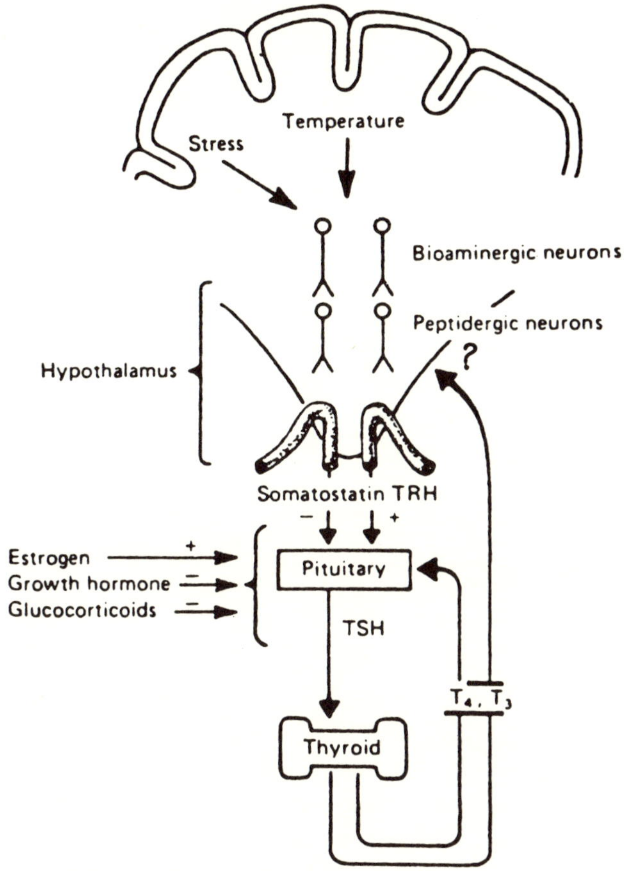

FIG. 3-9. HPT axis. From "Neuroendocrinology" by S. Reichlin, in R. H. Williams (Ed.), *Textbook of Endocrinology*, Philadelphia: Saunders, 1981, p. 612. Reprinted by permission.

has been described; thus in the middle of the sleep period there is a major episode of TSH release. In depressed patients, this TSH circadian rhythm and nocturnal release are absent (Golstein, VanCauter, Linkowski, Vanhaelst, & Mendlewicz, 1980).

Further, in some depressed subjects there is a failure to release TSH following exogenous TRH administration, which was first reported in 1972 (Prange, Wilson, Lara, Alltop, & Breese, 1972). A TRH stimulation test (TRH-ST) in a healthy control and a depressed patient are presented in Figure 3-10. TSH is measured in international microunits per milliliter. The study is conducted by drawing a baseline TSH level (0 minutes). Then TRH is given intravenously follow-

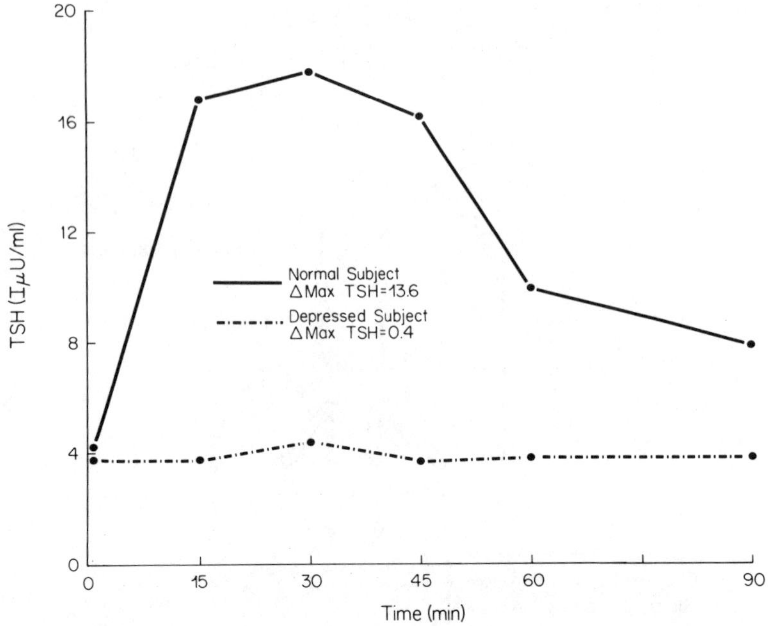

FIG. 3-10. The TRH-ST in a depressed and a normal subject.

ing the baseline sample. TSH levels are measured at 15-minute intervals for up to 90 minutes after the TRH infusion. As the normal control demonstrates, TRH causes a brisk secretion or release of TSH.

In healthy adults, TSH concentrations reach a maximum usually at 30 minutes after TRH infusion but almost always in the first 45 minutes, after which TSH levels return to near baseline at 120 to 180 minutes (Loosen, Mason, & Prange, 1982). In some depressed patients, this TSH response to TRH is absent or reduced. Note that while the depressed patient has a normal baseline TSH level, he or she has almost no response at all to TRH. The results of this test are usually reported as the difference between the highest TSH value after TRH administration minus the baseline value (Δ_{max} TSH). Δ_{max} TSH was 13.6 for the normal control and 0.4 for the depressed patient.

A Δ_{max} TSH of greater than or equal to 5.0 IμU/ml is considered normal, whereas a Δ_{max} TSH of less than 5.0 IμU/ml is blunted or abnormal (Loosen & Prange, 1982). The TRH stimulation test (TRH-ST) in psychiatric inpatients reveals that 30% to 60% of depressed patients (whether bipolar or unipolar) are blunted (Loosen & Prange, 1982). Similarly, bipolar patients in the mixed and manic phases will also have blunted TRH-ST responses (Kirkegaard, Bjorum, Cohn, &

Luridsen, 1978; Extein, Pottash, Gold, & Cowdry, 1982). TRH-ST blunting does not occur in schizophrenia, panic disorder, and other psychiatric illnesses, except for alcoholism and possibly anorexia nervosa (Loosen & Prange, 1982).

The TRH-ST was developed by clinical endocrinologists to aid the clinician in diagnosing thyroid disorders. The various available studies of the TRH-ST in psychiatric patients have used widely divergent TRH-ST techniques and methods to assess the results. Most psychiatric investigators use the TRH-ST technique developed by endocrinology.

Patients are typically studied in the midmorning (8 a.m. to 10 a.m.) in the recumbent position after an overnight fast. After one or two baseline TSH determinations (separated by 15 minutes), an intravenous challenge of TRH over 10–60 seconds is administered. Serum TSH levels are determined by RIA. The major source of variation of the TRH-ST technique is accounted for by TRH dose and TSH level sampling time. The dose of TRH used in psychiatric investigations includes 200 μg, 400 μg, 500 μg, or 600 μg. The TSH response to TRH is linear between 100 and 400 μg, above which a plateau is reached in the dose–response curve (Anderson *et al.*, 1971; Burger & Patel, 1977). Hence, among the various studies submaximal, maximal, and supramaximal doses of TRH have been used. After TRH administration, TSH levels are obtained at one or more times including 10, 15, 20, 30, 40, 45, 60, 90, 120, 150, and/or 180 minutes.

The results of the TRH-ST have been expressed in various ways, including: (1) the absolute level of TSH achieved at a certain time interval after TRH administration (usually 30 minutes); (2) the increment in TSH level at a certain time interval relative to baseline (Δ TSH); or (3) the maximum increment in TSH level relative to baseline observed in the first 60 to 90 minutes following TRH (Δ_{max} TSH).

In studies of psychiatric patients, the Δ_{max} has been most commonly used. Investigators have attempted to classify patients as either blunted or normal. While some argue for a Δ_{max} TSH threshold of 7.0 IμU/ml (Extein, Pottash, & Gold, 1981; Extein *et al.*, 1982), most (Loosen & Prange, 1982; Loosen *et al.*, 1982) argue for a more conservative 5.0 IμU/ml threshold value based on normal control data. Because of these methodological differences, results from different centers are very difficult to compare. Hence the literature on the TRH-ST in psychiatric patients is ostensibly confusing and often contradictory.

The TRH-ST is generally accepted as a measure of pituitary TSH stores (Haigler, Pittman, Hershman, & Baugh, 1971; Ormston, Garry, Cryer, Bersen, & Hall, 1971; Sawin & Hershman, 1976). Regardless of which TSH measure is used, the TRH-ST is an attempt to derive a simple index of the pituitary reserve of TSH. The best available or ideal measure of total TSH release is the area under the curve above baseline, which describes the change in TSH level with time (Wilkin, Baldet, Papachristou, & Jaffiol, 1979). Since this procedure requires several and frequent TSH determinations over a long time period, it is both impractical and costly.

We recently conducted a study in a psychiatrically ill population to identify the most accurate and simple index of pituitary TSH reserves. We found that Δ_{max} TSH based on four blood samples at 0 minutes (baseline), and at 15, 30, and 45 minutes following TRH infusion yielded the most accurate simple index from the TRH-ST (Schlesser, Rush, Fairchild, Crowley, & Orsulak, 1983). Loosen *et al.* (1982) reports similar findings in normal adults.

The TRH-ST procedure we recommend follows. The test is performed 2 days prior to DST to avoid the possibility that dexamethasone may artificially blunt the TSH response to TRH. The patient is kept fasting after midnight. The TRH-ST begins between 8 a.m. and 10 a.m. hours with the patient recumbent. An intravenous catheter is inserted into the forearm vein and a slow drip of normal saline is used to keep the line open. Ten milliters of blood are obtained at baseline. Samples are drawn at 15, 30, and 45 minutes after TRH infusion. TRH (500 μg) is administered by intravenous push over 5 to 10 seconds after the baseline sample is obtained. Serum TSH is determined by RIA (Schlesser, Rush, Fairchild, Crowley, & Orsulak, 1983). Δ_{max} TSH is calculated by subtracting the baseline TSH level from the highest TSH value after TRH administration. Table 3-4 lists those conditions and situations that confound the TRH-ST. The optimal procedure is to keep patients drug-free for at least 7 days prior to the procedure. False augmentation occurs in hypothyroidism, as well as in patients taking lithium or estrogen.

Whether the blunted TRH-ST is state- or trait-dependent abnormality is not clear. Some studies indicate that the TRH-ST becomes normal in clinical remission, while other studies find that depressed patients may have the abnormality in depression and it persists into euthymia (Loosen & Prange, 1982).

The blunted TRH stimulation test observed in depressed subjects is considered a neuroendocrine abnormality (Loosen & Prange, 1982). The reasoning is as follows: It is offered that during the initial stages

TABLE 3-4. Confounds of the TRH-ST

False blunting
Hyperthyroidism
Cushing's disease or syndrome
Pseudo-Cushing's syndrome of alcoholism
Renal failure
Klinefelter's syndrome
Starvation
Somatostatin
Neurotensin
Dopamine
Thyroid hormone
Glucocorticoids
Aspirin (possible)
Tylenol (possible)
Hepatic-enzyme-inducing drugs (alcohol, barbiturates, benzodiazepines, and other sedative-hypnotics)
Sedative-hypnotic drug withdrawal (possible)
Narcotic drug withdrawal (possible)

False augmentation
Hypothyroidism
Lithium
Estrogens

of depression and mania there is activation of the HPT axis, as evidenced by slight elevations in T_4 and FTI, although their values remain within the normal range. Increased TRH secretion and hence increased TSH secretion is proposed to be responsible for this transient hypersecretion of thyroid hormone. After chronic exposure of the pituitary to slightly elevated levels of TRH, thyrotrope cells in the anterior pituitary may become hyporesponsive to TRH possibly due to down-regulation of TRH receptors, resulting in the blunted TSH response to TRH that is observed (Loosen & Prange, 1982).

The TRH-ST is moderately sensitive (40%) and specific (90%) for the diagnosis of depression and mania, although it may not be as sensitive nor as specific as the DST for the diagnosis of depression. Whether the TRH-ST predicts response to different antidepressant drugs is unknown and has not been studied to date. Much like the DST, failure to normalize or improve the TRH-ST after thymoleptic treatment may be predictive of a poor course or prognosis—early relapse, return of symptoms, suicide, or rehospitalization (Loosen & Prange, 1982). Thus, the TRH-ST may be a laboratory index of recovery from depression. Further studies are needed to decisively answer this question. Whether the TRH-ST is predictive of incipient depression has not been studied at all.

The TRH-ST has been proposed by some to be a useful diagnostic test for depression (Extein *et al.*, 1981) and for mania (Extein *et al.*, 1982). Although the TRH-ST has reasonable specificity in the control groups studied (schizophrenia, neuroses, personality disorders, normals), many psychopathological groups have not been studied. The sensitivity, which is around 40% in most studies, varies from 20% to 75% depending on the patient samples. Obviously, the sensitivity and specificity are dependent on the Δ_{max} TSH criterion for blunting. The lack of high sensitivity and partially studied specificity, as well as cost, may argue against its use as a diagnostic test. The issues of sensitivity, specificity, and other control variables such as the effects of sex, age, and various medications require further study. Keeping in mind the limitations of the TRH-ST, some clinicians may choose to use the test as a diagnostic test. If so, strict adherence to medical exclusion criteria and the careful definition of normal control values are recommended, just as with the DST.

Recent studies have applied both the DST and the TRH-ST to the same population of depressed patients. About 20% to 30% of depressed patients are positive on both tests, 20% to 30% are positive on the TRH-ST only, and another 20% to 30% are positive on the DST only. Collectively, the two tests may identify 80% to 90% of depressed inpatients, although the detection rate in outpatients is lower (Rush, *et al.*, 1983). If these early studies are replicated, and the two abnormalities are independent of each other, then the TRH-ST may add to the laboratory armamentarium for the diagnosis of depression.

Further research in the neuroendocrinology of depression will likely fall into two general categories. The first will include further clinical studies to define the implications of these neuroendocrine abnormalities for diagnosis, prognosis, and treatment selection. The second will consist of basic studies designed to establish the neurotransmitter and other basic brain mechanisms that underly these neuroendocrine abnormalities.

REFERENCES

Albala, A. A., Greden, J. F., Tarika, J., & Carroll, B. J. (1981). Changes in serial dexamethasone suppression tests among unipolar depressives receiving electroconvulsive treatment. *Biological Psychiatry, 16,* 551–560.

Anderson, M. S., Bowers, C. Y., Kastin, A. J., Schlalch, D. S., Schally, A. V., Snyder, P. J., Utiger, R. D., Wilber, J. F., & Wise, A. J. (1971). Synthetic thyrotropin-releasing hormone: A potent stimulator of thyroptopin secretion in man. *New England Journal of Medicine, 285,* 1279.

Burger, H. G., & Patel, Y. C. (1977). TSH and TRH: Their physiological regulation and the clinical application of the TRH. In L. Martin & G. M. Besser (Eds.), *Clinical neuroendocrinology*. New York: Academic Press.

Carroll, B. J. (1978). Neuroendocrine function in psychiatric disorders. In M. A. Lipton, A. DiMascio, & K. F. Killam (Eds.), *Psychopharmacology: A generation of progress*. New York: Raven Press.

Carroll, B. J. (1979). Neuroendocrine function in mania. In B. Shopsin (Ed.), *Manic illness*. New York: Raven Press.

Carroll, B. J. (1982). The dexamethasone suppression test for melancholia. *British Journal of Psychiatry, 140,* 292–304.

Carroll, B. J., Curtis, G. C., & Mendels, J. (1976a). Neuroendocrine regulation in depression: I. Limbic system adrenocortical dysfunction. *Archives of General Psychiatry, 33,* 1039–1044.

Carroll, B. J., Curtis, G. C., & Mendels, J. (1976b). Neuroendocrine regulation in depression: II. Discrimination of depressed from nondepressed patients. *Archives of General Psychiatry, 33,* 1051–1058.

Carroll, B. J., Feinberg, M., Greden, J. F., Tarika, J., Albala, A. A., Haskett, R. F., James, N. M., Kronfol, Z., Lohr, N., Steiner, M., de Vigne, J. P., & Young, E. (1981). A specific laboratory test for the diagnosis of melancholia. *Archives of General Psychiatry, 38,* 15–22.

Carroll, B. J., Greden, J. F., & Feinberg, M. (1981). Suicide, neuroendocrine dysfunction and CSF 5-HIAA concentrations in depression. In B. Angrist (Ed.), *Recent advances in neuropsychopharmacology: Proceedings of the 12th CINP Congress.* Oxford: Pergamon Press.

Carroll, B. J., Greden, J. F., Haskett, R., Feinberg, M., Albala, A. A., Martin, F. I. R., Rubin, R. T., Heath, B., Sharp, P. T., McLeod, W. L., & McLeod, M. F. (1980). Neurotransmitter studies of neuroendocrine pathology in depression. *Acta Psychiatrica Scandinavica* (Suppl.), *280,* 183–199.

Carroll, B. J., & Mendels, J. (1978). Neuroendocrine regulation in affective disorders. In E. J. Sachar (Ed.), *Hormones, behavior, and psychopathology,* New York: Raven Press.

Coryell, W., & Schlesser, M. A. (1981). Suicide and the dexamethasone suppression test in unipolar depression. *American Journal of Psychiatry, 138,* 1120–1121.

Extein, I., Pottash, A. L. C., & Gold, M. S. (1981). The thyrotropin-releasing hormone test in the diagnosis of unipolar depression. *Psychiatry Research, 39,* 311.

Extein, I., Pottash, A. L. C., Gold, M. S., & Cowdry, R. W. (1982). Using the protirelin test to distinguish mania from schizophrenia. *Archives of General Psychiatry, 39,* 77–81.

Giles, D. E., & Rush, A. J. (1982). Relationship of dysfunctional attitudes and dexamethasone response in endogenous and nonendogenous depression. *Biological Psychiatry, 17,* 1303–1314.

Goldstein, J., VanCauter, E., Linkowski, P., Vanhaelst, L., & Mendlewicz, J. (1980). Thyrotropin nyctohemeral pattern in primary depression: Differences between unipolar and bipolar women. *Life Sciences, 27* (18); 1695–1703.

Graham, P. M., Booth, J., Boranga, G., Galhenage, S., Myers, C. M., Teoh, C., & Cox, L. S. (1982). The dexamethasone suppression test in mania. *Journal of Affective Disorders, 4,* 201–211.

Greden, J. F., Albala, A. A., Haskett, R. F., James, N. M., Goodman, L., Steiner, M., & Carroll, B. J. (1980). Normalization of dexamethasone suppression test: A laboratory index of recovery from endogenous depression. *Biological Psychiatry, 15,* 449–458.

Greden, J. F., de Vigne, J. P., Albala, A. A., Tarika, J., Buttenheim, M., Eiser, A., & Carroll, B. J. (1982). Serial dexamethasone suppression tests among rapidly cycling bipolar patients. *Biological Psychiatry, 17,* 455–461.

Greden, J. F., Gardner, R., King, D., Grunhaus, L., Carroll, B. J., & Kronfol, Z. (1983). Dexamethasone suppression tests in antidepressant treatment of melancholia. *Archives of General Psychiatry, 40,* 493–500.

Greden, J. F., Kronfol, Z., Gardner, R., Feinberg, F., Mukhopadhyay, S., Albala, A. A., & Carroll, B. J. (1981). Dexamethasone suppression test and selection of antidepressant medications. *Journal of Affective Disorders, 3,* 389–396.

Grossman, A., Perry, L., Schally, A. V., Rees, L. H., Nieuwenhuyzen-Kruseman, A. C., Tomlin, S., Coy, D. H., Comaru-Schally, A., & Besser, G. M. (1982). New hypothalamic hormone, corticotropin-releasing factor, specifically stimulates the release of adrenocorticotropic hormone and cortisol in man. *Lancet, 1,* 921–922.

Gwirtsman, H., Gerner, R. H., & Sternbach, H. (1982). The ovenight dexamethasone suppression test: Clinical and theoretical review. *Psychiatry, 43,* 321–327.

Haigler, E. D., Pittman, J. A., Hershman, J. M., & Baugh, C. M. (1971). Direct evaluation of pituitary thyrotropin reserve utilizing synthetic TRH. *Journal of Clinical Endocrinology and Metabolism, 33,* 573.

Holsboer, F., Liebl, R., & Hofschuster, E. (1982). Repeated dexamethasone suppression test during depressive illness. *Journal of Affective Disorders, 4,* 93–101.

Holsboer, F., Steiger, A., & Maier, W. (1983). Four cases of reversion to abnormal dexamethasone suppression test response as indicator of clinical relapse: A preliminary report. *Biological Psychiatry, 18,* 911–916.

Janowsky, D. C., El Yousef, M. C., & Davis, J. M. (1972). Cholinergic–adrenergic hypothesis of mania and depression. *Lancet, 2,* 632–635.

Kirkegaard, C., Bjorum, N., Cohn, D., & Luridsen, U. B. (1978). Thyrotropin-releasing hormone (TRH) stimulation test in manic-depressive illness. *Archives of General Psychiatry, 35,* 1017–1021.

Loosen, P. T., Mason, G. A., & Prange, A. J., Jr. (1982). The TRH test in normal subjects: Methological considerations. *Psychoneuroendocrinology, 7,* 147–153.

Loosen, P. T., & Prange, A. J., Jr. (1982). Serum thyrotropin response to thyrotropin-releasing hormone in psychiatric patients: A review. *American Journal of Psychiatry, 139,* 405–416.

Ormston, B. J., Garry, R., Cryer, R. J., Bersen, G. M., & Hall, R. (1971). TRH as a thyroid function test. *Lancet, 2,* 10.

Papakostas, Y., Fink, M., Lee, J., Irwin, P., & Johnson, L. (1981). Neuroendocrine measures in psychiatric patients: Course and outcome with ECT. *Psychiatry Research, 4,* 55–64.

Prange, A. J., Jr., Wilson, I. C., Lara, P. P., Alltop, L. B., & Breese, G. R. (1972). Effects of thyrotropin-releasing hormone in depression. *Lancet, 2,* 999–1002.

Reichlin, S. (1981). Neuroendocrinology. In R. H. Williams (Ed.), *Textbook of endocrinology* (6th ed.). Philadelphia: W. B. Saunders.

Rose, R. M., & Sachar, E. (1981). Psychoendocrinology. In R. H. Williams (Ed.), *Textbook of endocrinology* (6th ed.). Philadelphia: W. B. Saunders.

Rush, A. J., Giles, D. E., Roffwarg, H. P., & Parker, C. R. (1982). Sleep EEG and dexamethasone suppression test findings in outpatients with unipolar major depressive disorders. *Biological Psychiatry, 17,* 327–340.

Rush, A. J., Schlesser, M. A., Giles, D. E., Crowley, G. T., Fairchild, C., & Altshuler, K. Z. (1982). The effect of dosage on the dexamethasone suppression test in normal controls. *Psychiatry Research, 7,* 277–285.

Rush, A. J., Schlesser, M. A., Giles, D. E., Orsulak, P., Parker, C. R., Weissenburger, J., Crowley, G. T., Khatami, M., & Vasavada, N. *The dexamethasone suppression test as a diagnostic test.* Manuscript submitted for publication.

Rush, A. J., Schlesser, M. A., Roffwarg, H. P., Giles, D. E., Orsulak, P. J., & Fairchild, C. (1983). Relationships among the TRH, REM latency and dexamethasone suppression tests: Preliminary findings. *Journal of Clinical Psychiatry, 44,* 23–29.

Sachar, E. J., Hellman, L., Roffwarg, H. P., Halpern, F. S., Fukushima, D. K., & Gallagher, T. F. (1973). Disrupted 24-hour patterns of cortisol secretions in psychotic depression. *Archives of General Psychiatry, 28,* 19–24.

Sawin, S. T., & Hershman, J. M. (1976). The TSH response to TRH in young adult men: Intraindividual variation and relation to basal TSH and thyroid hormones. *Journal of Clinical Endocrinology and Metabolism, 42,* 809.

Schlesser, M. A., & Rush, A. J. (1982, May). DST status in relation to desipramine response. *Abstract of the Society of Biological Psychiatry,* Toronto, p. 79.

Schlesser, M. A., & Rush, A. J. (1981, May). Serial changes in hypothalamic–pituitary–adrenal axis activity among depressed patients receiving ECT. *Abstract of the Society of Biological Psychiatry,* New Orleans, p. 69.

Schlesser, M. A., Rush, A. J., Fairchild, C., Crowley, G., & Orsulak, P. (1983). The thyrotropin-releasing hormone stimulation test: A methodological study. *Psychiatry Research, 9,* 59–67.

Schlesser, M. A., Rush, A. J., Orsulak, P., & Crowley, G. (1983, July). Serial measurement of hypothalamic–pituitary–adrenal axis activity in rapid cycling bipolar subjects. *Abstract of the VIIth World Congress of Psychiatry,* Vienna, p. 496.

Schlesser, M. A., Winokur, G., & Rush, A. J. (1981, June–July). The dexamethasone suppression test in schizoaffective psychosis. *Abstract of the IIIrd World Congress of Biological Psychiatry.* Stockholm, p. 363.

Schlesser, M. A., Winokur, G., & Sherman, B. M. (1979). Genetic subtypes of unipolar primary depressive illness distinguished by hypothalamic–pituitary–adrenal axis axtivity. *Lancet, 1,* 740–741.

Schlesser, M. A., Winokur, G., & Sherman, B. M. (1980). Hypothalamic–pituitary–adrenal axis activity in depressive illness. *Archives of General Psychiatry, 37,* 737–743.

Vale, W., Spiess, J., Rivier, C., & Rivier, J. (1981). Characterization of a 41-residue ovine hypothalamic peptide that stimulates secretion of corticotropin and β-endorphin. *Science, 213,* 1394–1397.

Wilkin, T. J., Baldet, L., Papachristou, C., & Jaffiol, C. (1979). The TRH test: Which is the best index of TSH release? *Annales d'Endocrinologie, 40,* 495.

4

Norepinephrine and Depression

JAMES W. MAAS

Over the past two decades we have greatly increased our understanding of the biological processes in affective disorders (i.e., depression and mania). Several areas in which altered biological processes are known to be relevant are reviewed elsewhere in this volume. This chapter focuses, for the most part, on issues revolving about clinical studies of catecholamine metabolism in depression.

I will first review early findings which suggested that catecholamine metabolism and/or disposition might be altered in patients with depression, and then consider the theoretical and practical problems relevant to interpreting measures of catecholamines and their metabolites. I will also review clinical studies dealing with catecholamines in depression, more specifically norephinephrine (NE), and will indicate those findings about which there appears to be some agreement as well as those about which there is controversy. The final section summarizes research findings relevant to the use of NE and its metabolites as predictors of response to specific antidepressants.

(In the 1950s a small but significant number of patients being treated for hypertension with a rauwolfia alkaloid developed depressions clinically indistinguishable from the naturally occurring disorders (Ayd, 1958; Faucett, Litin, & Achor, 1957; Jensen, 1959; Lemieux, Davignon, & Genest, 1956). At about the same time it was observed that patients with tuberculosis being treated with iproniazid developed elevations in mood above and beyond those expected from an improvement in physical health alone. Concurrent work revealed that iproniazid was a monomine oxidase inhibitor (Zeller, Barsky, Fouts, Kirchheimer, & VanOrden, 1952), and its administration was associated with an increase in brain biogenic amines, such as catecholamines (CA) and serotonin (5-HT), whereas the rauwolfia alkaloid

JAMES W. MAAS. Department of Psychiatry, University of Texas Health Science Center, San Antonio, Texas.

reserpine depleted brain of these amines (Shore, 1962). These findings suggested the possibility that increases in brain amines might be associated with states of hypomania or mania, whereas decrements in these amines could be associated with depression (Jacobsen, 1964).

This possibility was further strengthened when it was found that tricyclic antidepressants, such as imipramine, produced a blockade of the reuptake of NE and 5-HT and, therefore, might be expected to produce an increased amount of amine at the synapse (Glowinski & Axelrod, 1964; Maas, 1975). Additional findings about the effects of a variety of depressant and stimulating pharmacological agents were also consistent with the suggestion that brain biogenetic amines had a role in the regulation of mood (Schildkraut & Kety, 1967).

These clinical and basic neuropsychopharmacological data prompted a series of clinical investigations into the possible role of NE in the pathogenesis of depression. In order to understand the approaches that were taken in these clinical studies, let us briefly review the data relevant to the metabolism of NE in the brain (see Figure 4-1). For concentrations within the physiological range, there is a barrier to the movement of NE, epinephrine (E), metanephrine (M), and normetanephrine (NM) out of, as well as into, the brain (Glowinski, Kopin, & Axelrod, 1965; Maas & Landis, 1966; Weil-Malherbe, Whitby, & Axelrod, 1961). Epinephrine is present in brain in specific neuronal systems (Hokfelt, Fuxe, Goldstein, & Johansson, 1961), but the quantity found in the whole brain is far less than that of NE (Gunne, 1962). Vanillylmandelic acid (VMA) is a minor metabolite in the brain, whereas 3-methoxy-4-hydroxyphenylglycol (MHPG) is a major metabolite, with the ratios of MHPG to VMA being approximately 10:1. The formation of dihydroxyphenylglycol (DHPG) has been less well studied, but it appears that the ratio of MHPG to DHPG in the primate brain is of the order of 5:1 (Karoum, Neff, & Wyatt, 1976; Maas & Landis, 1968; Sjoquist, 1975). In the rat brain MHPG is almost totally conjugated, whereas in man it is present principally, if not totally, in the free form (Maas, Landis, & Dekirmenjian, 1976; Schanberg, Breese, Schildkraut, Gordon, & Kopin, 1968).

For reasons apparent from the above comments, clinical studies of NE metabolism in affective illness have tended to focus on the measurement of MHPG in either urine or cerebrospinal fluid (CSF). Before reviewing these studies, some comments about the appropriateness of these approaches, given recent research data, should be made.

Much research effort has been directed toward obtaining an estimate of the contribution of MHPG by brain to plasma MHPG or

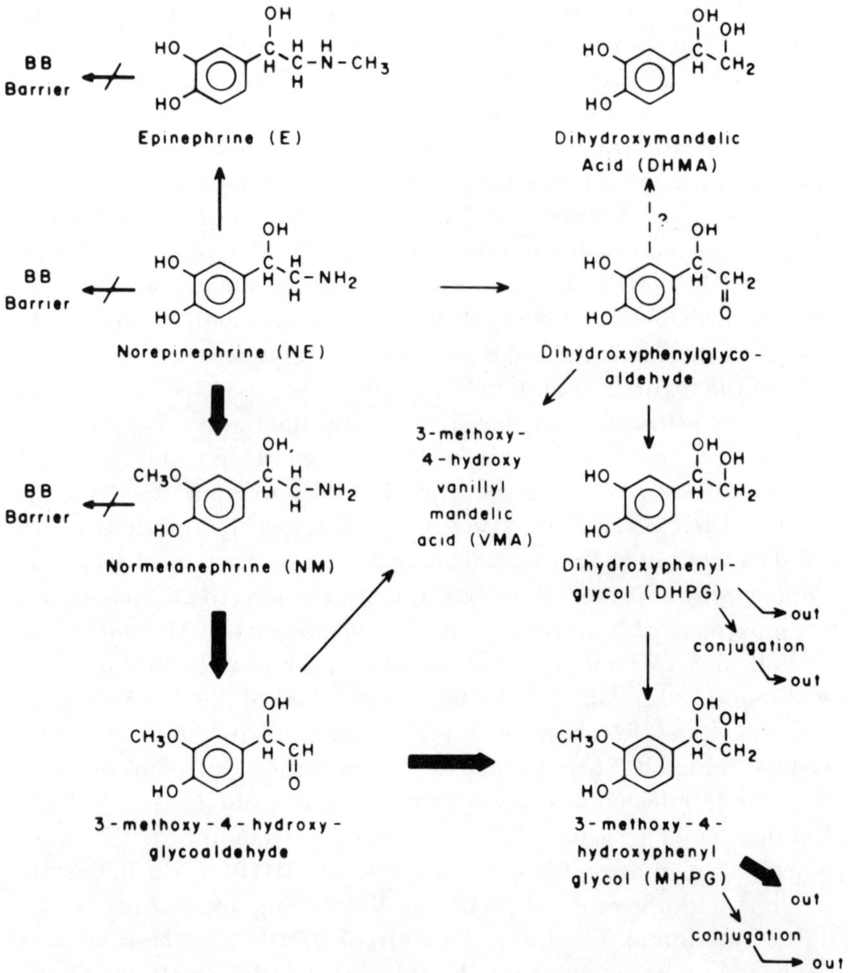

FIG. 4-1. Routes of metabolism of norepinephrine.

urinary MHPG, and this remains an area of controversy. Using a simple "overflow" model, it appears that in the rat the amount is quite small, 5% to 30% (Bareggi, Marc, & Morselli, 1974; Breese *et al.*, 1972; Helmeste, Stancer, Coscina, Takahashi, & Warsh, 1979; Karoum, Wyatt, & Costa, 1974), whereas in primates, including man, estimates range between 20% and 65% (Maas, Dekirmenjian, Garver, Redmon, & Landis, 1973; Maas, Hattox, Greene, & Landis, 1979). The interpretation of these estimates is further complicated by the fact that an (appreciable quantity of MHPG may be converted to VMA, with the estimates ranging from 27% to 50%)(Blombery, Kopin, Gordon, Markey, & Ebert, 1980; La Brosse, 1970; Mardh, Sjoquist, & Anggard, 1981).

The direct application of this "overflow model," which simplistically relies on estimates of how much MHPG originates in brain and how much originates in body pools other than the brain, is also made difficult by the recent demonstration that central nervous system (CNS) noradrenergic cell bodies have major descending tracts in the spinal cord. These tracts probably have a role in the regulation of outflow in the sympathetic nervous system. Thus, activity in CNS noradrenergic neurons is probably related to impulse flow in the sympathetic nervous system. Hence, changes in plasma or urinary levels of NE and metabolites may provide indices of CNS noradrenergic function even though, in the case of NE for example, the direct contribution to peripheral pools of NE by brain is nil (Maas & Leckman, 1983).

In CSF no ventriculolumbar gradient for MHPG has been found. Spinal cord transections in humans are associated with no change in CSF MHPG, and a block of CSF flow between higher and lower centers is associated with no decrement in lumbar CSF MHPG (Chase, Gordon, & Ng, 1973; Post, Goodwin, Gordon, & Watkin, 1973). These data, as well as estimates of the rate of MHPG clearance in the spinal cord (Wolfson & Escriva, 1976), suggest that lumbar CSF MHPG may not provide a good estimate of NE metabolism by brain. It has also been noted that CSF MHPG is continuously lost through capillaries within the spinal cord; that is, the deeper the site of the metabolite production the smaller proportion expected to reach CSF. For this reason, the degree to which lumbar CSF MHPG will reflect NE metabolism has been questioned (Kessler, Fenstermacher, & Patlak, 1976).

Despite these problems and caveats, a number of studies dealing with MHPG in depressed and healthy subjects have resulted in data having heuristic value. Some of these studies are reviewed next.

In 1968, preliminary results were reported indicating that a diagnostically heterogeneous group of depressed patients had significantly less MHPG in their urine than did a healthy group of controls. In contrast, the quantities of NM and M found in the urine of both groups were not significantly different (Maas, Fawcett, & Dekirmenjian, 1968a, 1968b). This initial report prompted a series of investigations to compare the amount of MHPG in the urine of various diagnostic subtypes of depression with each other as well as with the controls. Goodwin and Potter (1979) summarized these studies and found that by 1978 data were available from 312 depressed patients and 173 controls.

Examination of these data from individual studies as well as in the aggregate suggested that *as a group* depressed patients may not differ significantly from the normal controls in concentrations of urinary MHPG. However, when patients were divided into the unipolar and bipolar groupings, most investigators did find that bipolars as a group excreted less than normal amounts of urinary MHPG.

The recent findings of the six-university NIMH Collaborative Study of the Psychobiology of Depression—Biological Studies are relevant to this question (Maas *et al.*, 1980; Koslow *et al.*, 1983). In this study, 132 depressed patients and 80 normal healthy controls were studied. Urinary MHPG excretion rates did not differentiate between unipolars and bipolars and healthy controls. However, depressed patients as a group did have significantly elevated levels of NE, E, NM, M, and VMA compared to normal controls. This finding of no significant difference in MHPG between the groups, in the light of the evidence indicating that NE and E and all other metabolites were *elevated* in depressed patients, raises the possibility that in order to properly interpret MHPG excretion rates, other measures of adrenergic function may be essential.

In addition to the cross-sectional studies, five separate groups of investigators have studied the relationship of depression to urinary MHPG using a longitudinal approach. That is, they followed bipolar patients who cycled between depression, euthymia, and hypomania and compared urinary MHPG excretion rates during these phases in the same subjects. Four of the five groups found that these patients excreted *less* MHPG when depressed than when euthymic or hypomanic (Bond, Jenner, & Sampson, 1972; Greenspan *et al.*, 1970; Jones, Maas, Dekirmenjian, & Fawcett, 1973; Post *et al.*, 1977; Shopsin, Wilk, Gershon, Roffman, & Goldstein, 1974).

A more recent report indicated that in a group of patients followed for 10 months or longer, recovery from depression was associated with an increment in MHPG, whereas for those patients who did not recover the MHPG remained low (Pickar, Sweeney, Maas, & Heninger, 1978). These findings during the follow-up period were obtained during a drug-free state. In the aggregate, these findings indicate that urinary MHPG changes with the clinical state, and as such does not reflect some permanent characteristic of the patient.

The issue of whether the changes in patients followed longitudinally might be a function of activity level has been studied by different groups. One report suggested that changes in MHPG may be an artifact of decreased patient activity, whereas other investigators have found no differences in urinary levels of MHPG between agitated and retarded depressed patients (Ebert, Post, & Goodwin, 1972; Goodwin & Post, 1975; Greenspan *et al.*, 1970; Schildkraut, 1974). Another group also found that strenuous isotonic and isometric exercises by healthy subjects produced no significant changes in urinary MHPG, even though there were marked, and expected, changes in NE (Goode, Dekirmenjian, Meltzer, & Maas, 1973).

Some evidence suggests, however, that anxiety and MHPG levels may be related; that is, as anxiety levels increase, urinary MHPG increases (Sweeney, Maas, & Heninger, 1978). The relationship of these findings to the interpretation of the data obtained with depressed patients, however, is questionable, since most depressed patients are also quite anxious and, hence, it would be theoretically expected that MHPG levels would be elevated rather than decreased.

In addition to the diagnostic criteria used above to identify subgroups of depressed patients, a subcategorization has also been made, using biochemical and pharmacological criteria. The origins of these classifications and recent findings which are relevant to them are described next. In 1968 we reported that patients who previously had excellent therapeutic response to treatment with imipramine or desmethylimipramine had low pretreatment urinary MHPG values, whereas those patients who were unequivocal nonresponders to these medications had normal or higher than normal urinary MHPG values (Maas, Fawcett, & Dekirmenjian, 1968a). These findings were later replicated (Maas, Fawcett, & Dekirmenjian, 1972).

Concurrent with these studies relating pretreatment MHPG level to clinical response, a separate series of investigations were undertaken to see if one could predict the subsequent efficacy of treatment with imipramine by giving a trial of *d*-amphetamine. The serendipitous findings noted above as to a relationship between pretreatment MHPG and subsequent treatment response to impramine emerged just as these amphetamine drug response investigations were being pursued. For this reason, the preamphetamine urines of patients were assayed for MHPG. We found that those patients who had an elevation of mood after administration of *d*-amphetamine had *lower* predrug urinary MHPG values than did patients who did not have a brightening of mood after a trial of *d*-amphetamine (Fawcett,Maas, & Dekirmenjian, 1972). In addition, there was a positive and significant relationship between the positive mood induced by *d*-amphetamine and the presence of a subsequent response to imipramine (Fawcett & Siomopoulous, 1971).

In a separate study, Schildkraut (1973) noted that patients who had high or abnormal pretreatment values for urinary MHPG responded well to amitriptyline, whereas a lower MHPG value was associated with a failure to respond to amitriptyline.

These findings dealing with different responses to *d*-amphetamine and antidepressant drugs as a function of a pretreatment chemical measure were thought to have both theoretical and practical implications. From the theoretical standpoint, they suggested the possibility that there was a biochemically and pharmacologically identifiable subtype of depression associated with a disorder in NE metabolism and/or disposition; that is, the data were consistent with the notion that depression was a biochemically heterogeneous disorder. From the practical standpoint, these data suggested that there might be a biochemical and/or pharmacological test that would be helpful in choosing a particular tricyclic antidepressant for treatment.

Because of these theoretical as well as practical issues, studies of realtionships between pretreatment urinary MHPG and subsequent treatment response to a variety of tricyclic antidepressants have been undertaken by other investigative groups. Briefly, these data may be summarized as follows. There are five separate reports (Beckmann & Goodwin, 1975; Cobbin, Requin-Blow, Williams, & Williams, 1979; Maas, Fawcett, & Dekirmenjian, 1972; Maas *et al.*, 1982; Rosenbaum *et al.*, 1980) which indicate that a low pretreatment urinary MHPG is associated with an increased incidence of subsequent response to imipramine, whereas a high urinary MHPG is associated with decreased incidence of response to imipramine. (In general, in these studies "high" and "low" MHPG excretion rates do not refer to normative values but rather to high or low values relative to other patients within the group studied. For example, in the recent NIMH Collaborative Study, a patient was designated as being a high or low MHPG excretor if the urinary MHPG value was higher or lower respectively than the median value for all depressed patients.)

Similar findings have also been reported for the drugs maprotiline and nortriptyline (Hollister, Davis, & Berger, 1980; Rosenbaum *et al.*, 1980). For amitriptyline there have been a total of seven studies, four of which have demonstrated relationships between amitriptyline response and pretreatment urinary MHPG, whereas three others have not (Beckmann & Goodwin, 1975; Cobbin *et al.*, 1979; Coppen, Rama Rao, Ruthven, Goodwin, & Sandler, 1979; Gaertner, Kreuter, Scharek, Wiatr, & Breyer-Pfaff, 1982; Modai, Apter, Golomb, & Wijsenbeek, 1979; Sacchetti, Smeraldi, Cagnasso, Biondi, & Bellodi, 1976; Schildkraut, 1973).

Some of the complexities of these possible relationships between catecholamine metabolism and subsequent antidepressant drug response, however, are highlighted by the recent findings which have emerged from the NIMH Collaborative Study of Depression. In this study of 104 depressed patients, the relationships previously cited between pretreatment urinary MHPG and imipramine drug response were found. However, in addition, it was found that there were similar relationships between urinary NE and E and subsequent response to imipramine treatment. To further complicate the issue, it was also noted that when the patient groups were divided into bipolar and unipolar subtypes, the relationships noted were found only for the bipolar group. Moreover, when the bipolar group was further examined, trends approaching the level of statistical significance were noted between urinary VMA and CSF MHPG and the subsequent type of imipramine response. Thus, there appears to be possible a relationship between the preexisting state of adrenergic systems and drug response in a particular diagnostically definable subgroup of patients. As an additional, interesting sidelight, the collaborative study also found that low CSF 5-hydroxyindoleacetic acid (5-HIAA) was associated with a subsequent increased chance of response to imipramine, and that this occurred in unipolar but not bipolar patients.

In summary, the available data suggest the following:

1. Pretreatment urinary MHPG values, and probably other measures of the functional state of adrenergic systems, are associated with the type of response patients will have to imipramine. The possibility that this may also be true for maprotiline and nortriptyline requires further replication. The relationship between MHPG and subsequent response to amitriptyline remains uncertain because of the conflicting findings reported by different investigative groups.
2. Depression is probably a biochemically heterogeneous illness. Its subgroups may be definable by pharmacological and diag-

nostic markers in conjunction with other biochemical indicators of the functional state of adrenergic and serotonergic systems.

ACKNOWLEDGMENT

This work was supported in part by NIMH Collaborative Study Grant 7U01-MH38084-01, and by the Mary Yates Memorial Fund through the Hogg Foundation for Mental Health, University of Texas.

REFERENCES

Ayd, F. J., Jr. (1958). Drug-induced depression—fact or fallacy. *New York Medical Journal, 58,* 354–356.

Bareggi, S. R., Marc, V., & Morselli, P. L. (1974). Urinary excretion of 3-methoxy-4-hydroxyphenylglycol sulfate in rats after intraventricular injections of 6-OHDA. *Brain Research, 75,* 177–180.

Beckmann, H., & Goodwin, F. (1975). Antidepressant response to tricyclics and urinary MHPG in unipolar patients. *Archives of General Psychiatry, 32,* 17–21.

Blombery, P. A., Kopin, I. J., Gordon, E. K., Markey, S. P., & Ebert, M. H. (1980). Conversion of MHPG to vanillylmandelic acid. *Archives of General Psychiatry, 37,* 1095–1099.

Bond, P. A., Jenner, F. A., & Sampson, G. A. (1972). Daily variations of the urine content of MHPG in two manic-depressive patients. *Psychological Medicine, 2,* 81–85.

Breese, G. R., Prange, A. J., Howard, M. A., Lipton, M. A., McKinney, W. P., Beaman, R. E., & Bushness, P. (1972). 3-Methoxy-4-hydroxyphenylglycol excretion and behavioral changes in rat and monkey after central sympathectomy with 6-hydroxydopamine. *Nature New Biology, 240,* 286–287.

Chase, T. N., Gordon, E. D., & Ng, L. K. Y. (1973). Norepinephrine metabolism in the central nervous system of man: Studies using 3-methoxy-4-hydroxyphenethyleneglycol in cerebrospinal fluid. *Journal of Neurochemistry, 21,* 581–587.

Cobbin, D. M., Requin-Blow, B., & Williams, L. R., & Williams, O. R. (1979). Urinary MHPG levels and tricyclic antidepressant drug selection. *Archives of General Psychiatry, 36,* 1111–1118.

Coppen, A., Rama Rao, V. A., Ruthven, C. R. J., Goodwin, B. L., & Sandler, M. (1979). urinary 4-hydroxy-3-methoxyphenylglycol is not a predictor for clinical response to amitriptyline in depressive illness. *Psychopharmacology, 64,* 95–97.

Ebert, M. H., Post, R. M., & Goodwin, F. K. (1972). Effect of physical activity on urinary MHPG excretion in depressed patients (letter). *Lancet, 2,* 766.

Faucett, R. L., Litin, E. M., & Achor, R. W. P. (1957). Neuropharmacologic action of rauwolfia compounds and its psychodynamic implications. *Archives of Neurology and Psychiatry, 77,* 513–518.

Fawcett, J., Maas, J. W., & Dekirmenjian, H. (1972). Depression and MHPG excretion: Response to dextroamphetamine and tricyclic antidepressants. *Archives of General Psychiatry, 26,* 246–251.

Fawcett, J., & Siomopoulous, V. (1971). Dextroamphetamine response as a possible predictor of improvement with tricyclic therapy in depression. *Archives of General Psychiatry, 25,* 247–255.

Gaertner, H. J., Kreuter, F., Scharek, G., Wiatr, G., & Breyer-Pfaff, U. (1982). Do urinary MHPG and plasma drug levels correlate with response to amitriptyline therapy? *Psychopharmacology, 76,* 236–239.

Glowinski, J., & Axelrod, J. (1964). Inhibition of uptake of tritiated noradrenaline in the intact rat brain by imipramine and structurally related compounds. *Nature, 204,* 1318–1319.

Glowinski, J., Kopin, I. J., & Axelrod, J. (1965). Metabolism of [^{3}H] norepinephrine in rat brain. *Journal of Neurochemistry, 12,* 25–30.

Goode, D. J., Dekirmenjian, H., Meltzer, H. Y., & Maas, J. W. (1973). Relation of exercise to MHPG excretion in normal subjects. *Archives of General Psychiatry, 29,* 391–396.

Goodwin, F. K., & Potter, W. Z. (1979). Norepinephrine metabolite studies in affective illness. In E. Usdin, I. Kopin, & J. Barchas (Eds.), *Catecholamines: Vol. 2. Basic and clinical frontiers.* (pp. 1863–1865). New York: Pergamon Press.

Goodwin, F. K., & Post, R. M. (1975). Studies of amine metabolites in affective illness and schizophrenia: A comparative analysis. In D. X. Freedman (Ed.), *Biology of the major psychoses: A comparative analysis* (pp. 299–332). New York: Raven Press.

Greenspan, J., Schildkraut, J. J., Gordon, E. K., Baer, L., Aronoff, M. S., & Durell, J. (1970). Catecholamine metabolism in affective disorders: III. 3-Methoxy-4-hydroxyphenylglycol and other catecholamine metabolites in patients treated with lithium carbonate. *Journal of Psychiatric Research, 7,* 171–183.

Gunne, L. M. (1962). Relative adrenaline content in brain tissue. *Acta Physiologica Scandinavica, 56,* 324–333.

Helmeste, D. M., Stancer, H. G., Coscina, D. V., Takahashi, S., & Warsh, J. J. (1979). The contribution of CNS to plasma MHPG in the rat. *Life Sciences, 25,* 601–606.

Hokfelt, T., Fuxe, K., Goldstein, M., & Johansson, O. (1974). Immunohistochemical evidence for the existence of adrenaline neurons in the rat brain. *Brain Research, 66,* 235–251.

Hollister, L. E., Davis, K. L., & Berger, P. A. (1980). Subtypes of depression based on excretion of MHPG and response to nortriptyline. *Archives of General Psychiatry, 37,* 1107–1110.

Jacobsen, E. (1964). The theoretical basis of the chemotherapy of depression. In E. B. Davies (Ed.), *Depression: Proceedings of the symposium held at Cambridge.* Cambridge: Cambridge University Press.

Jensen, K. (1959). Depression in patients treated with reserpine for arterial hypertension. *Acta Psychiatrica Neurologica Scandinavica, 34,* 195–204.

Jones, F., Maas, J. W., Dekirmenjian, H., & Fawcett, J. A. (1973). Urinary catecholamine metabolites during behavioral changes in a patient with manic-depressive cycles. *Science, 179,* 300–302.

Karoum, F., Neff, N. H., & Wyatt, R. J. (1967). Distribution and turnover rate of vanillylmandelic acid and 3-methoxy-4-hydroxyphenylglycol in rat brain. *Journal of Neurochemistry, 27,* 33–35.

Karoum, F., Wyatt, R. J., & Costa, E. (1974). Estimation of the contribution of peripheral and central noradreneregic neurones to urinary 3-methoxy-4-hydroxyphenylglycol in the rat. *Neuropharmacology, 13,* 165–176.

Kessler, J. A., Fenstermacher, J. D., & Patlak, C. S. (1976). 3-Methoxy-4-hydroxyphenethyleneglycol (MHPG) transport from the spinal cord during spinal subarachnoid perfusion. *Brain Research, 102,* 131–141.

Koslow, S. H., Maas, J. W., Bowden, C. L., Davis, J., Hanin, I., & Javaid, J. (1983). Cerebrospinal fluid and urinary biogenic amines and metabolites in depression, mania, and healthy controls: A univariate analysis. *Archives of General Psychiatry, 40,* 999–1010.

LaBrosse, E. H. (1970). Catecholamine metabolism in neroblastoma: Kinetics of conversion of ^{3}H-3-methoxy-4-hydroxyphenylglycol to ^{3}H-3-methoxy-4-hydroxymandelic acid. *Journal of Clinical Endocrinology, 30,* 580–589.

Lemieux, G., Davignon, A., & Genest, J. (1965). Depressive states during rauwolfia therapy for arterial hypertension. *Canadian Medical Association Journal, 74*, 522–526.

Maas, J. W. (1975). Biogenic amines and depression. *Archives of General Psychiatry, 32*, 1357–1361.

Maas, J. W., Davis, J., Hanin, I., Kocsis, J. H., Redmond, D. E., Bowden, C. L., & Robins, E. (1982). Pre-treatment neurotransmitter metabolites in response to imipramine and amitriptyline treatment. *Psychological Medicine, 12*, 37–43.

Maas, J. W., Dekirmenjian, H., Garver, D., Redmond, D. E., Jr., & Landis, D. H. (1973). Excretion of catecholamine metabolites following intraventricular injection of 6-hydroxydopamine in the *Macaca speciosa. European Journal of Pharmacology, 23*, 121–130.

Maas, J. W., Fawcett, J. A., & Dekirmenjian, H. (1968a). *Catecholamine metabolism and the depressive states.* Paper presented at the annual meeting of the American Psychiatric Association, Boston.

Maas, J. W., Fawcett, J. A., & Dekirmenjian, H. (1968b). 3-Methoxy-4-hydroxyphenethyleneglycol (MHPG) excretion in depressive states. *Archives of General Psychiatry, 19*, 129–134.

Maas, J. W., Fawcett, J. A., & Dekirmenjian, H. (1972). Catecholamine metabolism, depressive illness, and drug response. *Archives of General Psychiatry, 26*, 252–262.

Maas, J. W., Hattox, S. E., Greene, N. M., & Landis, D. H. (1979). 3-Methoxy-4-hydroxyphenethyleneglycol (MHPG) production by human brain in vivo. *Science, 205*, 1025–1027.

Maas, J. W., Koslow, S., Davis, J., Katz, M., Mendels, J., Robins, E., Stokes, P., & Bowden, C. (1980). An overview: Biological component of the NIMH Clinical Research Branch collaborative considerations. *Psychological Medicine, 10*. 759–776.

Maas, J. W., & Landis, D. H. (1966). A technique for assaying the kinetics of norepinephrine metabolism in brain in vivo. *Psychosomatic Medicine, 28*, 247–256.

Maas, J. W., & Landis, D. H. (1968). In vivo studies of the metabolism of norepinephrine in the central nervous system. *Journal of Pharmacology and Experimental Therapeutics, 163*, 147–162.

Maas, J. W., Landis, D. H., & Dekirmenjian, H. (1976). The occurrence of free vs. conjugated MHPG in non-human and human primate brain. *Psychopharmacology Communications, 2*, 403–410.

Maas, J. W., & Leckman, J. F. (1983). Relationships between central nervous system noradrenergic function and plasma and urinary MHPG and other norepinephrine metabolites. In J. W. Maas (Ed.), *MHPG: Basic mechanisms and psychopathology* (pp. 33–43). New York: Academic Press.

Mardh, G., Sjoquist, B., Anggard, E. (1981). Norepinephrine membranes in man using deuterium labeling: The conversion of 4-hydroxy-3-methoxyphrenylglycol to 4-hydroxy-3-methoxymandelic acid. *Journal of Neurochemistry, 36*, 1181–1185.

Modai, I., Apter, A., Golomb, M., & Wijsenbeek, H. (1979). Response to amitriptyline and urinary MHPG in bipolar depressive patients. *Neuropsychobiology, 5*, 181–184.

Pickar, D., Sweeney, D. R., Maas, J. W., & Heninger, G. R. (1978). Primary affective disorder, clinical state change, and MHPG excretion: A longitudinal study. *Archives of General Psychiatry, 35*, 1378–1383.

Post, R. M., Goodwin, F. K., Gordon, E., & Watkin, D. M. (1973). Amine metabolites in human cerebrospinal fluid: Effects of cord transsection and spinal fluid block. *Science, 179*, 897–899.

Post, R. M., Stoddard, F. J., Gillin, J. C., Buchsbaum, M., Runkle, D. C., Black, R. E., & Bunney, W. E., Jr. (1977). Slow and rapid alterations in motor activity, sleep and biochemistry in a cycling manic-depressive patient. *Archives of General Psychiatry, 34*, 470–477.

Rosenbaum, A. H., Schatzberg, A. F., Maruto, T., Orsulak, P. J., Cole, J. O., Grab, E. L., & Schildkraut, J. J. (1980). MHPG as a predictor of antidepressant response to imipramine and maprotiline, *American Journal of Psychiatry, 137*, 1090–1092.

Sacchetti, E., Smeraldi, E., Cagnasso, M., Biondi, P. A., & Bellodi, L. (1976). MHPG, amitriptyline and affective disorders: A longitudinal study. *International Pharmacopsychiatry, 11*, 157–162.

Schanberg, S. M., Breese, G. R., Schildkraut, J. J., Gordon, E. K., & Kopin, I. J. (1968). 3-Methoxy-4-hydroxyphenylglycol sulfate in brain and cerebrospinal fluid. *Biochemical Pharmacology, 17*, 2006–2008.

Schildkraut, J. J. (1973). Norepinephrine metabolites as biochemical criteria for classifying depressive disorders and predicting responses to treatment: Preliminary findings. *American Journal of Psychiatry, 130*, 695–698.

Schildkraut, J. J. (1974). Catecholamine metabolism and affective disorders. In E. Usdin & S. Snyder (Eds.), *Frontiers in catecholamine research* (pp. 1165–1171). New York: Pergamon Press.

Schildraut, J. J., & Kety, S. (1967). Depressions and biogenic amines and emotion. *Science 156*, 21–30.

Shopsin, B., Wilk, S., Gershon, S., Roffman, M., & Goldstein, M. (1974). Collaborative psychopharmacologic studies exploring catecholamine metabolism in psychiatric disorders. In E. Usdin & S. Snyder (Eds.), *Frontiers in catecholamine research* (pp. 1173–1179). New York: Pergamon Press.

Shore, P. A. (1962). Release of serotonin and catecholamines by drugs. *Pharmacology Reviews, 14*, 531–550.

Sjoquist B. (1975). Mass fragmentographic determination of 4-hydroxy-3-methoxymandelic acid in human urine, cerebrospinal fluid, brain and serum using a deuterium-labelled internal standard. *Journal of Neurochemistry, 24*, 199–201.

Sweeney, D. R., Maas, J. W., & Heninger, G. R. (1978). State anxiety, physical activity and urinary 3-methoxy-4-hydroxyphenethyleneglycol excretion. *Archives of General Psychiatry, 35*, 1418–1423.

Weil-Malherbe, H., Whitby, L., & Axelrod, J. (1961). The uptake of circulating ^{3}H-norepinephrine by the pituitary gland and various areas of the brain. *Journal of Neurochemistry, 8*, 55–64.

Wolfson, L. I., & Escriva, A. (1976). Clearance of 3-methoxy-4-hydroxyphenylglycol in the cerebrospinal fluid. *Journal of Neurology, 26*, 781–784.

Zeller, E. A., Barsky, J., Fouts, J. R., Kirchheimer, W. F., & VanOrden, L. S. Influence of isonicotinic acid hydrazide (INH) and 1-isonicotinic-2-isopropyl hydrazide (IIH) on bacterial and mammalian enzymes. *Experientia, 8*, 349–350.

5

Adrenergic–Cholinergic Balance and Affective Disorders

DAVID S. JANOWSKY
S. CRAIG RISCH

Introduction

In 1972, a cholinergic–adrenergic balance hypothesis of affective disorders was proposed (Janowsky, El-Yousef, Davis, & Sekerke, 1972a). This hypothesis suggests that affect may be dictated by the relationship between the central cholinergic and adrenergic neurotransmitters. According to this hypothesis, depression is a manifestation of a cholinergic predominance, while mania is a manifestation of an adrenergic predominance. In the intervening years since this hypothesis was first published, considerable information has accumulated that supports the role of adrenergic–cholinergic interactions (cholinergic hypersensitivity) in the regulation of mood and of affective disorders. Some data have also been accumulated that are inconsistent with this hypothesis. This chapter reviews and updates the status of this hypothesis by presenting primarily clinical research data that supports the role of acetylcholine in the regulation of mood.

Behavioral Effects of Cholinomimetic Drugs

Animal Studies

As reviewed previously (Janowsky *et al.*, 1972a), central nervous system catecholaminergic and cholinergic system perturbations produce divergent behavioral and neurochemical effects in both human and

DAVID S. JANOWSKY and S. CRAIG RISCH. Departments of Psychiatry, Veterans Administration Medical Center, San Diego, and University of California, San Diego, La Jolla, California.

animal studies. Centrally active cholinomimetics, given systemically, consistently produce depressant and inhibitory behavioral effects, including increased lethargy, decreased locomotion, and decreased self-stimulation, while centrally active sympathomimetics and anticholinergic agents produce behavioral arousal, hyperactivity, increased self-stimulation and stereotypic behaviors (Janowsky, El-Yousef, Davis, & Sekerke, 1972a, 1972b). Furthermore, adrenergic and cholinergic agents behaviorally antagonize each other with respect to locomotion, self-stimulation, and stereotypic behaviors (Janowsky *et al.*, 1972b).

Human Studies

Evidence supportive of adrenergic-cholinergic behavioral interactions similarly comes from descriptions of the behavioral effects of centrally acting cholinesterase inhibitors in humans. Rowntree, Neven, and Wilson (1950), studying normals, depressives, and manics; Gershon and Shaw (1961) observing insecticide-poisoned normals; and Bowers, Goodman, and Sim (1964) observing normals, all reported that cholinesterase inhibitors exert anergic-inhibitory effects. They also reported that these agents intensified and induced depressive symptoms. Janowsky, El-Yousef, Davis, and Sekerke (1973a) and Janowsky, El-Yousef, and Davis (1974), in a similar set of studies, gave intravenous physostigmine, a centrally and peripherally active cholinesterase inhibitor, and neostigmine, a cholinesterase inhibitor that does not cross the blood-brain barrier, to psychiatric patients. Physostigmine (in contrast to neostigmine or placebo) rapidly exerted inhibitory behavioral effects which included anergy, lethargy, feelings of tiredness, psychomotor retardation, the perception of having no thoughts or decreased thoughts, feelings of being drained, and social withdrawal. These symptoms were rapidly antagonized by atropine—a centrally active antimuscarinic agent. These data suggest that the above symptoms ensue as a result of a muscarinic cholinergic mechanism.

Janowsky *et al.* (1974) also found that physostigmine caused a dramatic, brief, and atropine-reversible reduction in hypomanic and manic symptoms in bipolar patients in the manic or hypomanic phase. Neither placebo nor neostigmine produced these changes. After physostigmine administration, however, manics became significantly less talkative, active, euphoric, happy, cheerful, grandiose, and friendly, and they showed a decrease in flight of ideas. These patients also reported inhibitory symptoms, such as being anergic, feeling drained and apathetic, and having "no thoughts." Modestin, Hunger, and Schwartz (1973) and Modestin, Schwartz, and Hunger (1973) subsequently also reported a lessening of manic symptoms following infusion of physostigmine; and Davis, Berger, Hollister, and Defraites (1978) reported that physostigmine had dramatic antimanic effects, particularly in patients with low hostility/irritability. Carroll, Frazer, Schless, and Mendels (1973) and Shopsin, Janowsky, Davis, and Gershon (1975) also showed a decrease in euphoria/irritability and motor activity in manic patients following physostigmine.

Shopsin *et al.* (1975) studied the sequential effects of relatively high doses of physostigmine in three manic patients. All initially developed the "physostigmine inhibitory syndrome." In addition, in two, a late rebound into "hypermania" occurred, with exacerbation of mania beyond baseline levels. These authors suggested that this rebound phenomena might be due to compensatory increases in catecholaminergic activity, based on animal data showing a similar postphysostigmine rebound (Fibiger, Lynch, & Cooper, 1971).

Physostigmine also appears to cause a depressed (sad) mood. Several groups (Davis *et al.*, 1978; Gershon & Shaw, 1961; Janowsky *et al.*, 1972a; Modestin, Hunger, & Schwartz, 1973; Modestin, Schwartz & Hunger, 1973; Rowntree *et al.*, 1950) found induction and/or intensification of depressive symptoms in actively ill bipolar, manic-phase patients with physostigmine, as well as a worsening of depression in groups of unipolar depressed, and schizoaffective, depressed-phase patients (Janowsky *et al.*, 1974). Furthermore, Risch *et al.* (1983b) and Nurnberger *et al.* (1982a, 1982b) found that both normals and depressed patients, given the cholinergic agonist arecoline, also developed depression and other forms of negative affect, including hostility, confusion, and anxiety. Physostigmine caused a depressed mood in the majority of a group of euthymic, bipolar patients maintained on lithium (Oppenheimer, Ebstein, & Belmaker, 1979). Janowsky, Judd, and Groom (1982) Risch *et al.* (1981a) also recently noted that some normals given physostigmine or arecoline (Janowsky *et al.*, 1982) became depressed, anxious, hostile, and confused. In addition, normals having had marijuana pretreatment became profoundly depressed after receiving physostigmine (El-Yousef, Janowsky, Davis, & Rosenblatt, 1973; Davis, Hollister, & Overall, 1976), an effect that is atropine-reversible.

A depressed mood has also been observed in subjects who received acetylcholine precursors, including deanol, choline, and lecithin.

Davis, Hollister, and Berger (1979), and Tamminga, Smith, Change, Haraszti, and Davis (1976) found that depressive symptoms increased in some schizophrenic patients with tardive dyskinesia who were treated with choline, a phenomenon that was atropine-reversible. Others have noted that, in a subgroup of these cases, depressed mood was a side effect of choline or lecithin treatments that were employed as attempts to reverse the memory deficits of Alzheimer's disease (Bajada, 1982).

Casey (1979) observed that a depressed mood and, in some cases, paradoxical hypomania occurred in some deanol-treated tardive dyskinetic patients. Thus, precursors of acetylcholine appear to induce a depressed mood—a finding that is consistent with the adrenergic-cholinergic balance hypothesis, although the induction of hypomanic symptoms is not consistent with such a simple explanation of mood regulation. On the other hand, Cohen, Lipinsky, and Altesmar (1982) and Cohen, Miller, Lipinsky, and Pope (1980) reported that the acetylcholine precursor, lecithin, leads to antimanic effects on manic patients. Thus, the ultimate role of acetylcholine precursors in the direction of mood regulation remains to be established, although mood effects appear to occur.

Are Patients with Affective Disorders Uniquely Supersensitive to the Behavioral Effects of Cholinomimetic Agents?

Patients with affective disorders may be more sensitive to the mood-depressing effects of cholinomimetics than normals or other patient groups. Janowsky *et al.* (1974) noted that while most psychiatric inpatients developed an inhibitory/anergic syndrome following physostigmine administration, those patients with depression, mania, or schizoaffective disorders, when compared with schizophrenics without a significant mood component to their illness, became significantly more sad and depressed.

Janowsky *et al.* (1982) and Risch, Kalin, and Janowsky (1981b) have recently studied the possibility that there is a selective, exaggerated responsiveness in affect disorder patients to the mood depressant effect of intravenous physostigmine infusion. They found that rater-evaluated behavioral inhibition and self-rated anxiety, depression, hostility, confusion, and elation subscales showed significantly greater increases in negative affects in affective disorder than in other psychiatric patient groups after physostigmine infusion. Similarly, Casey (1979) noted that those patients with a strong history of affective disorder selectively showed increased affective symptoms while receiving deanol for tardive dyskinesia.

With respect to normals, Davis *et al.* (1976) and Greden (1982) noted no significant increases in depression in a group of normals receiving physostigmine, thus suggesting a relative lack of responsiveness to physostigmine in normals. Similarly, it was also noted (Oppenheimer *et al.*, 1979) that a significant proportion of euthymic bipolar patients receiving lithium became depressed after receiving physostigmine, while normal controls who received physostigmine did not. On the other hand, Risch *et al.* (1981a) found statistically significant increases in self- and observer-rated negative affect on the Brief Psychiatric Rating Scale, Profile of Mood States, and Activation–Inhibition rating scales in nine normals receiving 0.033 mg/kg intravenous physostigmine.

Furthermore, the effects of physostigmine (0.022 mg/kg) in normals, screened using a SADS interview so as to have no history of affect disorder, were evaluated by Janowsky *et al.* (1982). In 20 normal males, overall statistically significant increases in self- and observer-rated negative affect and anergia were found. Preliminary analysis of these results, compared with those of similarly treated affective-disorder patients, suggested that the affective-disorder group was somewhat more reactive to physostigmine than were normals, but not nearly as dramatically nor statistically significantly as when they were compared with non-affective-disorder patients.

The possibility that physostigmine may behaviorally differentiate patients with affective disorder diagnoses also receives support from the work of Edelstein, Schultz, Hirschowitz, Kanter, and Garver (1982). These investigators used physostigmine to differentiate schizophrenic patients who were responsive to lithium carbonate therapy from those who were not. They found that patients who responded to physostigmine with a clearing of psychotic symptoms were significantly *more* likely to respond to a trial of lithium, presumably because they represented affective-disorder variants.

Physiologic Studies

In addition to the above behavioral studies, evidence exists that physiological hyperresponsiveness to cholinomimetics occurs in affective-disorder patients. Sitaram (1983), Sitaram *et al.* (1981), and Sitaram,

Nurnberger, Gershon, and Gillin (1980) found that REM latency (an acetylcholine-sensitive sleep parameter which is decreased by acetylcholine and other cholinergic agonists, and which is decreased in depression), was shortened significantly more following arecoline infusion in patients with an affective disorder episode or a family history of affective disorder, than in normals. This hypersensitivity appears to be genetically linked, as noted in monozygotic twin studies (Nurnberger *et al.*, 1982a). It occured whether or not the patients were drug-free for a period of months. Sitaram, Nurnberger, Gershon, and Gillin (1982) also found a similar differentiation between patients with and without a personal or family history of affective disorder.

Sitaram (1983) has also shown an increased degree of pupillary constriction following instillation of the cholinergic agonist, pilocarpine, in the eyes of patients with affective-disorder diagnoses, as compared with normals. Also suggestive of a hypersensitivity phenomenon, Janowsky *et al.* (1982) reported that affective-disorder patients were more likely to have nausea and emesis after a physostigmine infusion than were normals or non-affective-disorder patients. Similarly, Berger, Lund, Browisch, and von Zerssen (1983) found that physostigmine-induced awakening from sleep occurred more often in affective-disorder patients than in normals, and Hanin (1983) observed high red-blood-cell choline levels in a subpopulation of depressed patients.

Neuroendocrine Studies

Neuroendocrine strategies may also reflect a differential sensitivity to cholinomimetic drugs. The differential effects among diagnostic groups of acetylcholine-active drugs on neuroendocrine function may provide clues as to the role of acetylcholine in affective disorders, and/or provide diagnostic markers of these disorders. There is animal evidence that acetylcholine may regulate prolactin, growth hormone, ACTH, cortisol, and β-endorphin secretion (for a review see Risch & Janowsky, 1983).

Several recent clinical studies (Davis & Davis, 1979; Janowsky *et al.*, 1982; Risch, Janowsky, Judd, & Huey, 1982b; Risch *et al.*, 1981b, 1982a, 1983a; Risch, Cohen, Janowsky, Kalin, & Murphy, 1981c) have explored the effects of acetylcholine on neuroendocrine activity in man. Physostigmine infusion significantly increases serum prolactin, ACTH, cortisol, growth hormone, and β-endorphin in normals and in psychiatric patients, as well as reversing dexamethasone suppression of cortisol in normals (Carroll *et al.*, 1978, 1980; Doerr & Berger, 1983). Furthermore, affective-disorder patients show significantly greater increases in β-endorphin, ACTH, and prolactin levels after physostigmine infusion (0.022 mg/kg) than do normals and other psychiatric patients (Janowsky *et al.*, 1982; Risch *et al.*, 1981b, 1982a, 1982b; Risch & Janowsky, 1983). Although affective-disorder patients have significantly and dramatically elevated prolactin levels after physostigmine, compared with other psychiatric patients, when affective-disorder patients are compared with normals, the differences are statistically significant, but not dramatic.

Thus, it appears that physostigmine-induced increases in hypothalamic–pituitary–adrenal function occur and that these parallel other phenomena noted in endogenous depression, such as increased afternoon cortisol secretion and cortisol resistance to suppression by dexamethasone (Carroll *et al.*, 1978). While physostigmine-induced changes in ACTH and β-endorphin may ultimately have diagnostic implications similar to the observations in hypothalamic–pituitary–adrenal function noted by others in affective-disorder patients, current data do suggest that the hypothalamic–pituitary–adrenal alterations seen in depression have a cholinergic component (Risch *et al.*, 1983a).

While considerable converging evidence suggests that hypersensitivity to cholinomimetic drugs occurs in affective disorders, some caution is indicated in interpreting these findings. First, cholinomimetic drugs could cause their anergic and dysphoric effects by inducing nausea, or a syndrome akin to motion sickness. However, two observations have been made which are inconsistent with such an etiology for physostigmine's mode of action. In a subgroup of inpatients, physostigmine infusion caused increased negative affect, anergia, and increased pulse and blood pressure without causing any nausea or emesis whatsoever, although lightheadedness and dizziness did occur (Janowsky *et al.*, 1982). Recently, arecoline given to normals and affective disorder patients caused affective changes, as well as increases in ACTH, cortisol, and β-endorphin, while nausea did not often develop. The subjects were not able to distinguish arecoline from placebo (Risch *et al.*, 1983b).

It is also possible that the relatively dramatic differences in responsiveness between affective-disorder patients and other psychiatric patients described above lies in a resistance to muscarinic agents in non-affective-disorder patients, rather than a hypersensitivity in affective disorders. Consistent with this interpretation, Nurnberger *et al.* (1982a, 1982b) have found no blood pressure, cortisol, prolactin, growth hormone, and behavioral differences between the effects of arecoline in normals and euthymic affect-disorder patients. Similarly, M. Berger (1982) did not find a hypersensitivity to physostigmine reversal of dexamethasone suppression in depressives.

Muscarinic Receptors in Affective-Disorder Patients

Several recent studies have suggested a difference between affective-disorder patients, non-affective-disorder patients, and normal subjects with respect to muscarinic receptor function. Nadi, Nurnberger, and Gershon (1984) have reported that fibroblasts, grown in culture from affective-disorder patients and their mood-disordered relatives, have more muscarinic-cholinergic (QNB) binding sites than non-affective-disorder controls, but no differences in their affinity for the ligand. Similarly, Meyerson *et al.* (1982) have noted that samples from the frontal cortex of individuals who committed suicide have more muscarinic (QNB) receptor binding activity than matched brains from people dying from accidents or having been murdered, although a similar study by Stanley (1984) showed negative results. These findings represent the first direct evidence that cholinergic function may be altered and possibly increased in affective-disorder patients.

Monoamine-Acetylcholine Interactions

A pharmacologic-behavioral model for naturally occurring catecholaminergic-cholinergic central nervous system (CNS) regulation of mood may be found in the interactions and reciprocal effects of psychostimulants (which increase catecholaminergic activity) and cholinomimetics (which increase cholinergic activity). Janowsky *et al.* (1972b) and others have noted that methylphenidate-induced stereotyped behavior and increased locomotion in rats (thought to represent a hyperdopaminergic phenomenon) is effectively antagonized by physostigmine, but not by the non-centrally-active cholinomimetic, neostigmine. These findings are compatible with the observation that physostigmine rapidly down regulates cortical β-adrenergic receptors (Groom, Janowsky, & Risch, 1983).

Likewise, methylphenidate-induced psychomotor stimulation in manic and schizophrenic patients (i.e., increased talkativeness, elevated mood, and interpersonal interactions in manics, or activation of psychosis in schizophrenics) is rapidly antagonized by physostigmine, but not by neostigmine. Conversely, physostigmine's inhibitory-depressant effects can be reversed by methylphenidate (Janowsky *et al.*, 1973b). Possibly related to the ability of physostigmine to antagonize methylphenidate-induced psychomotor stimulation is the observation that physostigmine caused a rapid, dramatic drop in serum MHPG in a manic patient, presumably reflecting a drop in CNS noradrenergic activity, temporally associated with induction of a tearful depressed state and improvement in manic thinking (Ostrow, Halaris, Dysken, & Davis, 1980).

Furthermore, a reciprocal relationship apparently exists between a subject's response to a psychostimulant and his separate response to a cholinomimetic agent. In one study, a negative correlation was noted between amphetamine-induced behavioral excitation in a given subject and the ability of arecoline, given on another occasion, to decrease REM latency (Nurnberger *et al.*, 1982b). Janowsky *et al.* (1982) also found that in psychiatric patients, the effects of 0.5 mg/kg of oral methylphenidate correlate inversely with the effects of physostigmine (0.022 mg/kg). They noted that patients who have intense behavioral inhibition and negative affect in response to physostigmine tended to show lower elevations of self-rated positive mood ratings and improvement in psychomotor and cognitive performance, as well as increased depression and anxiety after methylphenidate ingestion. Similarly, Siever, Risch, and Murphy (1981) showed that in a mixed group of affective disorder and normal subjects, those with the most dramatic physostigmine and arecoline-induced anergy and negative affect also showed a blunted growth hormone response to the noradrenergic agonist, clonidine.

Thus, the interaction and reciprocal relationship between cholinomimetics and psychostimulants, as they affect or relate to each other in man, could suggest an adrenergic–cholinergic continuum model of behavior, in which behavior ranges from catecholaminergic activation (increased thoughts, cheerfulness, talkativeness, mania, and the like) to cholinergic inhibition (decreased thoughts, dysphoria, lethargy, anergy, and depression). Clinically, such a continuum could determine a normal individual's relative aggressiveness, talkativeness, and activation, and in manic–depressives, such a balance could determine whether a psychiatric patient was activated and manic, or motor-retarded and depressed.

In addition to the above catecholaminergic–cholinergic balance hypothesis of affective disorders, it is possible that serotonergic–cholinergic balance may also regulate affect. Platelet serotonin uptake was lowered after physostigmine, but not after placebo infusion. Since platelet serotonin uptake often is low in depression, physostigmine lowers platelet serotonin uptake in the direction that occurs naturally in patients with depression (Rausch, Janowsky, Risch, Huey, & Swanson, 1982).

Cholinergic–Anticholinergic Behavioral Effects of Psychotropic Drugs

Mood Effects of Anticatecholaminergic Agents

Observations that many sympatholytic–antihypertensive medications such as methyldopa, propranolol, clonidine, and reserpine, which can cause depression, also have cholinomimetic properties (Janowsky *et al.*, 1972a), is supportive for a role for adrenergic–cholinergic balance in the regulation of affect. In animals, reserpine can cause parasympathetic somatic effects, including lacrimation, miosis, diarrhea, and tremor, and such behavioral effects as sedation, decreased locomotor activity, decreased self-stimulation, decreased conditioned responses, and antagonism of methylphenidate-induced increased stereotyped gnawing behavior.

Similarly, in humans, the central side effects of reserpine and other antiadrenergic–cholinomimetic antihypertensives are similar to those of centrally active parasympathetic agents, and include mood depression, vivid nightmares, lethargy, and sleepiness. Also, Van Putten and May (1978) have shown that antipsychotic drugs, which block central dopamine and increase acetylcholine turnover, can cause some of the components of depression in selected patients. These investigators reported that a subgroup of schizophrenics treated with antipsychotic drugs developed an "akinetic depression" that was reversed with anticholinergic drugs.

Mood Effects of Centrally Active Anticholinergic Agents

There is also some evidence that centrally active anticholinergic drugs have mood-elevating properties. Anticholinergic, antiparkinsonian drugs, used to treat drug-induced parkinsonian symptoms, have been reported to cause feelings of euphoria, associated with a sense of well-being, increased sociability, and even a reversal of depressed feelings (Jellinec, Gardos, & Cole, 1981; Smith, 1980). These euphoric effects can occur in patients who have not previously taken neuroleptics. Furthermore, one report exists suggesting that the anticholinergic agent, procyclidine, caused a switch from depression to mania in a bipolar patient (Coid & Strang, 1982).

Further, several reports suggest that high doses of atropine or other anticholinergics may alleviate depression. One recent report suggests that tricyclic-antidepressant-induced central anticholinergic syndrome may alleviate depression (Abood & Meduna, 1958; English, 1962; Finkelstein, 1961; Hoch & Mauss, 1932; Safer & Allen, 1971). Jimerson, Nurnberger, Simmons, and Gershon (1982) also have reported that trihexyphenidyl may have antidepressant properties. Further, Kasper, Moises, and Beckman (1981) have observed similar antidepressant effects with biperiden, especially in patients with endogenous depression who have a nonsuppressing dexamethasone suppression test. Unfortunately, these studies have been poorly controlled to date.

Conversely, neuroleptic-treated patients may develop some aspects of depression, including a depressed mood and hypoactivity several weeks after discontinuing anticholinergic medications (Jellinec *et al.*, 1981). These symptoms are preventable and/or reversible with continued anticholinergic treatment, and may represent muscarinic receptor hypersensitivity.

Treatment Implications

The adrenergic–cholinergic hypothesis provides several potential and already explored therapeutic applications. In recent years, oral physostigmine has become available (O'Neal, Jones and Feldman Company, Maryland Heights, Mo.). Oral physostigmine can be given at frequent intervals. It has been shown to be effective when given in 1.0–2.0 mg doses every 2 hours (during wakefulness) in the treatment of hereditary ataxias and related syndromes (Kark, Rodriguez-Budelli, Blass, & Spence, 1979). Oral physostigmine has been used in Alzheimer's disease patients in similar doses with equivocal results (Bajada, 1982). To date, we know of no reports of oral physostigmine being used as a treatment for mania, but this possibility is certainly worthy of study, since circumvention of the need for parenteral physostigmine would make physostigmine therapy for mania more practical.

Acetylcholine precursors also may have potential therapeutic value in the treatment of mania. Preliminary reports by Cohen *et al.* (1980, 1982) suggest that lecithin may have antimanic properties. It is also possible that directly acting centrally active muscarinic agonists, such as pilocarpine, oxotremorine, and arecoline may have clinically useable antimanic properties.

In the recent past, a number of techniques to enhance the effectiveness of acetylcholine precursors such as choline, lecithin, and possibly deanol have been developed by gerontologists and others. These techniques may have potential in the treatment of mania. A combination of physostigmine and lecithin appears to exert a synergistic effect on cholinergic function, as manifested by effects on memory (Peters & Levin, 1982). The combined use of an acetylcholine precursor such as lecithin, along with a centrally acting cholinesterase inhibitor such as physostigmine, might also be expected to have augmented antimanic effects. Similarly, reserpine in doses of 1.0–2.0 mg/day, and possibly propranolol, have been found to have antimanic properties, and both of these agents not only block and/or decrease central adrenergic activity, but also increase absolute and relative central and peripheral parasympathetic effects (Janowsky *et al.*, 1972a). Indeed, animal studies show an increase in physostigmine toxicity following reserpine pretreatment, a phenomenon that is prevented by antimuscarinic pretreatment (Janowsky, Pechnick, & Janowsky, 1976).

It is thus possible that a combination of a cholinergic agonist or a cholinesterase inhibitor and a centrally acting antiadrenergic agent such as methyldopa, reserpine, or propranolol would be especially effective as an antimanic treatment, since such a treatment would shift adrenergic-cholinergic balance toward a cholinergic predominance. Similarly, it is possible that a cholinomimetic drug such as physostigmine, given chronically, would be followed by tolerance development. A potential way to avoid the postulated development of endogenous adrenergic activity would be to give manics a catecholamine-depleting drug, such as reserpine, methyldopa, or a similar antiadrenergic drug, while simultaneously treating the mania with a cholinesterase inhibitor, acetylcholine precursor, or cholinergic agonist.

Along the same lines, another potential treatment for mania could involve the coadministration of marijuana or tetrahydrocannabinol plus physostigmine, or other centrally active cholinesterase inhibitors, acetylcholine precursors, or cholinergic agonists, since physostigmine plus marijuana has been shown to have synergistic toxic and depressant-anergic effects (El-Yousef *et al.*, 1973; Rosenblatt, Janowsky, & El-Yousef, 1972).

As described above, there is some evidence that centrally active anticholinergic compounds may have efficacy as antidepressant agents, at least in the treatment of some depressions. As a correlate of the above, it is generally thought that psychostimulants are not consistently useful as antidepressants, probably due to the development of tolerance. However, in the short run, these compounds can exert euphoric effects in some depressives and, indeed, these euphoric effects have been used to predict lithium and/or imipramine/desipramine efficacy.

Furthermore, withdrawal from chronic amphetamine administration causes a series of symptoms, usually thought due to catecholamine depletion, consisting of depression, anergy, lethargy, and somnolence. These psychostimulant withdrawal symptoms bear a remarkable resemblance to the effects of centrally acting cholinomimetics. It is possible that they represent cholinomimetic effects of acetylcholine, compensatorially caused by the chronic administration of amphetamine, unmasked upon amphetamine withdrawal, and serve to cause tolerance to psychostimulant antidepressant effects (Janowsky *et al.*, 1972a). If so, atropine or scopolamine should effectively antagonize postamphetamine depression, and a combination of a centrally active anticholinergic drugs and a psychostimulant might prove to be an effective antidepressant regimen.

With respect to diagnosis, a number of studies have explored the possibility that there is a selective and exaggerated responsiveness in affect disorder patients to the neuroendocrine, behavioral, and physiological effects of intravenous cholinomimetic drugs (Berger, Lund, Bronisch, & von Zerssen, 1982; Janowsky *et al.*, 1981; Risch *et al.*, 1981a, 1981b, 1981c, 1982a, 1982b; Risch & Janowsky, 1983; Sitaram, 1983; Sitaram *et al.*, 1980, 1981). Thus, the responses to cholinomimetic challenges may ultimately have diagnostic utility. Furthermore, if arecoline's enhanced ability to shorten REM latency, or if QNB binding increases in depressives are truly trait markers of affective disorders, it may be possible to prospectively diagnose patients with affective disorders. At the extreme, the latter tests could be used to determine if a given individual should be prospectively treated with lithium and/or an antidepressant drug in times of stress.

Discussion

Considerable clinical evidence suggests that the cholinergic nervous system, alone and/or interacting with serotonin, catecholamines, or other neurotransmitters, may have an important role in the regulation of affect. Nevertheless, as with all currently proposed biological hypotheses as to the etiology of affective disorders, there exist alternative explanations, as well as some data that are inconsistent with the adrenergic-cholinergic balance hypothesis.

For example, antidepressant drugs do not all have equal degrees of anticholinergic activity, and indeed trazodone, an effective antidepressant, has virtually no anticholinergic properties (Risch & Janowsky, 1981). Furthermore, it is possible that pharmacologically induced changes in acetylcholine may be the cause of perturbations in other than the adrenergic and cholinergic systems. Pharmacologically induced acetylcholine alterations could cause a "model depression," perturbing the governing neurotransmitters of depression in affect disorder patients (e.g., GABA, serotonin, dopamine, vasopressin, or norepinephrine), but at the same time endogenous acetylcholine may not directly cause depression.

However, even if cholinomimetics can only cause a model depression, understanding this phenomena may ultimately offer a window into understanding the pathophysiology of affective disorders, and may have useful treatment implications. Thus, understanding the "downstream" implications of cholinomimetics' mood depressant effects may give clues to the actual neurobiology of affective disorders. Alternatively, it is not beyond possibility that acetylcholine or adrenergic-cholinergic balance actually is involved in the etiology or the expression of affect.

Finally, at a more general level, the above reviewed information is consistent with a role for acetylcholine in the overall regulation of the effects of stress, of which affective disorders may be but one possible outcome (Anisman & Zacharko, 1982). Supportive of this concept is animal evidence that central acetylcholine turnover increases and muscarinic receptor activity decreases with stress, and that this effect is exaggerated in a strain of stress-sensitive rats (Gilad, Gilad, & Shenkman, 1982). Furthermore, blood pressure and pulse rate increases; increases in neurohormones, including epinephrine, ACTH, cortisol, β-endorphin, prolactin, growth hormone, and vasopressin; and increases in anxiety, depression, fatigue, hostility, and analgesia frequently occur following exposure to naturally occurring nonpharmacological aversive stressors, as well as following cholinomimetic administration (Brezenoff & Giuliano, 1982; Janowsky, Risch, Judd, Huey, & Parker, 1981; Risch *et al.*, 1981). Such parallels suggest that acetylcholine, along with other neurotransmitters such as norephinephrine, GABA, and serotonin, may be a major modulator of the behavioral, neuroendocrine, and cardiovascular manifestations of stress (Janowsky & Risch, 1984).

REFERENCES

Abood, L. C.; & Meduna, L. L. (1958). Some effects of a new psychotogen in depressive states. *Journal of Nervous and Mental Disease, 127,* 546–550.

Anisman, H., & Zacharko, R. M. (1982). Depression: The predisposing influence of stress. *The Behavioral and Brain Sciences, 5,* 89–137.

Bajada, S. (1982). A trial of choline chloride and physostigmine in Alzheimer's dementia. In S. Corkin, K. Davis, J. Growden, E. Usdin, & R. Wurtman (Eds.), *Alzheimer's disease: A report of progress.* New York: Raven Press.

Berger, M., Lund, R., Bronisch, T., & von Zerssen, D., Berger, M. (1982). Unpublished observations. Der Einfluss eines Cholinergikums auf den REM-Schlaf gesunder probanden und depressiver Patienten. In H. Beckman (Ed.), *Fortschritte Psychiatrischer Forschung.* Bern: Huber.

Berger, M., Lund, R., Bronisch, T., & von Zerssen, D. (1983). REM latency and endogenous depression and the cholinergic REM induction test. *Psychiatry Research, 10,* 113–123.

Bowers, M. G., Goodman, E., & Sim, V. M. (1964). Some behavioral changes in man following anticholinesterase administration. *Journal of Nervous and Mental Disease, 138,* 383–389.

Brezenoff, H. E., & Giuliano, R. (1982). Cardiovascular control by cholinergic mechanisms in the central nervous system. *Annual Review of Pharmacology and Toxicology, 22,* 341–381.

Carroll, B. J., Frazer, A., Schless, A., & Mendels, J. (1973). Cholinergic reversal of manic symptoms. *Lancet, 1,* 427–428.

Carroll, B. J., Greden, J. F., Haskett, R., Feinberg, M., Albala, A. A., Martin, F. I. R., Rubin, R. T., Heath, B., Sharp, P. T., McLeod, W. L., & McLeod, M. F. (1980). Neurotransmitter studies of neuroendocrine pathology in depression. *Acta Psychiatrica Scandinavica, Supplementum, 280,* 183–199.

Carroll, B. J., Greden, J. F., Rubin, R. T., Haskett, R., Feinberg, M., & Schteingart, D. (1978). Neurotransmitter mechanism of neuroendocrine disturbances in depression. *Acta Endocrinologica Supplementum, 220,* 14.

Casey, D. E. (1979). Mood alterations during deanol therapy. *Psychopharmacology,* 187–191.

Cohen, B. M., Lipinsky, J. F., & Altesmar, R. F. (1982). Lecithin in the treatment of mania. *American Journal of Psychiatry, 138,* 1162–1164.

Cohen, B. M., Miller, A. L., Lipinsky, J. F., & Pope, H. G. (1980). Lecithin in mania: A preliminary report. *American Journal of Psychiatry, 137,* 242–243.

Coid, B., & Strang, M. (1982). Mania secondary to procyclidine ("Kemadrin") abuse. *British Journal of Psychiatry, 141,* 81–84.

Davis, K. L., Berger, P. A., Hollister, L. E., & Defraites, E. (1978). Physostigmine in man. *Archives of General Psychiatry, 35(1),* 119–122.

Davis, K. L., & Davis, B. M. (1979). Acetylcholine and anterior pituitary hormone secretion. In K. L. Davis & P. A. Berger (Eds.), *Brain acetylcholine and neuropsychiatric disease.* New York: Plenum Press.

Davis, K., Hollister, L. E., & Berger, P. A. (1979). Choline chloride in schizophrenia. *American Journal of Psychiatry, 136,* 1581–1584.

Davis, K. L., Hollister, L. E., & Overall, J. (1976). Physostigmine effects on cognition and affect in normal subjects. *Psychopharmacology, 51,* 23–27.

Doerr, P., & Berger, M. (1983). Physostigmine-induced escape from dexamethasone suppression in normal adults. *Biological Psychiatry, 18,* 261–268.

Edelstein, P., Schultz, J. R., Hirschowitz, J., Kanter, D. R., & Garver, D. L. (1982). Physostigmine and lithium response in the schizophrenias. *American Journal of Psychiatry, 38,* 1078–1081.

El-Yousef, M., Janowsky, D. S., Davis, J. M., & Rosenblatt, J. E. (1973). Induction of severe depression by physostigmine in marijuana intoxicated individuals. *British Journal of Addiction, 68,* 321–325.

English, D. (1962). Reintegration of affect and psychic-emergence with ditran. *Journal of Neuropsychiatry, 3,* 304–310.

Fibiger, H. D., Lynch, G. S., & Cooper, H. P. (1971). A biphasic action of central cholinergic stimulation on behavioral arousal in the rat. *Psychopharmacology, 20,* 366–382.

Finkelstein, B. (1961). Ditran, a psychotherapeutic advance: A review of one hundred and three cases. *Journal of Neuropsychiatry, 2,* 144–148.

Gershon, S., & Shaw, F. H. (1961). Psychiatric sequelae of chronic exposure to organophosphorous insecticides. *Lancet, 9,* 1371–1374.

Gilad, G. M., Gilad, V. H., & Shenkman, L. (1982). Modes of regulation of hippocampal cholinergic activity after stress. *Proceedings of the 13th Collegium Internationale Neuro-Psychopharmacologicum Congress, 1,* 268. (Abstract)

Greden, J. F. (1982). Personal communication.

Groom, G., Janowsky, D., & Risch, S. C. (1983). Physostigmine down-regulation of beta-adrenergic receptors. *Psychopharmacology Bulletin, 19,* 670–675.

Hanin, I. (1983). RBC choline as a potential marker in psychiatric and neurologic disease. In E. Usdin & I. Hanin (Eds.), *Proceedings of the Conference on Biologic Markers in Psychiatry and Neurology.* New York: Pergamon Press.

Hoch, P. H., & Mauss, W. (1932). Atropin Behandlung bei Geisteckvankheiten [Atropine treatment of depression]. *Archives of General Psychiatry, 97,* 546–552.

Janowsky, D. S., El-Yousef, M. K., & Davis, J. M. (1974). Acetylcholine and depression. *Psychosomatic Medicine, 36,* 248–257.

Janowsky, D. S., El-Yousef, M. K., Davis, J. M., & Sekerke, H. J. (1972a). A Cholinergic-adrenergic hypothesis of mania and depression. *Lancet, 2,* 6732–6735.

Janowsky, D. S., El-Yousef, M. K., Davis, J. M., & Sekerke, H. J. (1972b). Cholinergic antagonism of methylphenidate-induced stereotpyed behavior. *Psychopharmacologia, 27,* 295–303.

Janowsky, D. S., El-Yousef, M. K., Davis, J. M., & Serkerke, H. J. (1973a). Parasympathetic suppression of manic symptoms by physostigmine. *Archives of General Psychiatry, 28,* 542–547.

Janowsky, D. S., El-Yousef, M. K., Davis, J. M., & Serkerke, H. J. (1973b). Antagonistic effects of physostigmine and methylphenidate in man. *American Journal of Psychiatry, 1930,* 1370–1376.

Janowsky, D. S., Judd, L. L., & Groom, G. (1982). The influence of lithium on cholinergic function. *Proceedings of the 13th Collegium Internationale Neuro-Psychopharmacologicum Congress, 1,* 268. (Abstract)

Janowsky, D. S., Pechnick, R., & Janowsky, E. (1976). Lethal effects of reserpine plus physostigmine and neostigmine in mice. *Clinical and Experimental Pharmacology and Physiology, 3,* 483–486.

Janowsky, D. S., & Risch, S. C. (1984). Cholinomimetic and anticholinergic drugs used to investigate an acetylcholine hypothesis of affective disorders and stress. *Drug Development and Research, 4,* 125–142.

Janowsky, D. S., Risch, S. C., Judd, L. L., Huey, L. Y., & Parker, D. S. (1981). Cholinergic supersensitivity in affect disorder patients. Behavioral and neuroendocrine observations. *Psychopharmacology Bulletin, 17,* 129–132.

Jellinec, T., Gardos, G. & Cole, J. (1981). Adverse effects of antiparkinsonian drug withdrawal. *American Journal of Psychiatry, 138*(12), 1567–1571.

Jimerson, D. C., Nurnberger, J. I. Jr., Simmons, S., & Gershon, E. S. (1982). *Anticholinergic treatment for depression.* Paper presented at the American Psychiatric Association Meeting, Toronto.

Kark, R. A. P., Rodriguez-Budelli, M., Blass, J. P., & Spence, M. A. (1979). Oral physostigmine and inherited ataxias. In K. Davis & P. Berger (Eds.), *Brain acetylcholine and neuropsychiatric disease,* New York: Plenum Press.

Kasper, S., Moises, H. W., & Beckman, H. (1981). The anticholinergic biperiden in depressive disorders. *Pharmacopsychiatry, 14,* 195–198.

Meyerson, L. R., Wennogle, L. P., Abel, M. S., Coupet, J., Lippa, A. S., Rauh, C. E., & Beer, B. (1982). Human brain receptor alterations in suicide victims. *Pharmacology Biochemistry and Behavior, 17,* 159–163.

Modestin, J. J., Hunger, J., & Schwartz, R. B. (1973). Uber die depressogene wirkung von Physostigmine. *Archiv für Psychiatrie und Nervenkrankheiten, 218,* 67–77.

Modestin, J. J., Schwartz, R. B., & Hunger, J. (1973). Zur Frage der Beeinflussung Schizophrener Symptome Physostigmine. *Pharmakopsychiatrie, 9,* 300–304.

Nadi, N. S., Nurnberger, J. I. Jr., & Gershon, E. S. (1984). Muscarinic cholinergic receptors on skin fibroblasts in familial affective disorders. *New England Journal of Medicine, 311,* 225–230.

Nurnberger, J., Gershon, E. S., Sitaram, N., Gillin, J. C., Brown, G., Ebert, M., Gold, P., Jimerson, D., & Kessler, L. (1982a). Dextroamphetamine and arecoline as pharmacogenetic probes in normals and remitted bipolar patients. *Psychopharmacology Bulletin, 17,* 80–82.

Nurnberger, J. I., Jimerson, D. S., Simmons, S., Tamminga, C., Nadi, N. S., & Gershon, E. S. (1982b). *Responses to arecoline in normal twins and "well state" patients with affective disorder.* Paper presented at the Society of Biological Psychiatry Annual Convention, Toronto.

Oppenheimer, G., Ebstein, R., & Belmaker, R. (1979). Effects of lithium on the physostigmine-induced behavioral syndrome and plasma cyclic GMP. *Journal of Psychiatry Research, 14,* 133–138.

Ostrow, D. G., Halaris, A., Dysken, M. E., & Davis, J. M. (1980). *Ion transport and neurotransmitter function in major affective disorders.* Paper presented at the Society of Biological Psychiatry Annual Convention, Boston.

Peters, B. H., & Levin, H. S. Chronic oral physostigmine and lecithin administration in memory disorders of aging. (1982). In S. Corkin, K. Davis, J. Growden, E. Usdin, & R. Wurtman (Eds.), *Alzheimer's disease: A report of progress.* New York: Raven Press.

Rausch, J., Janowsky, D. S., Risch, S. C., Huey, L. Y., & Swanson, G. W. (1983). Physostigmine effect on platelet serotonin uptake. In B. Ho & E. Usdin (Eds.), *Serotonin in biological psychiatry.* New York: Raven Press.

Risch, S. C., Cohen, P. M., Janowsky, D. S., Kalin, N. H., Insel, T. R., & Murphy, D. L. (1981a). Physostigmine induction of depressive symptomatology in normal volunteer subjects. *Journal of Psychiatric Research, 4,* 89–94.

Risch, S. C., Cohen, R. M., Janowsky, D. S., Kalin, N. H., & Murphy, D. L. (1981c). Plasma beta-endorphin and cortisol elevations accompany the mood and behavioral effects of physostigmine in man. *Science, 109,* 1545–1546.

Risch, S. C., & Janowsky, D. S. (1981). Trazodone. *Psychiatric Annals, 11*(11), 47–55.

Risch, S. C., & Janowsky, D. S. (1983). Cholinergic-adrenergic balance in affective disorders. In R. M. Post & J. C. Ballenger (Eds.), *Neurobiology of the mood disorders.* Baltimore: Williams & Wilkins.

Risch, S. C., Janowsky, D. S., Judd, L. L., & Huey, L. Y. (1982b). Elevated plasma β-

endorphin concentrations in depression and cholinergically supersensitive release mechanisms. *Psychopharmacology Bulletin, 18,* 211–216.

Risch, S. C., Janowsky, D. S., Kalin, N. H., Cohen, R. M., Aloi, J. A., Murphy, D. L. (1983a). Cholinergic β-endorphin hypersensitivity association with depression. In I. Hanin & E. Usdin (Eds.), *Biological markers in psychiatry and neurology,* Oxford: Pergamon Press.

Risch, S. C., Janowsky, D. S., Siever, L. J., Judd, L. L., Huey, L. Y., Beckman, K. A., Cohen, R. M., & Murphy, D. L. (1982a). Cholinomimetic induced co-release of prolactin and beta-endorphin in man. *Psychopharmacology Bulletin, 18*(4), 21–25.

Risch, S. C., Kalin, N. H., & Janowsky, D. S. (1981b). Cholinergic challenges in affective illness, behavioral and neuroendocrine correlates. *Journal of Clinical Psychopharmacology, 1,* 186–192.

Risch, S. C., Siever, L. Y., Gillin, J. C., Janowsky, D. S., Sitaram, N., Weker, J., Cohen, R. M., & Murphy, D. L. (1983b). Differential mood effects of arecoline in depressed patients and normal volunteers. *Psychopharmacology Bulletin, 19*(4), 696–698.

Rosenblatt, J. E., Janowsky, D. S., & El-Yousef, M. K. (1972). The augmentation of physostigmine toxicity in the rat by delta-9-tetrahydrocannabinol. *Research Communications of Chemistry, Pathology and Pharmacology, 3,*(3), 479–482.

Rowntree, D. W., Neven, S., & Wilson, A. (1950). The effects of diisopropylfluorophosphonate in schizophrenia and manic depressive psychosis. *Journal of Neurology, Neurosurgery and Psychiatry, 13,* 47–62.

Safer, D. J., & Allen, R. P. (1971). The central effects of scopolamine in man. *Biological Psychiatry, 3,* 347–356.

Shopsin, B., Janowsky, D. S., Davis, J. M., & Gershon, S. (1975). Rebound phenomena in manic patients following physostigmine. *Neuropsychobiology, 1,* 180–187.

Siever, L. J., Risch, S. C., & Murphy, D. L. (1981). Possible concurrence of cholinergic receptor hypersensitivity and adrenergic receptor hyposensitivity in affective disorders. *Psychiatric Research, 5,* 108–109.

Sitaram, N. (1983). Pupillary changes following cholinomimetics. In E. Usdin & I. Hanin (Eds.), *Biologic changes in psychiatry and neurology.* New York: Pergamon Press.

Sitaram, N., Moore, A. M., Vanskiver, C., Blendy, J., Nurnberger, J. I., Gershon, E. S., & Gillin, J. C. (1981). Hypersensitive cholinergic functioning in primary affective illness. In G. Pepeu & H. Ladinsky (Eds.), *Cholinergic mechanisms, phylogenetic aspects, central and peripheral synapses and clinical significance.* New York: Plenum Press.

Sitaram, N., Nurnberger, J., Gershon, E., & Gillin, J. C. (1980). Faster cholinergic REM sleep induction in euthymic patients with primary affective illness. *Science, 208,* 200–202.

Sitaram, N., Nurnberger, J. I., Gershon, E. S., & Gillin, J. C. (1982). Cholinergic regulation of mood and REM sleep: A potential model and marker for vulnerability to depression. *American Journal of Psychiatry, 139,* 571–576.

Smith, J. A. (1980). Abuse of antiparkinsonian drugs: A review of the literature. *Journal of Clinical Psychiatry, 41,* 351–354.

Stanley, M. (1984). Cholinergic receptor binding in the frontal cortex of suicide victims. *American Journal of Psychiatry, 141,* 1432–1436.

Tamminga, C., Smith, R. C., Change, S., Haraszti, J. S., & Davis, J. M. (1976). Depression associated with oral choline. *Lancet, 2,* 905.

Van Putten, T. V., & May, P. A. (1978). "Akinetic depression" in schizophrenia. *Archives of General Psychiatry, 35,* 1101–1107.

6

The Sleep EEG in Diagnosis and Treatment of Depression

DAVID J. KUPFER

Introduction

Our current state of knowledge about affective disorders would lead us to conclude that these disorders entail a dysfunction in multiple systems and do not simply reflect alterations in mood. Since many of the core symptoms of affective disorder represent changes in regulatory systems, investigators have frequently searched for markers of vulnerability and have explored the interdependencies among aspects of biological and psychological functioning. Such an approach has yielded promising findings with regard to electroencephalographic (EEG) sleep abnormalities. Indeed, the study of EEG sleep in affective states is now affording us an opportunity to examine, along with other biological variables, notions of how aberrations in neurochemical and neuroendocrine pathways and circadian rhythms may be responsible for the various biological disturbances in depression.

Methodological Issues

Based on the studies performed in most sleep research settings in the 1970s and early 1980s, several methodological advances have been made (Table 6-1). Increased diagnostic precision, such as the introduction of the Research Diagnostic Criteria (RDC) and the development of more operational criteria in all diagnostic categories (e.g., DSM-III), particularly in affective disorders, have made it easier to select patients for research studies (Spitzer, Endicott, & Robins, 1978). Second, the

DAVID J. KUPFER. Department of Psychiatry, University of Pittsburgh School of Medicine and Western Psychiatric Institute and Clinic, Pittsburgh, Pennsylvania.

TABLE 6-1. Methodological Issues

1. Diagnostic precision (homogeneous samples).
2. Distinction of primary depression from medical-depressive syndromes.
3. Length of psychotropic-drug-free interval.
4. Entrainment and adaptation effects.
5. Computer-assisted analysis of phasic phenomena (e.g., REMs and delta activity) and their temporal distribution
6. Adequate control of age-related variability.
7. Stability of findings over time and across samples (replicability).

importance of ruling out medical–neurological syndromes prior to the investigation of primary depression has become increasingly recognized. Studies can now provide information on how sleep associated with both depression and medical–neurological disorders can be distinguished from the sleep of individuals with depression alone. Third, while considerable controversy exists about whether patients on any type of psychotropic medication can be studied and, if not, how long the drug-free period needs to be, an accepted compromise position has been the use of a 2-week, drug-free period. Some critics, such as Ian Oswald, have argued that a minimum of 6 drug-free weeks are necessary to allow for metabolism and excretion of psychotropic drugs before sleep studies are undertaken with patients. Studies done with intervals of less than 6 drug-free weeks could theoretically reflect residual drug-withdrawal phenomena, rather than phenomena related to the depressive psychopathology. However, a recent investigation in which placebo was administered and all-night sleep EEG studies were performed nightly over a period of 6 weeks, demonstrated that hospitalized patients with no significant clinical change showed sleep findings unaltered over the 6-week period (Coble, Kupfer, Spiker, Neil, & McPartland, 1979).

The fourth methodological issue involves adaptation to recording procedures. Studies in this decade have dealt with the issues of entrainment, setting novelty, and the stress of sleeping in a new environment in a more sophisticated way than studies conducted in the 1960s. Many recent studies have been conducted in the same hospital rooms in which patients reside for weeks before the sleep investigation. For inpatients, this procedure leads to considerable entrainment and diminishes the importance of such issues as adaptation and the stress of the first nights of sleep study raised in the early 1970s. While adaptational problems have been eased by these procedural revisions, studies often include additional procedures that are required for neuroendocrine and biochemical studies.

Finally, the studies of the 1970s generally relied on the sleep-staging scheme published in the late 1960s (Rechtschaffen & Kales, 1968) and usually reported whole-night values. These studies were important and their results well-replicated in the late 1970s and early 1980s. A newly emerging trend, however, is to examine the distribution of both stages and phasic phenomena in sleep throughout the night. Examination of the number and distribution of REM waves or the number and distribution of delta waves has necessitated an increased reliance on the computer, not so much for computerized stage scoring but for characterizing these phasic phenomena.

Areas of Consensus

With these methological issues in mind, let us turn to the four major areas of consensus that have emerged from clinical sleep research in the 1970s (Kupfer, 1982) (Table 6-2). First, nearly all depressed patients demonstrate a change in sleep continuity. The majority of such patients show hyposomnia (a sleep continuity disturbance usually asso-

TABLE 6-2. Glossary of EEG Sleep Variables

Sleep latency: Time from lights out until the appearance of Stage 2 sleep.

Early morning awakening: Time spent awake from the final awakening until the subject gets out of bed.

Awake: Time spent awake after sleep onset and before the final awakening in the morning.

Time spent asleep (TSA): Time spent asleep less any awake time during the night after sleep onset.

Awake/TSA: The percentage of awake time over time spent asleep.

TSA/total recording period (sleep efficiency): The ratio of time spent asleep to total recording period.

Sleep architecture: The various percentages of each stage of sleep: Stage 1, Stage 2, Stage 3, and Stage 4 (Stages 3 and 4 are combined to yield delta sleep), State 1 REM percentage and Stage 2 REM percentage (the portion of the night when REMs are present during Stage 1 and Stage 2 sleep, respectively).

REM latency: Number of minutes asleep until the onset of the first REM period.

REM activity (RA): Each minute of REM sleep is rated on a 9-point scale (0–8) for the relative amount of REM occurring; the sum for the whole night provides the REM activity.

RA/TSA (average REM activity): The ratio of REM activity to time spent asleep.

RA/REM time (REM density): The ratio of REM activity to REM time.

ciated with increased wakefulness and frequent early morning awakening) (Figure 6-1). A minority (15% to 20%) have hypersomnia, a feature usually associated with other psychophysiological phenomena such as anergia. Second, there is generally a reduction in slow-wave sleep in depressed states. This finding is usually reported as a decrease or absence of Stages 3 and 4 sleep. But since considerably more Stage 1 sleep is also present in the sleep of depressed patients, one might conclude equally well that the major change is an increase of the lighter stages of sleep, Stages 1 and 2, which excludes Stages 3 and 4. The next finding, prominent because it has been well-replicated and can be scored and interpreted with relative ease, is that of a shortened time from sleep onset to the first REM period. While the extent of this finding is somewhat contingent upon the criteria used to determine sleep onset, REM latency is definitely shortened in the majority of depressed states. The relationship of REM latency and the severity of the illness is also established.

Finally, the recent findings about the distribution of REM sleep have also received considerable attention. Our own work, as well as that of Gillin, Duncan, Pettigrew, and Thurmond (1979) and Vogel (1981), has demonstrated the distribution of REM sleep to be abnormal in depressed patients, when contrasted with normals and patients suffering from other psychiatric illnesses or sleep disorders. An increased amount of REM sleep is present in the first third to first half of the night in the depressed; even more apparent is a marked increase in the number of eye movements. It may be that a change in the REM density (the concentration of eye movements) is the most significant REM sleep alteration in the sleep of these depressed patients.

Unresolved Issues

Despite consensus on these four features, several key issues concerning sleep in depressive states remain unresolved. While it is true that sleep is generally associated with a change in the pattern of all depressed patients, it is unclear whether hyposomnia or hypersomnia will be found in bipolar depression syndromes. While the hyposomnic picture is found in mixed depressed states as well as in bipolar patients requiring hospitalization, in bipolar and/or manic outpatients the presence of hypersomnia seems to be a much more common feature. The interpretation of the available data suggests, therefore, that the sleep pattern of hyper- or hyposomnia may be reflected in the level of

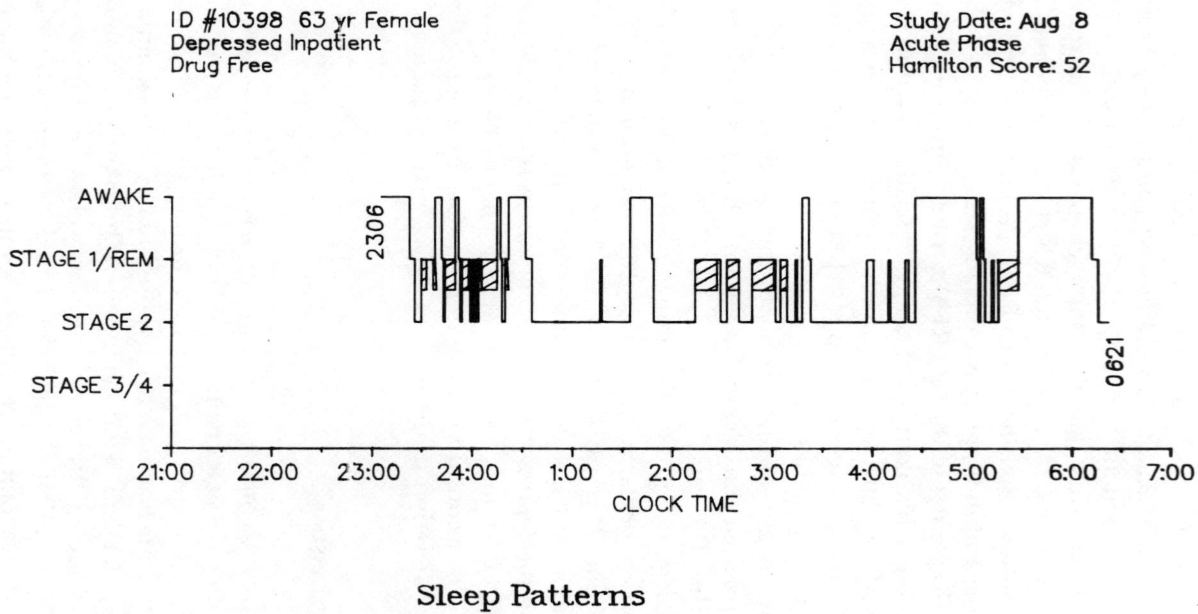

FIG. 6-1. All-night EEG sleep patterns of a 63-year-old depressed female.

severity with hyposomnia associated with increased levels of severity. This would agree with the observation that affective psychoses (delusional states) are usually associated with hyposomnia.

A number of unresolved questions also remain with respect to slow-wave sleep and the lighter stages of sleep. For example, little is known about the frequency and distribution of Stage 1 sleep in depressive disorders, other than that Stage 1 is associated with wakefulness and is found most commonly in patients with hyposomnia. With respect to slow-wave sleep, the data base on delta-wave amplitude, the number of slow waves, and the distribution of delta waves throughout the night in depressed patients is sparse. Thus, it may be premature to conclude that the reported reduction or even absence of Stages 3 and 4 is necessarily correct. Indeed, if the major change in slow-wave sleep during depresssion is a reduced amplitude of the average delta wave, it is possible that the total number of slow waves could be unchanged in depressive states. Further investigations need to be carried out with regard to these questions, in both depression and remission, and in comparison with matched controls.

We have recently tested the idea that abnormalities in sleep regulation, notably a weakened slow-wave sleep process, may be related to the pathophysiology of depression (Borbely & Wirz-Justice, 1982). Using automated delta-wave analytic techniques (Kupfer, 1983), we studied and compared the sleep patterns of 41 depressed patients and 23 normal controls under the age of 45. The data support the notion of a weakened S process in depressive states, with an absolute decrease in slow-wave sleep density in depressed patients throughout the night, particularly in the first half of the night. As illustrated in Table 6-3, normals showed a higher frequency of delta waves for each non-REM period throughout the night. The total delta-wave count was 5884 ($SD = 2473$) in normals versus 3058 ($SD = 1607$) counts in the depressed patients ($p < .001$). Comparisons based on manually scored

TABLE 6-3. Average Delta-Wave Count (Automated)

		Depressives ($n = 41$)	Normals ($n = 23$)	p
NREM period 1		17.6 ± 1.9	28.4 ± 2.9	.002
NREM period 2		17.9 ± 1.5	21.8 ± 2.2	NS
NREM period 3		7.8 ± 0.8	10.5 ± 1.7	NS
NREM period 4	($n = 33$)	6.0 ± 0.9	7.8 ± 1.0	NS
Average delta count		13.2 ± 1.0	16.9 ± 1.6	.03

sleep measures discriminated the two groups, but manual sleep staging did not accurately indicate the magnitude of the delta-wave "deficiency" in the depressed patients, especially in the earlier portions of the night (Figure 6-2). While one cannot generalize that this deficiency would be present if all delta waves were included, regardless of amplitude and wave length, it does strengthen the proposition that a delta-wave abnormality exists in depressed states.

REM Latency

Reduced REM latency is considered to be the most frequent and consistent sleep phenomenon found in depressed patients (Akiskal, Lemmi, Yerevanian, King, & Bulluomon, 1982). Nevertheless, issues dealing with its specificity to depression and certain depressive subtypes (e.g., primary vs. secondary) remain to be resolved (Table 6-4). Shortened REM latency has been considered to be a feature of primary depression rather than secondary depression; yet differences in REM latency have not discriminated primary from secondary depression when depression associated with alcoholism and drug abuse was included in the secondary depressed group (Spiker, Foster, Coble, Love, & Kupfer, 1977). It is also unclear whether it is increased severity, rather than type of depression, that accounts for the greater frequency of shortened REM latency reported in endogenous depressions. Finally, there remains the question of whether REM latencies have a bimodal distribution in depressed patients (Schulz, Lund, Cording, & Dirlich, 1979). Patients with particularly shortened REM latencies (under 20 minutes) seem to represent a group with a greater severity of illness and a greater resistance to treatment response (Coble, Kupfer, & Shaw, 1981). Our own data on depressed outpatients, however, suggest that, when age is taken into account, there is a continuous, rather than bimodal, distribution of reduced REM latency, ranging from 0 to 65 minutes.

Previous research has demonstrated that with the application of a cutoff of 50 minutes for REM latency, 70% to 75% of patients diagnosed with primary depression could be accurately identified (Gillin *et al.*, 1979; Kupfer, Foster, Coble, McPartland, & Ulrich, 1978). Using this arbitrary cutoff (50 minutes) for REM latency, data from our 1976 study showed an 83% sensitivity and a 74% specificity; a European study (Svendsen & Christensen, 1981) of 23 depressed patients showed a 92% sensitivity and 100% specificity.

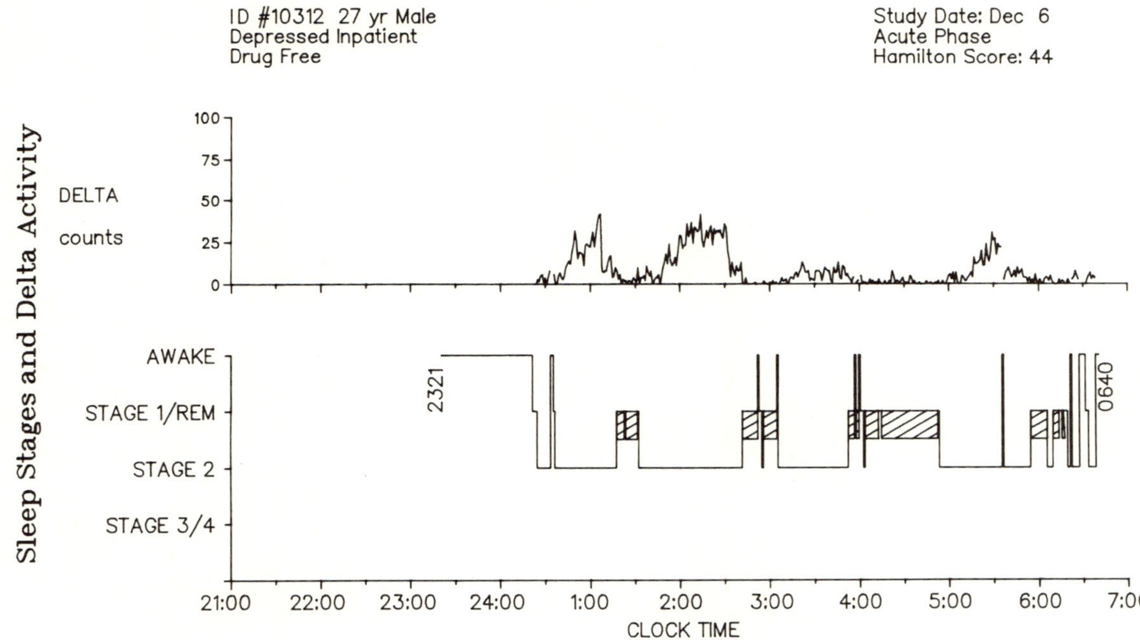

Sleep and Delta Patterns

FIG. 6-2. All-night EEG sleep pattern and automated delta activity of a 27-year-old depressed male.

TABLE 6-4. Short REM Latency

Melancholia
Endogenous depression
Unipolar/bipolar
Outpatients/inpatients
Schizoaffective disorders

These findings led us to question how age might affect levels of sensitivity and specificity and whether one REM latency cutoff score was appropriate for all age groups. Thus, the relationship of age and REM latency was examined in a sample of 87 depressed patients (18 to 60 years of age) (Ulrich, Shaw, & Kupfer, 1980). The group included 54 females and 33 males, with a mean age of 36.9 years (median age of 36.1). They were severely depressed, with a mean Hamilton Rating Scale score of 28.1 (range: 18–70). Mean duration since the first episode of depression was 8.4 years (median: 5.3 years) and the average length of the present episode was 66 weeks (median: 31.7 weeks). Since the mean number of previous episodes including manic episodes was 2.9 (median: 2.2), the group represents a population of recurrent and severely depressed individuals. The sample contained 20 delusional and 18 bipolar patients.

Examination of the overall group demonstrated a definite age trend for REM latency (Figure 6-3). In fact, when this sample of 87 patients was used to generate specific centile estimates for REM latency in age groups by 5-year increments, it became clear that values for REM latency obtained at one age range may not be comparable for another. A strong age trend existed, with the central estimates of REM latency ranging from 63.5 minutes in the youngest group to 23.9 minutes in the oldest. From Figure 6-3, it is apparent that extremely short REM latencies (i.e., less than 20–30 minutes) are more prevalent with increasing age.

REM Sleep Distribution

Another feature of sleep relevant to depression has to do with the distribution of REM sleep. At this point, very little is known about eye movement relationships and depression. While some evidence suggests that REM distribution is not as age-related as REM latency, the question remains open. The extent of the "V"-shaped distribution (increased eye movements in the first REM period and reduction in the second REM period) found in patients over 40 needs to be further examined to ascertain whether it is consistently present in younger depressed patients.

A recent study in this area, using automated counts, reported a redistribution and shift of REM activity into the first REM period in depressed patients under the age of 45, rather than an overall increase in REM activity, throughout the night (Kupfer, 1981). Total REM count for the depressed patients (n = 41) under the age of 45 was 674 (SD = 342) versus 564 (SD = 334) in the controls, a difference not reaching statistical significance. These data imply that an increase of REM activity in the first REM period may be present across the age spectrum and in most depressed patients.

It is clear that the average REM count for individual REM periods generally demonstrates considerable decreases in the second half of the

FIG. 6-3. REM latency over five age groups in nonpsychotic depressed inpatients and outpatients (n = 108) as contrasted to normals.

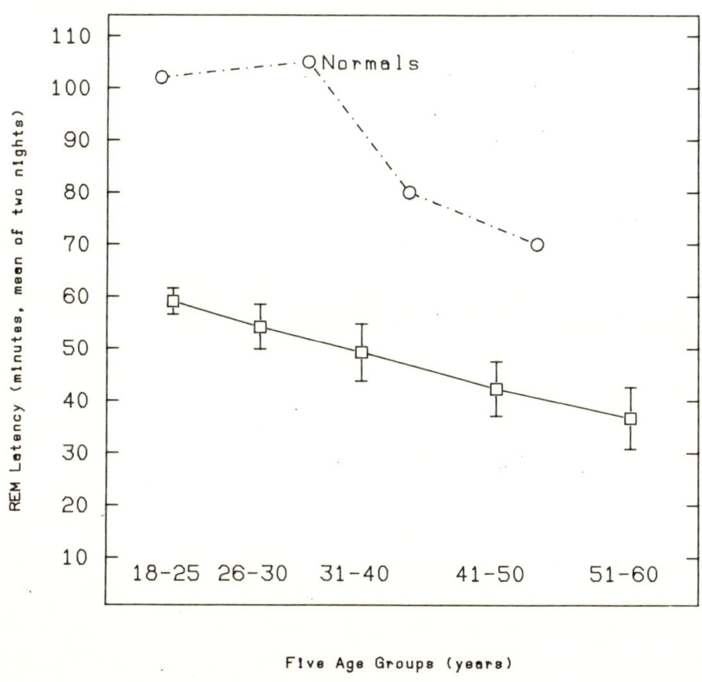

REM periods and has differentiated patients who subsequently do not respond well to amitriptyline. These findings (reported previously) suggest that, even as late as 6 hours into the night of sleep, significant differences among depressed patients are present, based on treatment responder groups. It also suggests that a reevaluation of the previous emphasis on REM abnormalities solely in the first hour or two of the night may be indicated (Kupfer, Shaw, Ulrich, Coble, & Spiker, 1982a).

Potential Clinical Applications

Sleep studies have several further potential clinical applications. Sleep studies could be used to improve differential diagnosis (to ascertain whether an affective disorder is present). Examples of this "diagnostic boundary" application include differentiating affective disorders from schizoaffective illness, borderline states, anxiety states, and dementias. Within the spectrum of affective disorders, sleep investigations could further our understanding of diagnostic subgroups, or even refine that clinical classification by creating new diagnostic subgroups.

The final potential and important application of sleep investigations is the extent to which sleep investigations can be used as a "test." Are one or more sleep variables sensitive or specific enough to somehow better predict diagnostic specificity, treatment, and prognosis? Aside from the issues of sensitivity and specificity, it may be necessary to construct normograms and tables. While this represents an admirable goal, it must be emphasized that short REM latency does not constitute the whole range of sleep abnormalities. Using sleep variables both as a test and to set up a discriminating system where it is either abnormal or not abnormal, a so-called yes–no situation, could severely constrict and reduce the richness of the sleep data. The use of a test should not in any way be confused with the notion of using sleep variables to contribute to our understanding of the pathophysiology of depression.

The sensitivity and specificity of sleep measures, as well as of other biological tests in psychiatry, have recently come under investigative scrutiny. Rush, Giles, Roffwarg, and Parker (1982) differentiated endogenous from nonendogenous patients by means of sleep measures, and Akiskal *et al.* (1982) similarly discriminated primary from secondary depressives (Table 6-5). Feinberg, Gillin, Carroll, Greden, and Zis (1982) developed a discriminant function based on sleep continuity variables from a population of unipolar depressives

Table 6-5. Sensitivity and Specificity of EEG Sleep Studies for Depression

Study	Criterion group (*n*)	Control group(s) (*n*)	Method	Sensitivity	Specificity
Gillin, Duncan, Pettigrew, & Thurmond (1979)	Primary inpatients (56)	Normals and insomniacs (59)	Discriminant analysis[a]	73.2	100
Rush, Giles, Roffwarg, & Parker (1982)	Endogenous outpatients (21)	Nonendogenous outpatients (18)	REM latency ≤62 min	76.0	72.0
Feinberg (1982)	Endogenous inpatients (33)	Nonendogenous inpatients (28)	Discriminant analysis[b]	61.0	93.0

[a]Six variables: Total sleep, total recording period, sleep efficiency, sleep latency, REM time, REM percent.
[b]REM latency and REM density.

and compared its sensitivity and specificity with a function based on REM latency and REM density derived from a mixed group of depressed patients. The function developed from the unipolar population identified only 40% of bipolar depressives (compared with 61% of the unipolaar), while the function based on REM measures (latency and density) correctly classified 73% of the bipolar and 72% of the unipolar depressives. If the sleep EEG is to assist in the differential diagnosis of bipolar versus unipolar disorder, discriminant functions derived and validated in populations containing both types of disorders are needed.

Such studies demonstrate acceptable sensitivity and specificity for EEG sleep studies. The findings are made more impressive in light of emerging evidence that a significant portion of depressives classified clinically as secondary, neurotic, or nonendogenous (and who would be therefore considered "false positives") actually have an atypical, subsyndromal, or otherwise complicated form of melancholic or vital depression (Akiskal *et al.*, 1980; Akiskal, Bitar, Puzantian, Rosenthal, & Walberg, 1978; Carroll, 1982).

Several groups also compared sleep EEG and dexamethasone suppression test (DST) results with regard to the questions of sensitivity and specificity. Rush *et al.* (1982) found REM latency to be more sensitive in depressed outpatients than the DST (76% vs. 38%), but of lower specificity (72% vs. 94%). Reduced REM latency was present in nearly all DST nonsuppressors. Feinberg (1982), in a melancholic population, found 72% agreement between DST and sleep studies.

What then is our current understanding of how sleep measures are relevant in affective disorders? The observation that shortened REM latency is generally present in depressive disorders and is inversely correlated with severity of the disorder has been confirmed. While these relationships are present if the spectrum of patients considered includes those with mild as well as with severe depression, the linear relationship between severity and REM latency is less prominent if only severe depressions (requiring hospitalization) are considered.

It appears, therefore, that shortened REM latency represents a threshold phenomenon and is a common factor in all depressive states, regardless of severity. REM latencies of less than 30–40 minutes relate less to severity directly than to age or the presence of delusions. Thus, a shortened REM latency is always suggestive of depression, but may not always correlate with severity. Severity is better reflected in measures of sleep continuity and REM distribution. Sleep continuity correlates highly with severity, even when age is controlled, as again confirmed in our latest investigation in younger depressives (Kupfer *et al.*, 1981).

Automated REM Sleep Analysis

The advent of automated analysis has made the case with regard to REM distribution considerably stronger. The shift of REM activity to the left or the earlier part of the night is more often found in depressed individuals who meet endogenous criteria and present with a higher level of severity. Furthermore, it would appear that such individuals tend to be more refractory to the usual treatment with tricyclics. Baseline measures of sleep, especially the distribution of REM sleep, assist in the prediction of treatment response. The greater the density of REM sleep in the first third of the night, the less likely it is that the individual is going to respond to the usual dose of tricyclic antidepressants.

This hypothesis was tested in a group of 74 depressed patients studied recently on the Clinical Research Unit at Western Psychiatric Institute and Clinic. Of the 74 patients, 68 were unipolar; 53 patients were diagnosed definitely endogenous by RDC, and 48 had a recurrent unipolar disease. Six were delusional. In addition, 17 patients showed psychomotor retardation, 23 showed psychomotor agitation, and eight were both agitated and retarded. The mean age was 37.3 ($SD = 12.9$ years) with an initial Hamilton Rating Scale for Depression (HRS-D) score of 37.2 ($SD = 7.3$) (sum of two raters). Fifty of the 74 patients were female. The median length of the current episode was 30.5 weeks and the median number of previous episodes was 2.2. Twenty-three of the patients had a clear-cut positive clinical response at the end of 4 weeks of treatment (HRS-D ≤ 12) (sum of two raters), whereas 29 of the remaining 52 patients were partial responders (HRS-D = 13–20). The remaining 22 patients were definite nonresponders (HRS-D > 20).

The initial analysis focused on the all-night time period divided into sleep hours, "hourly REM activity", as well as division of the night into halves (Figure 6-4). A significant interaction between hourly REM activity and clinical response was found ($F = 2.28$, $p < .01$), primarily due to the linear trend ($F = 4.95$, $p < .01$). When the REM activity was then examined by halves of the night, an interaction between clinical response and REM sleep by halves of the night was very significant ($F = 6.04$, $p < .004$) (Figures 6-5 to 6-7). Further analysis revealed that this interaction was largely due to the fact that nonresponders had a relative *decrease* in the REM activity in the second half of the night, while responders and partial responders showed a relative *increase* in REM activity in the second half of the night.

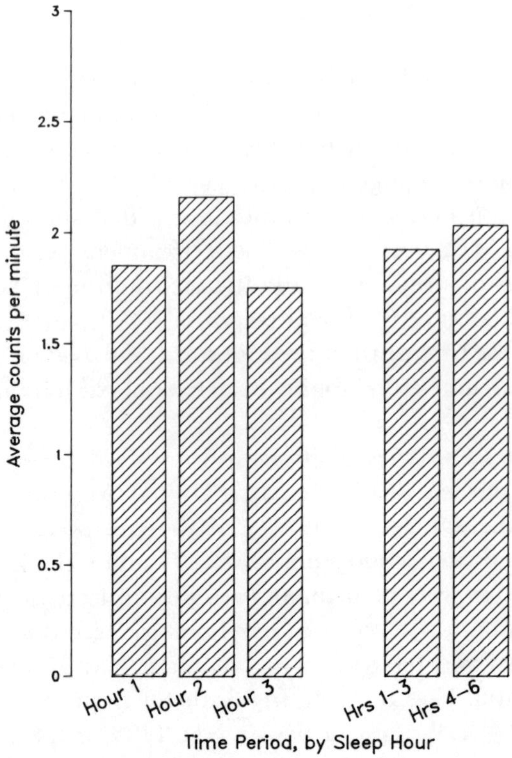

FIG. 6-4. Profile of *baseline* REM activity in 74 depressed patients who received amitriptyline.

With respect to the first 3 hours of REM sleep activity, the nonresponder group had clearly a significantly greater amount of REM activity. However, the three groups did not differ in REM activity in the second 3 hours of the night. While automated REM activity is related to the severity of illness ($r = .30$, $p < .005$), the distribution of REM activity by halves may help predict clinical response. Interestingly, REM activity in the first half of the night ($r = .37$, $p < .001$), but not in the second half of the night ($r = .12$, NS), was related to severity.

Which sleep EEG changes best correlate with the clinical episode of depression? Sleep discontinuity variables appear to correlate highly with the episode. The disruption of sleep stages with increased wakefulness is most prominent at the time that the episode is most severe, although various REM and slow-wave changes are also present. However, what order these sleep change alterations occur as improvement with treatment takes place and whether these are reversible is unclear.

Effects of Antidepressants

A schema of the immediate effects of various antidepressants on the sleep profile of depressed patients is shown in Table 6-6. In the short run, tricyclics suppress REM sleep—as reflected by their tendency to extend the inter-REM time interval. In essence, each of the non-REM (NREM) periods are prolonged, a prolongation probably associated with increased numbers of delta waves and decreased time awake. This NREM effect is associated with a REM effect, which tends to consolidate each of the REM periods into a more "intensive" REM period without reducing the length of each REM period. Thus, by the end of the night there will be fewer REM periods but no marked decrease in REM activity. This drug-sleep interaction is immediate and appears to be a threshold phenomenon with even 25 mg of amitriptyline.

On the other hand, monoamine oxidase inhibitors (MAOIs) appear to operate initially by a different mechanism. For example, one or

FIG. 6-5. Profile of *baseline* REM activity in 74 depressed patients (responders; $n = 23$) who received amitriptyline.

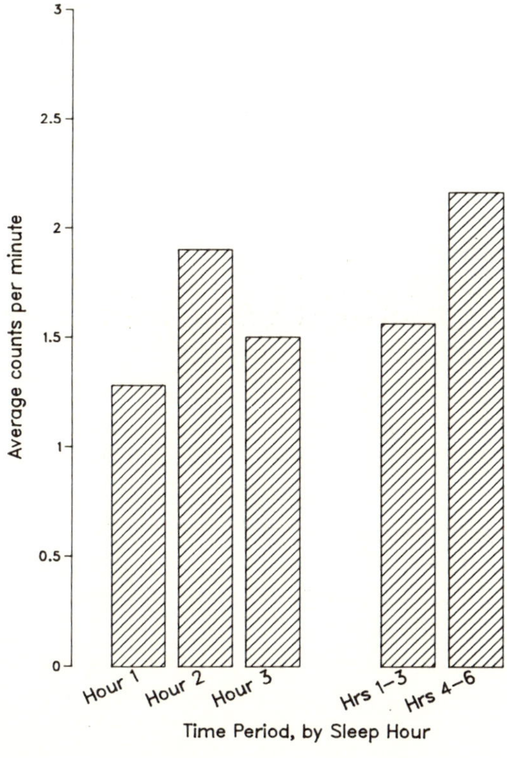

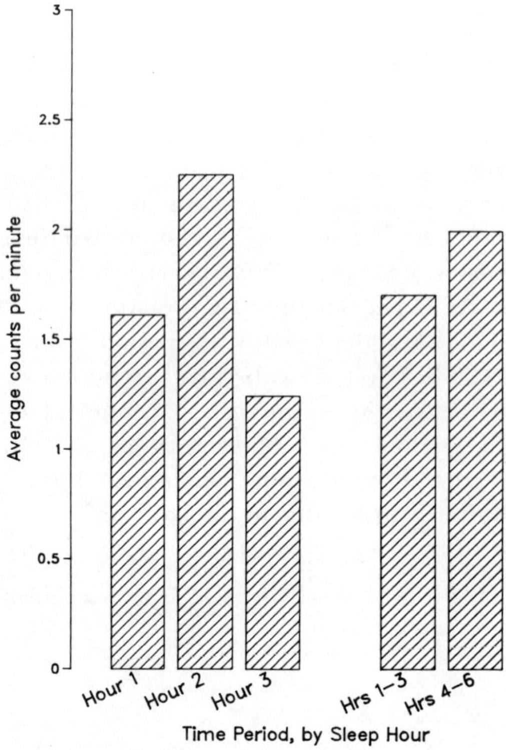

FIG. 6-6. Profile of *baseline* REM activity in 74 depressed patients (partial responders; $n = 29$) who received amitriptyline.

two doses of an MAOI does not profoundly affect any aspect of REM sleep. However, the effect of an MAOI on REM sleep is apparent within several days of administration. This effect is best described as a true suppressant effect: The length of REM periods appears to be abbreviated and broken by the action of an MAOI. There is an associated increase of EMG tone, tending to decrease the likelihood of long REM periods without stage shifts on actual awakenings. The prime alteration, therefore, is not one of extending NREM intervals as much as phasing out REM sleep further and further into the night. Eventually, at a certain threshold level (related to but not necessarily caused by inhibition of platelet MAOI), complete or almost complete REM suppression will be present.

Lithium carbonate manifests a drug–sleep action more similar to MAOIs than tricyclics: Lithium tends to shorten the length of REM

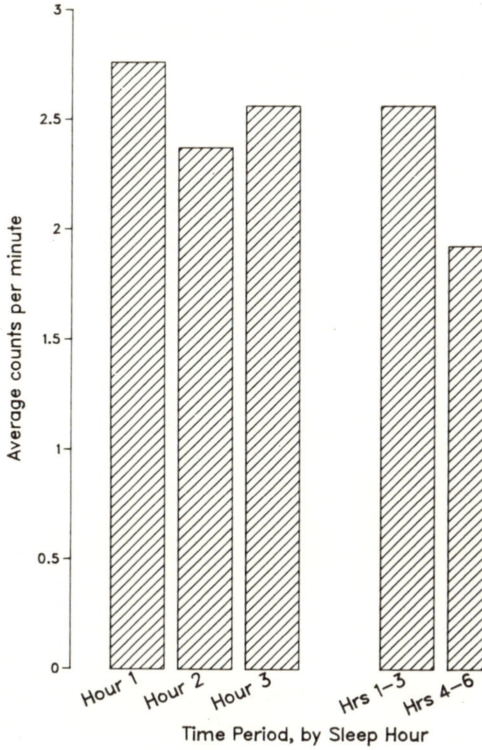

FIG. 6-7. Profile of *baseline* REM activity in 74 depressed patients (nonresponders; $n = 22$) who received amitriptyline.

TABLE 6-6. Effects of Antidepressants on the Sleep Profile of Depressed Patients

Immediate tricyclic antidepressant effects
1. Decrease in REM sleep percent
2. Decrease in REM activity
3. Reduction in sleep onset difficulty and intermittent awakenings
4. Increase in the number of delta waves
Chronic tricyclic antidepressant effects
1. Sustained decrease in REM sleep percent
2. Sustained improvement in sleep continuity

periods, rather than necessarily increase the NREM interval. Lithium does not lengthen REM latencies as profoundly as tricyclics or MAOIs. While REM latency may be lengthened by all three classes of drugs, tricyclics and MAOIs are most associated with a shift in the distribution of REM sleep. However, MAOIs may more powerfully shift the distribution of REM sleep from earlier to later in the night. Perhaps the patient who is relatively unresponsive to tricyclics and who shows a pronounced shift to the left of REM sleep will respond better to an MAOI electroconvulsive therapy (ECT) (ECT may also represent a powerful treatment modality associated with a shift of REM sleep). Finally, the few sleep studies on mania and hypomania reveal shortened REM latencies, although not necessarily accompanied by a shift to the left of REM distribution. In this sense, lithium carbonate may represent the most appropriate drug for this group.

Many of the central nervous system and behavioral effects of antidepressants take several days or even weeks to occur. Such delayed effects may be related to steady-state plasma levels of the drug of its active metabolites. On the other hand, antidepressant drug-induced sleep EEG changes are more immediate. The immediate administration of antidepressants is associated with profound changes in several major sleep parameters, including a delayed onset of the first REM period which is associated with decreased total REM sleep time, fewer REM periods, and a transient reduction in the number of rapid eye movements, as well as a transient increased number of delta waves (Kupfer, 1984). The continued administration of these compounds is associated with a persistence of these sleep alterations, except that the REM activity is restored to baseline levels.

While the immediate action of these compounds on sleep appears to produce changes in the direction of "normalization," even the continued administration of these compounds does not necessarily "correct" all sleep abnormalities. Nevertheless, normalization of REM latency, redistribution of REM activity with more REM activity in the second half of the night, improved sleep continuity, and increased numbers of delta waves are all consistent with the drug effect acting as a "corrective" influence.

It is important to separate effects related to sedation and those related to REM sleep. Our data support the notion that sedative effects of antidepressants are related to anticholinergic (mainly) or serotonergic (possibly) activity of the drugs. The action of amitriptyline (in contrast to zimelidine or desipramine) illustrates this point. The mild sedative action of nortriptyline supports its middle position. It is appealing to assume that the REM sleep abnormalities in depression are associated with decreased norepinephrine (NE) and increased acetylcholine (ACh). The administration of drugs that either increase NE or decrease ACh would alter this balance. If we assume that it is an additive effect, it is possible that drugs that operate on only one system may have as much of an effect as those drugs that affect both systems.

Treatment response predictions based on changes in EEG sleep variables have been derived from studies with amitriptyline. Three investigations, all utilizing amitriptyline, have established that the degree of REM suppression, as well as the degree of prolongation of REM latency, relates significantly to positive response (Kupfer *et al.*, 1980, 1981, 1982b). Baseline as well as immediate sleep EEG changes following antidepressant drug administration are apparently predictive of ultimate response. Individuals who experience a so-called "breakthrough" (a shortened REM latency that may be prolonged only transiently after the initial administration of a tricyclic antidepressant) appear likely to be refractory. Other nonresponders will show little or no lengthening of REM latency in the several days following initiation.

Are the sleep EEG changes that predict amitriptyline response applicable to other tricyclic antidepressants? Although no other prediction studies have been completed, data on the effects of other tricyclics on the sleep of normals and depressed patients point in the same direction. While it is tempting to generalize to all antidepressants the relationship clearly established with amitriptyline, EEG sleep, and clinical response, such a position should be resisted. As of now, it appears that all techniques utilized to treat depression (including nonpharmacological procedures such as sleep and REM deprivation) are associated with a degree of REM suppression. Whether there is a relationship between ultimate clinical response and immediate REM suppression for all forms of antidepressant treatment is unclear.

We do hypothesize that the persistent presence of REM suppression is a necessary but insufficient condition for clinical response (i.e., the REM suppression associated with administration of an MAOI is present when an MAOI is efficacious, but can also be present even when the drug is ineffective). However, the degree of REM suppression is related to the enhancement of NREM sleep. Therefore, increased opportunity for delta-wave generation may also relate to clinical response. Another possibility is that REM sleep suppression may result from an immediate alteration of receptor sites. This immediate alteration may differ from that found with more chronic administration of antidepressants, where it has been proposed that postsynaptic adrenergic sensitivity is reduced, while response to adrenergic stimulation is enhanced.

Sleep Measures and Clinical Changes

Sleep measures might also be of value in assessing response and course of illness over more extended time periods. Considerable interest has arisen identifying the residual sleep abnormalities in depressed patients currently in remission. Remitted formerly depressed persons who are at high risk for relapse may continue to demonstrate sleep abnormalities that are similar to those noted in the acute episode or that are somewhat between the abnormalities in the acute episode and the normal state. A second question is which sleep characteristics persist with remission independent of the prognostic value of these findings. Presently, reductions in delta (Stages 3 and 4) sleep do not appear to persist with clinical remission. The sleep continuity, while somewhat to considerably improved, still shows some disruption in remitted individuals. To date, a number of patients who are not in a clinical episode appear to have short REM latencies and some continue to demonstrate a leftward shift in REM distribution.

This discussion naturally leads to the third question—what is the order of sleep changes in the initial stages of a new episode? Our best hunch is that the short REM latency is the first finding that one will note in the early stages of a new episode, followed by a redistribution of REM sleep with an increased shift to the left. Thus, oscillations in REM latency seem to be most sensitive to the clinical course, changes in REM percent and sleep maintenance are sensitive to drug effect, and the onset of a new episode may be associated with a redistribution in REM activity. Stage 2 REM and the number of arousals are most common in the acute phase and REM density is at its highest during the phase of drug stabilization, as is REM latency. During relapse, the REM latencies are similar to the previous acute phase.

Finally, if there are sleep variables associated with the risk of relapse, do these variables represent vulnerability factors? That is, are they traits associated with a proneness to develop a new (first or recurrent) episode of depression? If such markers are detected, studies of relatives, especially younger individuals, who themselves may be at high risk to develop the actual disease, would be indicated. If we are to examine the sleep of a depressed individual in remission, is it similar to the sleep of a relative of a proband who had depression or another individual who is at high risk for affective disorders? Are we likely to observe a particular constellation of sleep variables that would correlate or represent this vulnerability factor? An important subset of this question relates to whether the baseline sleep of such an individual will be able to elicit this information, or whether some kind of pharmacological or biochemical probe will be needed to bring out this vulnerability factor (e.g., the use of arecoline as a provocative agent). Another suggestion would be to use a small dose of a tricyclic antidepressant, since it has been hypothesized that such a patient may possibly have a response different from that of individuals who are not at risk for depression.

While there are a number of unanswered questions regarding the use of EEG sleep measures in the prediction of treatment response among depressed patients, the significant correlation of a measure of sleep disturbance with a particular time in the course of the depressive episode might represent a powerful tool for understanding treatment course and prognosis in depression. Alterations in circadian rhythms in depressed patients have been suggested as explanations for various biological abnormalities associated with depression, including disturbances in sleep, motor activity, and endocrine function. It has also been proposed that sleep deprivation, which is capable of inducing transient remission of depression, slows or delays patients' circadian temperature rhythms. In a similar way, it has been suggested that procedures that advance the patient's environmental schedule relative to their circadian rhythms also abolish differences in timing and, therefore, improve depressed mood at least transiently. Other studies using cholinergic probes and "cholinergic REM induction test" have suggested that the action of physostigmine and arecoline on REM sleep timing (the onset of REM periods) points to a cholinergic mechanism which may be responsible for the short REM latency. At the present time, none of the proposed theories or hypotheses adequately explains the available data. Nevertheless, they represent important and innovative steps that may lead to an increased understanding of the pathophysiology of depression.

ACKNOWLEDGMENT

This work was supported in part by National Institute of Mental Health Grants MH-25642 and MH-30915, as well as a Grant from the John D. and Catherine T. MacArthur Foundation Research Network on the Psychobiology of Depression.

REFERENCES

Akiskal, H. S., Bitar, A. H., Puzantian, V. R., Rosenthal, T. L., & Walker, P. M. (1978). The nosological status of neurotic depression. *Archives of General Psychiatry, 35*, 756–766.

Akiskal, H. S., Lemmi, H., Yerevanian, B., King, D., & Bulluomon, J. (1982). The utility of the REM latency test in psychiatric diagnosis: A study of 81 depressed outpatients. *Psychiatry Research, 7*, 101–110.

Akiskal, H. S., Rosenthal, T. L., Haykal, R. F., Lemmi, H., Rosenthal, R. H., & Scott-Strauss, A. (1980). Characterological depressions: Clinical and sleep EEG findings separating subaffective dysthymias from character spectrum disorders. *Archives of General Psychiatry, 37*, 777–783.

Borbely, A. A., & Wirz-Justice, A. (1981). Sleep, sleep deprivation and depression. *Human Neurobiology, 1*, 205–210.

Carroll, B. J. (1982). The dexamethasone suppression test for melancholia. *British Journal of Psychiatry, 140*, 292–304.

Coble, P. A., Kupfer, D. J., & Shaw, D. H. (1981). Distribution of REM latency in depression. *Biological Psychiatry, 16*, 453–466.

Coble, P. A., Kupfer, D. J., Spiker, D. G., Neil, J. F., & McPartland, R. J. (1979). EEG sleep in primary depression: A longitudinal placebo study. *Journal of Affective Disorders, 1*, 131–138.

Feinberg, M. (1982). EEG studies of sleep and dexamethasone suppression test in the diagnosis of depression. In I. Hanin & E. Usdin (Eds.), *Biological markers in psychiatry and neurology* (pp. 241–251). New York: Pergamon Press.

Feinberg, M., Gillin, J. C., Carroll, B. J., Greden, J. F., & Zis, A. P. (1982). EEG studies of sleep in the diagnosis of depression. *Biological Psychiatry, 17*, 305–316.

Gillin, J. C., Duncan, W. C., Pettigrew, K. D., & Thurmond, A. J. (1979). Successful separation of depressed, normal and insomniac subjects by EEG sleep data. *Archives of General Psychiatry, 35*, 85–90.

Kupfer, D. J. (1982). Application of EEG sleep in the treatment of depression. In J. Mendlewicz & H. M. van Praag (Eds.), *Advances in biological psychiatry* (Vol. 6, pp. 387–396). New York: Pergamon Press.

Kupfer, D. J. (1983). Recent applications of automated sleep analysis in affective states. In C. Perris, D. Kemali, & M. Koukkou-Lehmann (Eds.), *Advances in biological psychiatry* (pp. 182–191). Zurich: Karger.

Kupfer, D. J. (1984). REM activity and delta abnormalities in affective states. *Research Communications in Psychology, Psychiatry and Behavior, 9*, 149 176.

Kupfer, D. J., Foster, F. G., Coble, P. A., McPartland, R. J., & Ulrich, R. F. (1978). The application of EEG sleep for the differential diagnosis of affective disorders. *American Journal of Psychiatry, 135*, 69–74.

Kupfer, D. J., Shaw, D. H., Ulrich, R. F., Coble, P. A., & Spiker, D. G. (1982a). Application of automated REM analysis in depression. *Archives of General Psychiatry, 39*, 569–573.

Kupfer, D. J., Spiker, D. G., Coble, P. A., Neil, J. F., Ulrich, R. F., & Shaw, D. H. (1980). Depression, EEG sleep and clinical response. *Comprehensive Psychiatry, 21*, 212–220.

Kupfer, D. J., Spiker, D. G., Coble, P. A., Neil, J. F., Ulrich, R. F., & Shaw, D. H. (1981). Sleep and treatment prediction in endogenous depression. *American Journal of Psychiatry, 138*, 429–434.

Kupfer, D. J., Spiker, D. G., Rossi, A., Coble, P. A., Ulrich, R. F., & Shaw, D. H. Recent diagnostic and treatment advances in REM sleep and depression. (1982b). In P. Clayton & J. Barrett (Eds.), *Treatment of depression: Old controversies and new approaches* (pp. 31–52). New York: Raven Press.

Rechtschaffen, A., & Kales, A. A. (1968). *A manual of standardized terminology, techniques and scoring for sleep stages of human subjects.* Washington, DC: Department of Health, Education and Welfare.

Rush, A. J., Giles, D.E., Roffwarg, H. P., & Parker, C. R. (1982). Sleep EEG and dexamethasone suppression test findings in outpatients with unipolar major depressive disorder. *Biological Psychiatry, 17,* 327–341.

Schulz, H., Lund, R., Cording, C., & Dirlich, G. (1979). Biomodal distribution of REM sleep latencies in depression. *Biological Psychiatry, 14,* 595–600.

Spiker, D. G., Foster, F. G., Coble, P. A., Love, D., & Kupfer, D. J. (1977). The sleep disorder in depressed alcoholics. *Sleep Research, 6,* 161.

Spitzer, R., Endicott, J., & Robins, E. (1978). Research diagnostic criteria. *Archives of General Psychiatry, 34,* 773–782.

Svensden, S., & Christensen, P. G. (1981). Duration of REM sleep latency as a predictor of effect of antidepressant therapy. *Acta Psychiatrica Scandinavica, 64,* 238–243.

Ulrich, R. F., Shaw, D. H., & Kupfer, D. J. (1980). Effects of aging on EEG sleep in depression. *Sleep, 3,* 31–40.

Vogel, G. W. (1981). The relationship between endogenous depression and REM sleep. *Psychiatric Annals, 11,* 423–428.

7

Brain Imaging in Affective Disorders

MONTE S. BUCHSBAUM
H. H. HOLCOMB
L. DELISI
E. HAZLETT

Introduction

The brain, the chief target organ for psychiatry, has up to now been studied through approaches that were necessarily indirect. Blood, urine, and cerebrospinal fluid, though valuable indicators of neurochemical and neuropharmacological activity, are removed in time and place from the disordered thought and diluted by the products of both functional and dysfunctional systems.

The dramatic response of psychiatric patients to psychoactive medication and the subtle but pervasive genetic transmission of liability continue to inspire biological approaches to the puzzles of psychopathology. From this, we might expect that a neurochemical dysfunction is involved in these illnesses and that a neurochemical test could diagnose the illness, predict treatment outcome, and assess longitudinal course. Unfortunately, despite the logical scientific basis of this approach, there has been great difficulty in discovering a reliable chemical indicator for affective disorders or schizophrenia. This difficulty may be due partly to biological heterogeneity of the disorders, along with the presence of several or even many biological deficits responsible for the symptom clusters associated with schizophrenia or affective disorder (Buchsbaum, Davis, & van Kammen, 1980; Buchsbaum & Haier, 1978).

No less severe may be the problems inherent in the indirect ap-

MONTE S. BUCHSBAUM and E. HAZLETT. Department of Psychiatry and International Institute on Brain and Behavior, Visual Imaging Center, University of California, Irvine, California.

H. H. HOLCOMB and L. DELISI. Laboratory of Psychology and Psychopathology, National Institute of Mental Health, Bethesda, Maryland.

proach of the clinical neuroscientist to the brain. He or she relies on peripheral fluids to assess central and regional neurochemical processes. Blood, urine, and cerebrospinal fluid, although valuable reflectors of the neurochemical and neuropharmacological activity of the brain, are removed in time and place from disordered thought processes and diluted by the products of functional and dysfunctional brain systems. Biopsy studies, which have aided the study of functional disorders of organs such as the liver, are destructive to the brain and less useful because of the brain's complex and varied structure. While autopsy studies can provide important regional cues, they present major difficulties for the depression researcher. Depression is a phasic disorder and the need for repeated biological measures over prolonged time intervals makes autopsy samples less useful than in diseases with a more continuous and progressive course, such as Parkinson's. Lastly, the experimental insights gained from experiments in animals that examine the pharmacology of individual cell groups in striatum or locus ceruleus, for example, cannot easily or unambiguously be applied in clinical populations.

New technologies are now making a specific regional approach to patients with the major psychoses possible. These include xenon-133 (^{133}*Xe*) *blood flow, electroencephalography* (*EEG*) and *evoked potential topography, x-ray transmission scanning* (*CAT or CT scans*), *nuclear magnetic resonance* (*NMR*) *imaging,* and *position emission tomography* (*PET*). These techniques so far have been more widely applied in schizophrenia than in affective illness. This may partly reflect a research emphasis on the illness with relatively poorer prognosis. Further, the motor, perceptual, and cognitive deficits in schizophrenia have suggested discrete cortical lesions to some investigators, just as schizophrenia's neuroleptic sensitivity suggested a basal ganglia locus to others.

However, there is no clear reason to believe that mood disturbance and noradreneric pathways are any less focal than the findings suggested in schizophrenia. Even cognitive deficits, long the province of schizophrenia research, are now being reported in affective illness, with rigorous neuropsychological tasks such as dichotic listening (Bruder, Sutton, Berger-Gross, Quitkin, & Davies, 1981). All of this indicates the need to apply these new regional approaches in depression.

The two main functional anatomic hypotheses of depression involve the nondominant cortex and catecholamine function in limbic reward systems. Nondominant hemispheric dysfunction (Flor-Henry,

1979; Ross & Rush, 1981) has been studied by taking advantage of natural lesions, administering carefully selected psychological tasks and left–right differences in EEG and evoked potentials. While there are extensive findings of unusual asymmetry in patients with affective illness, there are many conflicting lines of evidence. The tendency to use a single pair of EEG electrodes or single task as representative of an entire hemisphere's dysfunction must be an important factor in this uncertainty. Limbic reward systems have been even more inaccessible to direct regional study in man up to now. It is our plan here not to review these hypotheses, which have been well treated elsewhere, but to explore new techniques for systematically examining the entire brain on an anatomic as well as functional basis.

Blood Flow, Brain Work, and Regional Function

The major energy source for the brain is *glucose* and its use is closely related to local functional activity, *oxygen consumption,* and blood flow (Sokoloff, 1981). This coupling is not merely a generalized brain effect characterizing states such as coma or excitement, but is a localized mechanism affecting small brain areas. Before the development of PET techniques, cerebral blood flow was, together with the EEG, the major means of approaching regional brain function in clinical studies. In the earliest efforts, Kety *et al.*, (1948) studied the cerebral blood flow correlates of schizophrenia with their nitrous oxide technique for the whole brain. No differences between their 22 patients and normal controls were found, but they noted that "there remains the possibility that local disturbances confined to small but important regions may still occur since the method used yields only mean values for the entire brain." Using the Kety technique, Hoyer and Oesterreich (1975) did find whole brain blood flow increased in "productive" schizophrenics, but by this time regional approaches to blood flow had become possible.

Blood Flow

Regional cerebral blood flow can be studied with the ^{133}Xe washout technique. The isotope may be injected into the internal carotid artery or breathed as a mixture with oxygen and air. A battery of detectors arranged over the scalp picks up the appearance and disappearance of the radioactivity. Analysis of this clearance curve yields estimates of blood-flow rate under each detector. With intracarotid injection and detectors spaced at l-cm intervals, resolution in the range or 2 cm may result (see phantom data in Foit, Larsen, Hattori, Skinhj, & Lassen, 1980). Inhalation techniques yield somewhat lesser resolution, but avoid possible hazards associated with carotid injection. Recently, single-photon emission tomography has been introduced using ^{133}Xe or [^{123}I]iodoamphetamine (Comar *et al.*, 1979; Kuhl *et al.*, 1982), which yields a slice image with resolution somewhat less than that achieved with PET scanning but still allowing visualization of basal ganglia and major cortical regions.

In the first studies of schizophrenia, Ingvar and Franzen (1947b) measured cerebral blood flow in 31 patients with schizophrenia and 10 neurologically normal male alcoholics. They used the intra-arterial ^{133}Xe injection technique with 32 detectors to evaluate cortical flow. Subjects were tested resting, usually with their eyes closed. Control subjects had relatively higher frontal than posterior blood flow. Patients with schizophrenia had less frontal–posterior blood flow difference; low frontal flow was especially found in patients with symptoms of indifference, inactivity, and autism. Flow increases in postcentral temporal–occipital and parietal regions were associated with symptoms of disturbed cognition.

Chronic schizophrenics also showed smaller increases in frontal blood flow with simple tasks. In highly disturbed patients, the task of naming objects in pictures produced slight and nonsignificant frontal flow increases (Franzen & Ingvar, 1975). Controls showed large increases, although a somewhat more difficult task (Raven's Matrices) was used, which might have increased blood flow. However, postcentral flows increased about equally in both groups, tending to support the concept of hypofrontal function in schizophrenia. The blood flow in the frontal lobes was further explored in studies of "motor ideation" (Ingvar & Philipson, 1977). Regional-blood-flow maps were obtained at rest, while subjects imagined a slow rhythmic clenching of the right hand, and during actual hand movements. Again, at rest, the subjects had higher flows in frontal than postcentral regions. When they imagined hard movements, flow increases appeared in premotor frontal regions, especially in superior frontal, inferior frontal, and temporal pole regions.

Subsequent reports on cerebral blood flow using inhalation of ^{133}Xe in depression (Mathew *et al.*, 1980) and schizophrenia (Mathew, Duncan, Weinman, & Barr, 1982) showed decreases in blood flow in the whole right hemisphere in depression and whole left hemisphere in schizophrenia, but no regional analysis was presented. A similar reduction in blood flow in depressives was observed by Gustafson, Risberg, and Silfverskiold (1981). In a subsequent report, they suggest that normal depressive differences were largely due to age differences (blood flow decreases with age and the depressives were older than normals) or pCO_2 differences (Silfverskiold, Gustafson, Johansson, & Risberg, in press). They also observed the lowest blood flows in manics, a group younger than their depressives and with equal pCO_2 levels. However, medication status was uncontrolled and the greater use of neuroleptic medication in the manic group might have been decisive. Specific statistical regional comparisons for patient groups were not made, so assessment of the hypofrontal phenomenon of Ingvar and Franzen (1974a) was not directly possible. A frontal index based on the ratio of anterior five probes divided by the hemisphere mean was calculated on the manic group. Its value of 1.05 was comparable to that observed in young schizophrenics by Ingvar and Franzen (1974b) but corresponding values in normals of Silfverskiold *et al.* are not available.

Single-photon emission tomography was used by Rush, Schlesser, Stokely, Bonte, and Altshuler (in press) in patients with affective disorder, free of psychoactive medication for at least 7 days. Decreased blood flow was observed in patients with unipolar depression, consistent with the results of Mathew *et al.* (1980) and Silfverskiold *et al.* (in press). However, unlike the findings of Silfverskiold *et al.*, patients with manic or mixed phase bipolar (BP) illness had higher flows than controls. Despite obtaining regional data, all three groups did not analyze or separately report statistics on regional comparisons, preferring to average entire hemispheric data. Despite the elegant studies of many investigators (Ingvar & Philipson, 1977; Ingvar, Rosen, Eriksson, & Elmqvist, 1976; Roland, 1981) indicating effects of psychological tasks on regional blood flow, these authors do not mention a specific task or detail the experimental conditions under which the data were collected. Interpretation of left–right differences under these circumstances seems ambiguous.

Positron Emission Tomography Methods

The method of ^{133}Xe washout blood-flow measurement, like rheoencephalography and electroencephalography, is basically a two-dimensional technique. Flow values in the gray matter of the cortex or underlying white matter are assessed and plotted on a two-dimensional projection of the cortical surface. PET is a three-dimensional technique, developing consecutive slice images and assessing each cubic centimeter of brain tissue. The historical development of PET scanning technology is well reviewed by Phelps, Mazziotta, and Huang (1982). PET is a versatile approach utilizing the mathematics of x-ray transmission scanning (CT scans) to produce slice images of radioisotope distribution (Brownell, Budinger, & Lauterbur, & McGeer, 1982). This opens an unlimited vista of metabolic studies.

Positron emitters such as carbon-11 (^{11}C) or fluorine-18 (^{18}F) can be used to label glucose, amino acids, drugs, neurotransmitter precursors, and many other molecules and to examine their distribution and fate in discrete cell groups. What molecules should be imaged in psychiatry? The therapeutic success of tricyclics suggests examining their distribution. The blood-flow results suggest the dynamic imaging of local metabolism. These two types of PET imaging are only the beginning of the potential approaches to the varied problems in psychiatry and human behavior.

Metabolic Rate of Glucose

PET imaging of glucose metabolic rate rather than blood flow has both advantages and disadvantages for psychiatric studies. The Sokoloff technique (1982) uses an ^{18}F-labeled analogue of glucose, 2-deoxyglucose (FDG). FDG is taken up by the brain much as glucose itself. But glucose is rapidly metabolized to CO_2 and H_2O. Since CO_2 is a gas, it diffuses rapidly across tissues and prevents us from obtaining both high-resolution images and precise quantification of metabolic rates. The unusual structure of 2-deoxyglucose allows its metabolism to the first step in the glycolytic pathway (to 2-deoxyglucose-6-phosphate), but no further. Since its metabolism stops at this point, the cells are labeled in proportion to their glucose uptake. After injection of FDG, it is almost entirely taken up over the next 30–40 minutes, the majority consumed in the first 10.

This step can be accomplished in a separate, quiet, and controlled environment. The scan, started at 50 minutes, therefore reflects glucose use during the initial controlled period after injection, not the scan operation. Thus, psychological tasks, directed interviews about emotional subjects, or even REM sleep could be studied. The need to sustain the activity for 30 minutes, however, limits the time resolution and the habituated response to sensory stimulation could predominate in the glucose use image. Nevertheless, FDG has been the predominantly used tracer in psychiatric studies to date.

Tomographic Mapping of Glucose Use and Sensory Stimulation

As was observed in studies of blood flow and psychological tasks, local glucose use is highly sensitive to sensory stimulation. Visual stimulation in one hemifield is associated with increases in glucose use in the contralateral visual cortex (Greenberg *et al.*, 1981) and more glucose is used when two eyes are stimulated than when one eye is stimulated (Phelps, Kuhl, & Mazziotta, 1981a). As visual stimulation increased from eyes closed to simple white light, checkerboard pattern reversal, and viewing a park outside the laboratory, visual cortex glucose use increased twofold (Phelps *et al.* 1981a, 1981b). Somatosensory and auditory stimulation also increased glucose use in the primary sensory areas (Buchsbaum *et al.*, 1984; Buchsbaum, Holcomb, Johnson, King, & Kessler, 1983); Greenberg *et al.*, 1981). Whole brain glucose use was little changed by visual stimulation.

PET in Affective Disorders

The finding by Ingvar and co-workers (1974a) of a relative decrease in cerebral blood flow in the frontal lobes in schizophrenia suggested the utility of replicating these studies with measurement of glucose use by PET. In order for the studies to be comparable, we also tested our first subjects resting with their eyes closed, and computed frontal to whole hemisphere ratios of glucose use. In our initial study of eight off-medication patients with schizophrenia and six normal controls (Buchsbaum *et al.*, 1982a), the patients had significantly lower frontal/whole slice glucose ratios, consistent with Ingvar's findings and with preliminary PET reports (Farkas, *et al.* 1980; Widen *et al.*, 1981).

In replicating and extending this initial study, we felt that a comparison with affective disorders would be valuable for evaluating diagnostic specificity. Second, the "resting" condition left psychological activity uncontrolled and open to different self-imposed tasks or mood states in patients and control groups. Simple sensory stimula-

1A

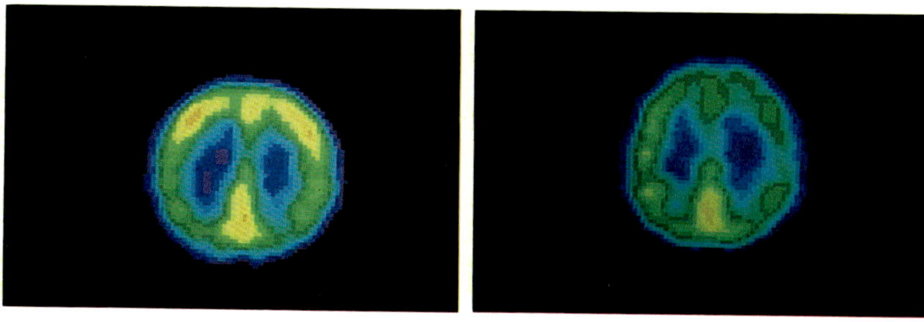

1B

2A

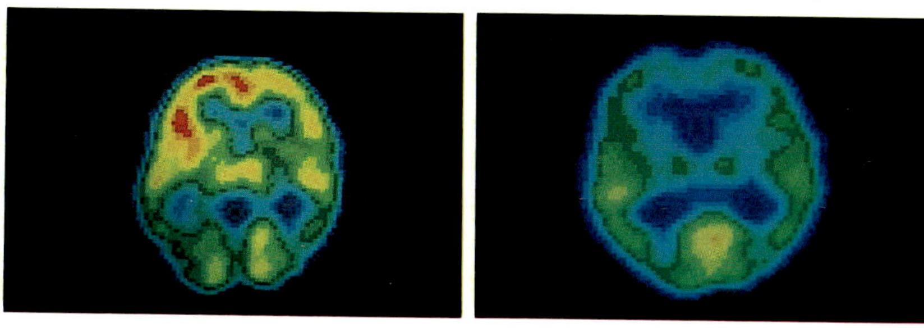

2B

FIG. 7-1A and 7-1B. Positron emission tomography with [^{18}F]-2-deoxyglucose (FDG). Slices are horizontal, parallel to the canthomeatal line (joining the outer canthus of eye and the external auditory meatus) and supraventricular level. Red, orange, and yellow are areas of relatively high glucose use, typically cerebral gray matter. Violet and blue indicate low glucose use, typically cerebral white matter and ventricles. A PET scan of a normal control (Figure 7-1A) and patient with affective disorder (Figure 7-1B) are shown. Both subjects are receiving shocks to their right forearm with eyes closed. Note that normal individual has high frontal glucose use and patient has less prominent frontal dominance.

FIG. 7-2A and 7-2B. PET images at midventricular level as shown in Figure 7-1. This horizontal slice is computed at 48 mm above canthomeatal (CM) line for both the normal control (Figure 7-2A) and affective-disorder patient (Figure 7-2B).

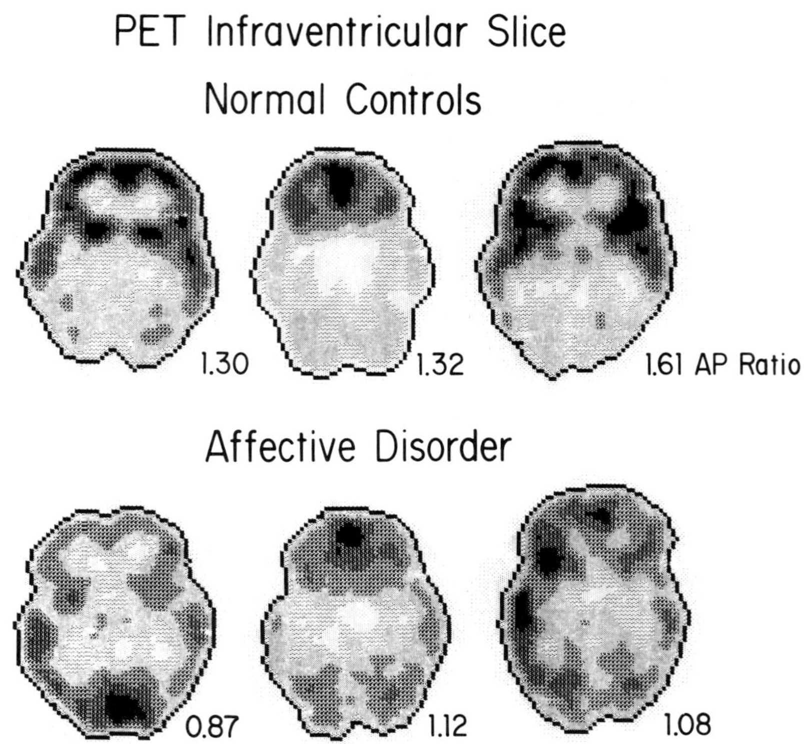

FIG. 7-3. PET images at infraventricular level displayed as nine-level dot density gray scale. Black indicates area of highest glucose use, and lighter shades are low glucose use. Three scans typical of normal controls and patients with affective disorder are shown. A ratio of anterior to posterior (AP) cortex glucose was calculated, as in Buchsbaum *et al.* (1982a), and is shown below and to the right of each slice.

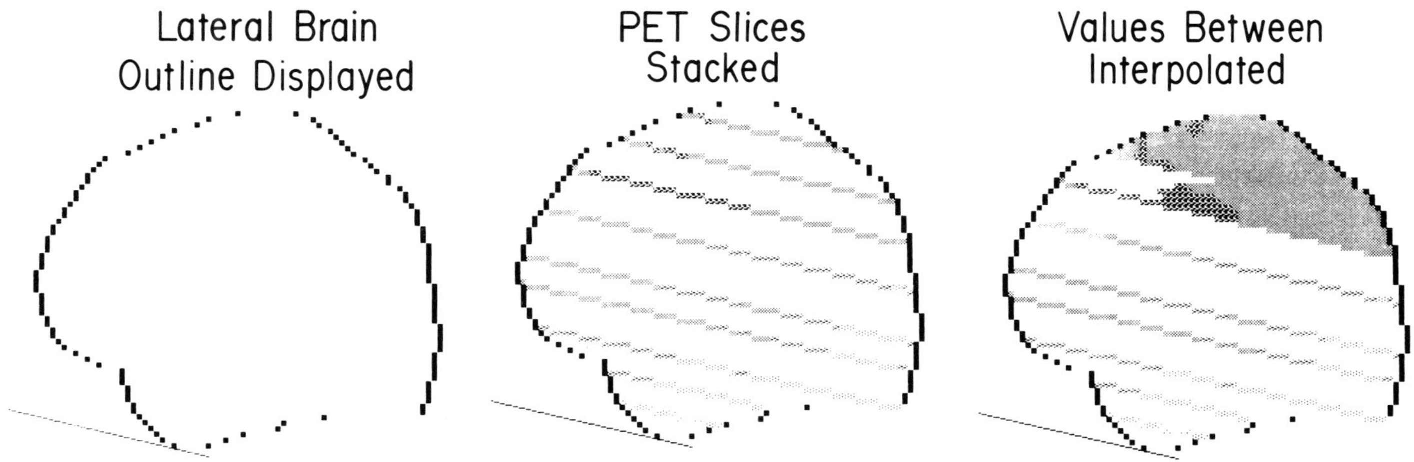

Fig. 7-4. Technique for creating lateral cortex surface views from slice images. Using the approximately equal-area lateral brain projection previously developed for electrophysiological topography (Buchsbaum *et al.*, 1982b), hemisphere cortical peels were placed on the brain lateral outline at the appropriate level. Slice level was expressed in percent of brain height. This was accomplished by identifying slice level as a percent of head height (measured perpendicular to the CM line to the top of the head) and translating this to approximate percent brain height from the atlas (Matsui & Hirano, 1978). An interpolation routine next approximated pixel values between the slice levels. This procedure has several features that make it suitable for schizophrenia and affective-disorder studies. First, it allows direct comparison with two-dimensional cerebral blood flow data previously studied. Second, it allows the computation of mean glucose use images for group comparisons with pixel-by-pixel statistics for exploratory analyses. Third, direct comparison of electrophysiological and glucographic topography becomes possible.

5A 5B

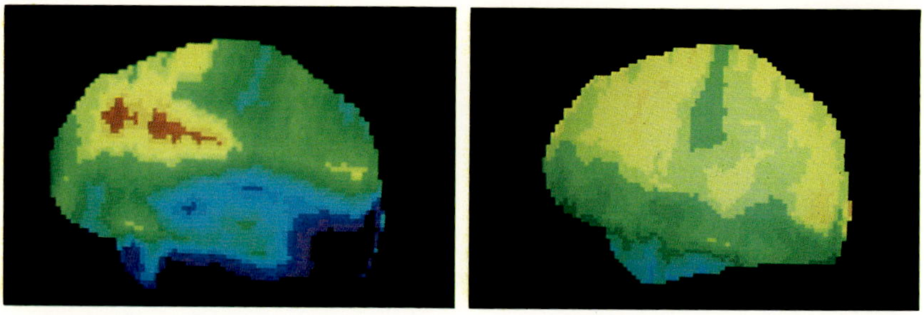

6A 6B 6C

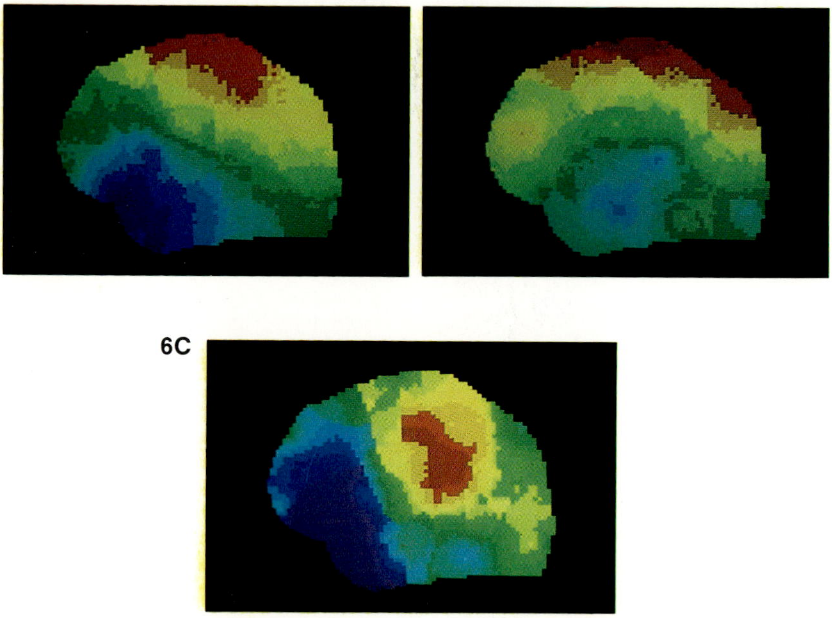

FIG. 7-5A and 7-5B. Left hemisphere lateral view of one normal control (Figure 7-5A) and patient with affective disorder (Figure 7-5B) receiving shocks to right forearm during glucose uptake. Normal shows prominent frontal glucose use and absence of occipital activity. In contrast, patient with affective illness has less prominent frontal activity. Data are expressed on normal scale. This was done as follows: The mean and *SD* of 2991 pixels in map was calculated; next, for each pixel we took the value, subtracted the mean, and divided by the *SD*. Thus, each map has a mean = 0.0, *SD* = 1.0.

FIG. 7-6A, 7-6B, and 7-6C. Group average—left hemisphere lateral EP topography for N120, intensity 3 shock component. Averages for 19 normal controls (Figure 7-6A) and 11 patients with affective disorder (Figure 7-6B) and *t* test (Figure 7-6C) between groups are shown. Averages were computed on a pixel-by-pixel basis as were *t* tests. Scale for averages is *SD* units (see caption for Figure 7-5) and scale for *t* test is adjusted so that $p < .05$, two-tailed, is red (normals higher) or violet (patients higher). Patients with affective illness showed a more diffuse and posterior pattern of relative activity (see also Table 7-1).

tion during the FDG uptake period that would avoid motor activity including eye movements, or tasks capable of solution by multiple and thus possibly multiarea strategies, seemed appropriate at this stage of PET development.

Affective Stimulation with Pain

In our second series of patients, we chose painful somatosensory stimulation of the right forearm as the condition. This was done because Ingvar *et al.* (1976) noted that frontal blood flow increased in subjects who received electrical skin stimulation; a smaller increase was observed in schizophrenics (see Figures 7-1 and 7-2). This was consistent with the observations by ourselves and others (Buchsbaum *et al.*, 1980; Davis & Buchsbaum, 1981; Davis, Buchsbaum, & Bunney, 1979; Davis, Buchsbaum, van Kammen, & Bunney, 1979) of diminished pain sensitivity in affective disorders as well as schizophrenia. Animal studies of bradykinin perfusion of the right lower extremity of cats also showed increases of left frontal, but not occipital, cerebral blood flow (Tsubokawa, Katayama, Ueno, & Moriyasu, 1981). We anticipated that in addition to a possibly enhanced hypofrontality in affective illness, we might observe some lateralized indication of the affective response to pain.

The patient group comprised 16 patients with schizophrenia (11 men, 5 women; mean age 28.3 ± 7.7) and 11 patients with affective disorder (7 men, 4 women, mean age 41.7 ± 9.9). They were hospitalized as inpatients at the National Institutes of Health (NIH) Clinical Center, Bethesda, Maryland, and the research ward branch of the Adult Psychiatry Branch at St. Elizabeth's Hospital, or were outpatients of the Maryland Psychiatric Research Center, Catonsville, Maryland. All patients were off psychoactive medicine for a minimum of 14 days and mean of 39.8 days for schizophrenics and 36.5 days for affectives. Patients on depot medication had days off medication counted, beginning from the second week following the last injection. All patients were in good physical health and none had significant abnormalities upon physical examination or laboratory tests. Diagnoses were made using DSM-III (APA, 1980) criteria by psychiatrists without knowledge of PET, electrophysiological, or CT results. All patients and controls received a semistructured research interview based on the Schedule for Affective Disorders and Schizophrenia (Endicott & Spitzer, 1978) or modified Present State Examination (Wing, Cooper,

& Sartorius, 1973). Diagnoses were based on all available information including chart review and consultation with the primary care staff for each patient.

The control subjects (13 men and 6 women; mean age 31.1 ± 10.5) were selected to match the ages and sexes of both schizophrenic and affective patient groups. Subjects were screened with a physical exam, laboratory measures, and interview. Individuals with a history of mental health problems in self or first-degree relatives were excluded. Neither control subjects nor patients overlap with our previous clinical report (Buchsbaum *et al.*, 1982a). No subject had an abnormal plasma glucose. Preliminary analyses of data on seven schizophrenics and ten normals from this larger sample has been reported at scientific meetings (Buchsbaum, Holcomb, Kessler *et al.*, 1983).

FDG Uptake Procedure

Subjects were seated in a darkened, acoustically isolated (floating slab) room. An intravenous line with 0.9% saline drip was inserted into the subject's right arm for isotope injection and another one into the subject's left arm for blood sampling. The left arm was wrapped in a hot pack for arteriolization of venous blood. Intravenous lines were started well in advance of the FDG injection and subjects were allowed to relax for 20–40 minutes before isotope injection to avoid imaging this stimulation. At 5–10 minutes before the FDG injection, room lights were extinguished; subjects were asked to close their eyes, and they remained so for 35–40 minutes after isotope injection. Subjects were not spoken to during uptake and remained quiet and cooperative. Subjects were continuously observed to insure that their eyes were closed. A small, low-level lamp illuminating the left arm area, was kept on for blood sampling. Somatosensory stimulation was administered to the right forearm and was the same used for other pain experiments with evoked potential recording (Buchsbaum, Davis, Coppola, & Naber, 1981a, 1981b). About 20–40 minutes before injection, subjects completed a psychophysical pain rating (Buchsbaum *et al.*, 1981a). This consisted of a series of 93 stimuli presented at 3-second intervals ranging from barely perceptible to unpleasant.

Beginning at the time of FDG injection, a sequence of electrical stimuli was started. This consisted of 1/second single, constant-current shocks ranging in intensity from barely perceptible to unpleasant presented in a random order to the right forearm. Six to seven sets of

256 stimuli were presented (4-minute blocks with 5–15 second pause) and 16-channel evoked potential (EP) recordings obtained.

EEG was recorded from 16 channels all on the left side, including all 10–20 system locations, midline F_z-C_z-P_z-O_z, and four additional electrode locations added to provide greater resolution of the posterior cortex. These are placed at the centers of squares formed by connecting P_2-P_2-O_z-O_1 (PO), C_3-C_z-P_z-P_3 (CP), T_3-C_3-P_3-T_5 (TCP), and F_7-F_3-C_3-T_3 (FTC). For the cortical mapping experiments, EPs were first detrended using linear regression and then digitally filtered to remove frequencies below 4 Hz and above 30 Hz, as described (with different bandpass) elsewhere (Lavine, Buchsbaum, & Schechter, 1980). Eye movements and artifacts were monitored using lead F_{p1}; trials exceeding a threshold were automatically excluded from the average for all leads. Individuals exceeding a 50% trial loss on any condition were excluded. The 16 values were then used to interpolate values over the entire scalp area as described elsewhere (Buchsbaum *et al.*, 1982b). EPs were measured as described elsewhere (Buchsbaum, Post, & Bunney, 1977) by area integration for P100 (76–112 msec), N120 (116–152 msec), and P200 (168–240 msec). Average maps were calculated from amplitude averages for each of the 16 leads.

Patients were then transferred to the scanning room. PET scan measurements of local cerebral glucose use by PET were obtained at six or seven levels (Ortec Ecat II) at 50–90 minutes following FDG injection and reflected glucose use during the rest or stimulation period. The transverse PET glucose images were reconstructed into a lateral cortical equal-area projection developed for EEG topographic mapping (Figure 7-3). Using digital techniques, consecutive PET slices have a 1-cm-thick cortical strip peeled off, conformed to the lateral brain view, and values between strips interpolated (Figure 7-4). The result is two simultaneously obtained electrophysiological and metabolic lateral views of brain function displayed in gray; scale values were represented by dot density (Figure 7-5).

The results were analyzed with a four-way analysis of variance (ANOVA) with independent groups (normals and affectives) and repeated measures for slice level (supra-, mid-, and infraventricular), hemisphere (right, left), and anteroposterior position (four sectors). Normals and patients both showed a significant anteroposterior gradient in glucose use, with highest values in the frontmost sector. Patients with affective illness showed less of an anteroposterior gradient especially at superior levels, which was statistically confirmed by ANOVA (Table 7-1). Absolute glucose levels in patients, which were

TABLE 7-1. Supra-, Mid-, and Infraventricular Glucose Use

		Normals (n = 19)		Affectives (n = 11)	
Height[a]		Mean	*SD*	Mean	*SD*
Supraventricular (61%)	1	21.9	6.23	25.9	6.69
	2	20.6	6.14	25.5	6.86
	3	19.3	5.72	23.6	6.84
	4	19.9	5.66	25.7	7.75
Midventricular (41%)	1	19.0	5.89	23.2	7.14
	2	20.1	6.02	23.6	6.99
	3	17.4	5.53	22.0	6.99
	4	16.6	5.07	20.8	6.21
Infraventricular (29%)	1	18.3	5.43	21.7	6.79
	2	16.5	5.71	20.3	7.07
	3	14.9	4.60	18.8	5.96
	4	14.2	4.48	18.9	7.63

[a]Height is percent of head height measured from canthomeatal line to top of head.

Note. TSQ level by anterioposterior poosition by group, $F = 3.64$. Other effects include: $df = 6{,}23$; $p < .01$. Group $F = 3.63$, $df = 1{,}28$; p = NS. Level TSQ, $F = 51.9$, $df = 2{,}27$; $p < .01$. Anteroposterior position TSQ, $F = 21.0$, $df = 3{,}26$; $p < .01$. Level by group, hemisphere by group, anteroposterior by group = NS.

actually higher in posterior regions rather than lower in frontal regions, were the largest contributors to the effect. Neither group differences in whole brain glucose use nor left–right asymmetries reached statistical significance. These results are consistent with our earlier reports of a relative hypofrontal function in schizophrenia, compared with controls and extend the finding to the affective illness, the other group of major psychoses.

Limitations of Current Studies

These results are preliminary and represent our first examination of a continuing series of patients and normals. The most notable limitations include small sample size, the methods of dissecting the cortex, the limited resolution of current PET images, and the failure to take into account wide individual differences in brain anatomy, pain tolerance, and patients' current symptomatology. Nevertheless, because the PET provides a new and very powerful approach to functional measurement of cerebral function, it seemed appropriate to report a working summary of the data at this time.

Smaller and more precisely positioned sectors and boxes may yield more striking and reliable lateralized effects. Other sites in limbic areas may also be more salient for the affective effects of pain stimulation and will be explored.

Evoked potential maps for the N120 component were chosen for preliminary analysis because of our finding of the relationship of this component to pain stimulation. EP maps were normalized within each subject so that topographic contour features rather than merely amplitude could be examined; *t* tests were done on a pixel-by-pixel basis; mean and *t* tests show a more diffuse EP pattern with parietal differences (Figure 7-6).

Regional EEG differences in affective disorder were also explored by Shagass, Roemer, and Straumanis (1982) in one of the few reports to assess topographic phenomena statistically. Multivariate analysis revealed groups more different over posterior than anterior cortical areas, although EEG was not recorded from anterior F_{p1} and F_3. Our finding of a posterior distribution of somatosensory response and *t* test differences is consistent with this and the relative shift from frontal to posterior regions of glucose use.

The lack of differences between patients with schizophrenia and those with affective disorder deserves careful consideration. Factors possibly contributing to failing to confirm true differences include the relatively small affective disorder sample size, diagnostic heterogeneity within both the schizophrenia and the affective group, mood heterogeneity, lack of salience of pain stimulation for underlying biological deficits, and the limited number of brain structures tested. However, the reduced anteroposterior gradient could be a generalized feature of the psychoses. Other more extensively studied biological markers, including smooth pursuit eye movements (Holzman & Levy, 1977), platelet monoamine oxidase, and attentional deficits, show considerable overlap between the groups and the anteroposterior ratio may be no exception to this pattern. These biological measures may indicate the communality between schizophrenia and affective illness.

X-Ray CT Scanning

X-ray CT scanning produces a slice image of x-ray density. Bone cerebral calcification and fluid filled sulcal and ventricular spaces are well visualized, but gray and white matter differing little in x-ray density are barely differentiated on standard clinical studies. Thus, it is a technique most successfully used to examine brain size and cortical shrinkage rather than soft tissue modification. Evidence of enlarged ventricular size in schizophrenia has been found by several investigators (Johnstone, Crow, Frith, Husband, & Kreel, 1976; Weinberger, Torrey, Neophytides, & Wyatt, 1979). Depression has been much less studied than schizophrenia, but similar ventricular enlargement was found (Pearlson & Veroff, 1981). In an older subgroup with a higher incidence of endogenous features, Jacoby and Levy (1980) also found ventricular enlargement. At 2-year follow-up, mortality was significantly higher in this subgroup (Jacoby, Levy, & Bird, 1981).

Nuclear Magnetic Resonance Imaging

NMR imaging is based on reception of radiofrequencies emitted by nuclei of different elements in the brain following application of a magnetic field (Brownell *et al.*, 1982; Coleman, Drayer, & Jaszczak, 1982; James *et al.*, 1982). Using principles similar to x-ray CT scan reconstruction, a slice image can be obtained. The first clinical use has been to image the hydrogen nucleus; mostly in H_2O, it provides a water distribution picture. Since gray and white matter differ significantly in water content, gray matter structures may be more easily separated. Examples may be seen in patients with various tumors (Hawkes, Holland, Moore, & Worthington, 1980) but no psychiatric studies have been done. The technique has a potential for going beyond anatomic studies and measuring other nuclei such as ^{31}P cell energy metabolism, and NMR-sensitive labeled pharmaceuticals. But the low concentrations of these nuclei make the production of high-resolution slice images currently unattainable.

Conclusion

Biological diagnostic tests in depression are a rapidly developing approach, with a large series of scientific studies supporting their validity. PET studies are just beginning. It is the promise of the technique for investigation of specific brain structures in the future that makes it noteworthy at this time. In a combination with new clinical anatomical imaging techniques, such as EEG topography, NMR (Brownell *et al.*, 1982), and insights from animal data obtained with radioautography, a level of scientific approach previously unattainable will be realized.

ACKNOWLEDGMENTS

The complex technical nature of this project required the cooperation of many collaborating groups. Clinical research unit collaborators with their nursing at NIMH (R. Post and R. Cohen) medically supported off-medication patients and furnished clinical and diagnostic information. The NIH Clinical Center, Department of Nuclear Medicine (R. Kessler, R. Margolin), oversaw the [^{18}F] 2-deoxyglucose synthesis; conducted tests of purity, sterility, and pyrogenicity (Drs. R. Channing and R. Manning); and operated the scanner (J. Bird and C. Strauss). L. Sokoloff furnished a basic program for glucose computation for radioautographic animal data, which was adapted by us for PET use (J. Cappelletti and M. S. Buchsbaum, a PASCAL version) and applied to the data. J. Wu reconstructed the individual lateral images, and R. Ball developed the pixel-by-pixel statistical programs. S. Donovan provided bibliographic research and manuscript preparation.

REFERENCES

American Psychiatric Association. (1980). *Diagnostic and statistical manual of mental disorders* (3rd ed.). Washington, DC: Author.

Brownell, G. L., Budinger, T. F., Lauterbur, P. C., & McGeer, P. L. (1982). Positron tomography and nuclear magnetic resonance imaging. *Science, 215*, 619–626.

Bruder, G., Sutton, S., Berger-Gross, P., Quitkin, M., & Davies, S. (1981). Lateralized auditory processing in depression: Dichotic click detection. *Psychiatry Research, 4*, 253–266.

Buchsbaum, M. S., Cappelletti, J., Ball, R., Hazlett, E., King, A. C., Johnson, J., Wu, J., DeLisi, L. E., Holcomb, H. H., Zimmerman, S. D., & Kessler, R. (1984). PET image measurement in schizophrenia and affective disorders. *Annals of Neurology, 15* (Suppl.), S157–S165.

Buchsbaum, M. S., Davis, G. C., Coppola, R., & Naber, D. (1981a). Opiate pharmacology and individual differences: I. Psychophysical pain measurements. *Pain, 10*, 357–366.

Buchsbaum, M. S., Davis, G. C., Coppola, R., & Naber, D. (1981b). Opiate pharmacology and individual differences: II. Somatosensory evoked potentials. *Pain, 10*, 367–377.

Buchsbaum, M. S., Davis, G. C., & van Kammen, D. P. (1980). Diagnostic classification and the endorphin hypothesis of schizophrenia: Individual differences and psychopharmacological strategies In C. Baxter & T. Melnechuk (Eds.), *Perspectives in schizophrenia research* (pp. 177–194). New York: Raven Press.

Buchsbaum, M. S., & Haier, R. J. (1978). Biological homogeneity, symptom heterogeneity and the diagnosis of schizophrenia. *Schizophrenia Bulletin, 4*, 473–475.

Buchsbaum, M. S., Holcomb, H. H., Johnson, J., King, A. C., & Kessler, R. (1983). Cerebral metabolic consequences of electrical stimulation in normal individuals. *Human Neurobiology, 2*, 35–38.

Buchsbaum, M. S., Holcomb, H. H., Kessler, R., Johnson, J., King, A. C., Cappelletti, J., Bisserbe, J. C., van Kammen, D. P., Selub, S., Wu, J., Manning, R. G., & Channing, M. (1983). Lateralized asymmetries in glucose uptake assessed by positron emission tomography in patients with schizophrenia and normal controls. In P. Flor-Henry & J. Gruzelier (Eds.), *Hemispheric asymmetries of function in psychopathology* (Vol. 2, pp. 559–568). New York: Elsevier.

Buchsbaum, M. S., Ingvar, D. H., Kessler, R., Waters, R. N., Cappelletti, J., van Kammen, D. P., King, A. C., Johnson, J., Manning, R. G., Flynn, R. W., Mann, L. S., Bunney, W. E., Jr., & Sokoloff, L. (1982a). Cerebral glucography with positron tomography. *Archives of General Psychiatry, 39*, 251–259.

Buchsbaum, M. S., Post, R. M., & Bunney, W. E., Jr. (1977). Average evoked responses in a rapidly cycling manic-depressive patient. *Biological Psychiatry, 12,* 83–99.

Buchsbaum, M. S., Rigal, F., Coppola, R., Cappelletti, J., King, A. C., & Johnson, J. (1982b). A new system for gray-level surface distribution maps of electrical activity. *Electroencephlography and Clinical Neurophysiology, 53,* 237–242.

Coleman, R. E., Drayer, B. P., & Jaszczak, R. J. (1982). Studying regional brain function. *Journal of Nuclear Medicine, 23,* 266–270.

Comar, D., Zarifian, E., Verhas, M., Soussaline, F., Maziere, M., Berger, G., Loo, H., Cuche, C., Kellershohn, C., & Deniker, P. (1979). Brain distribution and kinetics of ^{11}C-chloropromazine in schizophrenics. *Psychiatry Research, 1,* 23–29.

Davis, G. C., & Buchsbaum, M. S. (1981). Pain sensitivity and endorphins in functional psychoses. In T. A. Ban, F. A. Freyhan, P. P. Ichot, & W. Poldinger (Eds.), *Modern problems of pharmacopsychiatry* (pp. 99–108). Basel: Karger.

Davis, G. C., Buchsbaum, M. S., & Bunney, W. E., Jr. (1979). Analgesia to painful stimuli in affective illness. *American Journal of Psychiatry, 136,* 1148–1151.

Davis, G. C., Buchsbaum, M. S., van Kammen, D. P., & Bunney, W. E., Jr. (1979). Analgesia to pain stimuli in schizophrenics reversed by naltrexone. *Psychiatry Research, 1,* 61–69.

Endicott, J., & Spitzer, R. L. (1978). A diagnostic interview: The schedule for affective disorders and schizophrenia. *Archives of General Psychiatry, 35,* 837.

Farkas, T., Reivich, M., Alavi, A., Greenberg, J. H., Fowler, J. S., Mac Gregor, R. R., Christman, D. R., & Wolf, A. P. (1980). The application of ^{18}F 2-deoxy-2-fluoro-D-glucose and positron emission tomography in the study of psychiatric conditions. In J. V. Passonneau, R. A. Hawkins, W. D. Lust, & F. A. Welsh (Eds.), *Cerebral metabolism and neural function* (pp. 403–408). Baltimore: Williams & Wilkins.

Flor-Henry, P. (1979). On certain aspects of the localization of the cerebral systems regulating and determining emotion. *Biological Psychiatry, 14,* 677–698.

Foit, A., Larsen, B., Hattori, S., Skinhj, E., & Lassen, N. A. (1980). Cortical activation during somatosensory stimulation and voluntary movement in man: A regional cerebral blood flow study. *Electroencephalography and clinical neurophysiology, 50,* 426–436.

Franzen, G., & Ingvar, D. H. (1975). Absence of activation in frontal structures during psychological testing of chronic schizophrenics. *Journal of Neurology, Neurosurgery and Psychiatry, 38,* 1027–1032.

Greenberg, J. H., Reivich, M., Alavi, A., Hand, P., Rosenquist, A., Rintelmann, W., Stein, A., Tusa, R., Dann, R., Christman, D., Fowler, J., MacGregor, B., & Wolf, A. (1981). Metabolic mapping of functional activity in human subjects with the (^{18}F) fluorodeoxyglucose technique. *Science, 212,* 678–680.

Gustafson, L., Risberg, J., & Silfverskiold, P. (1981). Cerebral blood flow in dementia and depression. *Lancet, i,* 275.

Hawkes, R. C., Holland, G. N., Moore, W. S., & Worthington, B. S. (1980). Nuclear magnetic resonance (NMR) tomography of the brain: A preliminary clinical assessment with demonstration of pathology. *Journal of Computer Assisted Tomography, 4,* 577–586.

Holzman, P. S., & Levy, D. L. (1977). Smooth pursuit eye movements and functional psychoses: A review. *Schizophrenia Bulletin, 3,* 15–27.

Hoyer, S., & Oesterreich, K. (1975). Blood flow and oxidase metabolism of the brain in patients with schizophrenia. *Psychiatria Clinica, 8,* 304–313.

Ingvar, D. H., & Franzen, G. (1974a). Abnormalities of cerebral blood flow distribution in patients with chronic schizophrenia. *Acta Psychiatrica Scandinavica, 50,* 425–462.

Ingvar, D. H., & Franzen, G. (1974b). Distribution of cerebral activity in chronic schizophrenia. *Lancet, 2,* 1484–1486.

Ingvar, D. H., & Philipson, L. (1977). Distribution of cerebral blood flow in the dominant hemisphere during motor ideation and motor performance. *Annals of Neurology, 2,* 230–237.

Ingvar, D. H., Rosen, I., Eriksson, M., & Elmqvist, D. (1976). Activation patterns induced in the dominant hemisphere by skin stimulation. In Y. Zotterman (Ed.), *Sensory functions of the skin* (pp. 549–559). London: Pergamon Press.

Jacoby, R. J., & Levy, R. (1980). Computed tomography in the elderly: III. Affective disorder. *British Journal of Psychiatry, 139,* 288–292.

Jacoby, R. J., Levy, R., & Bird, J. M. (1981). Computed tomography and the outcome of affective disorder: A follow-up study of elederly patients. *British Journal of Psychiatry, 139,* 288–292.

James, A. E., Jr., Price, R. R., Rollo, F. D., Patton, J. A., Erickson, J. J., Coulam, C. M., & Partain, C. L. (1982). Nuclear magnetic resonance imaging: A promising technique. *Journal of the American Medical Association, 247,* 1331–1334.

Johnstone, E. C., Crow, T. J., Frith, C. D., Husband, J., & Kreel, L. (1976). Cerebral ventricular size and cognitive impairment in chronic schizophrenia. *Lancet, ii,* 924–926.

Kety, S. S., Woodford, R. B., Harmel, M. H., Freyhan, F. A., Appel, K. E., & Schmidt, C. F. (1948). Cerebral blood flow and metabolism in schizophrenia. *American Journal of Psychiatry, 104,* 765–770.

Kuhl, D. E., Barrio, J. R., Huang, S. C., Selin, C., Ackermann, R. F., Lear, J. L., Wu, J. L., Lin, T. H., & Phelps, M. E. (1982). Quantifying local cerebral blood flow by *N*-isopropyl-*p*[^{123}] iodoamphetamine (IMP) tomography. *Journal of Nuclear Medicine, 23,* 196–203.

Lavine, R. A., Buchsbaum, M. S., & Schechter, G. (1980). Human somatosensory evoked responses: Effects of attention and distraction on early components. *Physiological Psychology, 8,* 405–408.

Mathew, R. J., Duncan, G. C., Weinman, M. L., & Barr, D. L. (1982). Regional cerebral blood flow in schizophrenia. *Archives of General Psychiatry, 39,* 1121–1124.

Mathew, R. J., Meyer, J. S., Frances, D. J., Semchuk, K. M., Mortel, K., & Cleghorn, J. L. (1980). Cerebral blood flow in depression. *American Journal of Psychiatry, 137,* 1449–1450.

Matsui, T., & Hirano, A. (1978). *An atlas of the human brain for computerized tomography.* Tokyo: Igaku-Shoin.

Pearlson, G. D., & Veroff, A. E. (1981). Changes in computerized tomographic scan changes in manic depressive illness. *Lancet, i,* 470.

Phelps, M. E., Kuhl, D. E., & Mazziotta, J. C. (1981a). Metabolic mapping of the brain's response to visual stimulation: Studies in humans. *Science, 211,* 1445–1448.

Phelps, M. E., Mazziotta, J. C., & Huang, S. C. (1982). Study of cerebral function with positron computed tomography. *Journal of Cerebral Blood Flow and Metabolism, 2,* 113–162.

Phelps, M. E., Mazziotta, J. C., Kuhl, D. E., Nuwer, M., Packwood, J., Metter, J., & Engel, J., Jr. (1981b). Tomographic mapping of human cerebral metabolism: Visual stimulation and deprivation. *Neurology, 31,* 517–529.

Roland, P. E. (1981). Somatotopical tuning of postcentral gyrus during focal attention in man (A regional cerebral blood flow study). *Journal of Neurophysiology, 46,* 744–754.

Ross, E. D., & Rush, A. J. (1981). Diagnosis and neuroanatomical correlates of depression in brain-damaged patients. *Archives of General Psychiatry, 38,* 1344–1354.

Rush, A. J., Schlesser, M. A., Stokely, E., Bonte, F. R., & Altshuler, K. Z. (in press). Cerebral blood flow in depression and mania. In M. S. Buchsbaum, E. Usdin, W. E. Bunney, Jr., & D. Ingvar (Eds.), *Brain imaging in psychiatry and neurology: Positron emission tomography and other techniques.* Pacific Grove, CA: Boxwood Press.

Shagass, C., Roemer, R. A., & Straumanis, J. J. (1982). Relationships between psychiatric diagnosis and some quantitative EEG variables. *Archives of General Psychiatry, 39,* 1423–1435.

Silfverskiold, P., Gustafson, L., Johansson, B. A., & Risberg, J. RCBF in affective disorders (in press). In M. S. Buchsbaum, E. Usdin, W. E. Bunney, Jr., & D. Ingvar (Eds.), *Psychiatry and neurology: Positron emission tomography and other techniques.* Pacific Grove, CA: Boxwood Press.

Sokoloff, L. (1981). Relationships among local functional activity, energy metabolism, and blood flow in the central nervous system. *Federation Proceedings, 40,* 2311–2316.

Sokoloff, L. (1982). The radioactive deoxyglucose method. *Advances in neurochemistry* (pp. 1–81). New York: Plenum.

Tsubokawa, T., Katayama, Y., Ueno, Y., & Moriyasu, N. (1981). Evidence for involvement of the frontal cortex in pain-related cerebral events in cats: Increase in local cerebral blood flow by noxious stimuli. *Brain Research, 217,* 179–185.

Weinberger, D. F., Torrey, E. F., Neophytides, A. N., & Wyatt, R. J. (1979). Lateral cerebral ventricular enlargement in chronic schizophrenia. *Archives of General Psychiatry, 36,* 935.

Widen, L., Bergstrom, M., Blomquist, C., Brismar, T., Ehrin, E., Elander, S., Eriksson, K., Erikson, L., Greitz, T., Litton, J., Malmborg, P., Nilsson, L., Sedvall, G., & Ugglas, M. (1981, July). *Glucose metabolism in patients with schizophrenia: Emission computed tomography measurements with 11-C-glucose.* Paper presented at meeting of the International Congress of Biological Psychiatry, Stockholm.

Wing, K., Cooper, J. E., & Sartorius, N. (1973). *Present State Examination.* Cambridge, England: Cambridge University Press.

8

Receptor Studies in Diagnosis and Treatment of Depression

DAVID L. GARVER
FRANK P. ZEMLAN

Introduction

The classical catecholamine and indolamine hypotheses of depressive disorders suggest that depression is associated with a paucity of norepinephrine (NE) or serotonin (5-HT) at certain critical central nervous system (CNS) synapses. The evidence supporting such amine hypotheses has been indirect. The NE hypothesis is supported by the findings of low urinary 3-methoxy-4-hydroxyphenylglycol (MHPG) in some types of depression (see Chapter 4), blunted growth hormone response to insulin hypoglycemia, and preferential antidepressant response to antidepressant drugs (such as imipramine, desipramine, and maprotiline), which inhibit the reuptake of NE, and thereby increase the amount of NE acting on the postsynaptic receptor. The 5-HT hypothesis is supported by the finding of a group of depressives with low cerebrospinal fluid (CSF) 5-hydroxyindoleacetic acid (5-HIAA) who responded favorably following a precursor load with 5-hydroxytryptophan and antidepressant agents that preferentially inhibit reuptake of 5-HT, such as amitriptyline (Garver & Davis, 1979).

The introduction of new antidepressant drugs (such as iprindole or mianserin) that neither inhibit neurotransmitter reuptake nor inhibit monoamine oxidase (MAO) and compounds (such as amphetamine or cocaine) that inhibit NE and 5-HT reuptake (see Chapter 11) but do not have antidepressant properties, have raised fundamental

DAVID L. GARVER. Department of Psychiatry, Pharmacology and Cell Biophysics, University of Cincinnati College of Medicine, Cincinnati, Ohio.

FRANK P. ZEMLAN. Department of Psychiatry, Physiology and Biophysics, University of Cincinnati College of Medicine, Cincinnati, Ohio.

problems for both our concepts of the biology of affective illness and our understanding of the relevant mechanisms of action of antidepressant drugs (Charney, Menkes, & Heninger, 1981b).

But even more disturbing to the traditional concepts of synaptic deficiencies of NE and 5-HT was the realization that the time course for a clinically significant antidepressant response (2–3 weeks) was quite different from the time course for the uptake inhibition-related increase of synaptic NE or 5-HT. Inhibition of neurotransmitter reuptake takes hours, or at most a few days, after the initiation of drug treatment. The 2-week time course discrepancy between reuptake inhibition and clinical improvement, in addition to the "atypical" antidepressants (i.e., iprindole and mianserin), which do not affect reuptake, demanded fresh approaches to both the study of the relevant mechanism of action of the antidepressants (Cooper, Bloom, & Roth, 1982) and the study of the biologic nature of depressive illness.

These fresh approaches have been based on new concepts of both pre- and postsynaptic neurons. Presynaptic neuronal activity is regulated in part by autoreceptors. When stimulated, these autoreceptors reduce the amount of neurotransmitter released by the presynaptic neuron. Regulation of postsynaptic neuronal activity is not only by release of neurotransmitter onto postsynaptic receptors, but also involves the linkage of the activated receptor with its transmembrane catalytic moiety (such as adenylate cyclase) and the activity of phosphorylated kinases that phosphorylate membrane proteins and functionally alter resting potentials, inhibiting or facilitating neuronal activity (Cooper *et al.*, 1982) (Figure 8-1).

β-Adrenergic Supersensitivity and Depression

The classical NE deficiency hypothesis of depression was turned "upside down" in the seminal discovery by Ventulani and Sulser (1975) that chronic, but not acute treatment with a variety of antidepressant drugs—including tricyclics, monoamine oxidase inhibitors (MAOIs), and iprindole—as well as electroconvulsive therapy (ECT) caused a down-regulation of the postsynaptic NE-induced cyclic AMP (cAMP) response in limbic forebrain tissue. Although acutely administered antidepressant drug has no effect on NE-stimulated cAMP production, after 10–20 days of drug treatment the postsynaptic neuron was able to generate only a blunted cAMP response to NE agonist stimulation.

Reduction of NE-stimulated cAMP has now been reported follow-

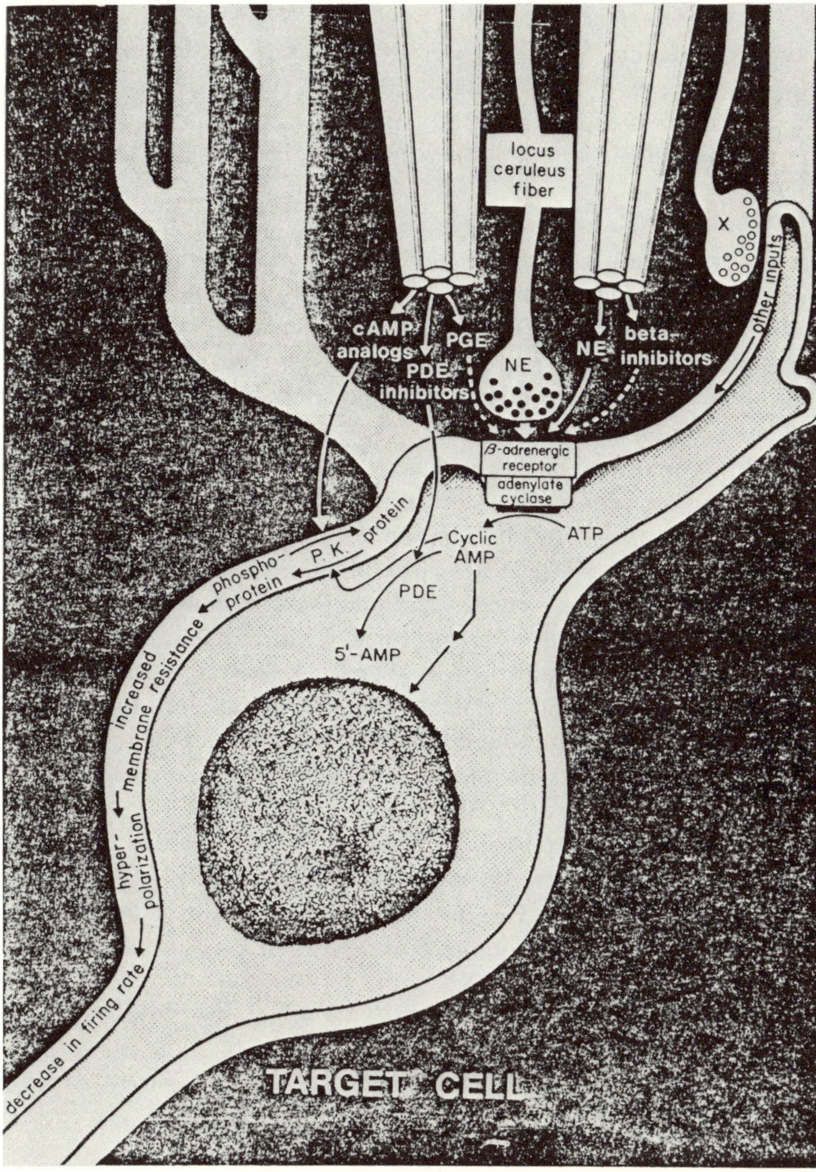

FIG. 8-1. Schematic diagram summarizing events linked with the activation of the postsynaptic β-adrenergic receptor complex. From *The Biochemical Basis of Neuropharmacology* by J. R. Cooper, F. E. Bloom, & R. H. Roth, New York: Oxford University Press, 1982, p. 342. Reprinted by permission.

ing long-term treatment with a variety of typical and atypical antidepressant agents, as well as with MAOIs and ECT by various investigators. Selective 5-HT uptake inhibitors such as zimelidine and clomipramine are identical to NE uptake inhibitors in producing such postsynaptic β-adrenergic down-regulation (Table 8-1) (Charney *et al.*, 1981b).

The subtype of adrenergic receptor at which NE causes cAMP generation is not fully understood. Isoproterenol, which is a β-adrenergic agonist, causes only half of the cAMP production seen with NE stimulation, suggesting that a non-β component of NE induced cAMP generation is present in most tissues. Only the non-β component appears to be decreased by chronic mianserin or zimelidine treatment (Mishra, Janowsky, & Sulser, 1980).

β-Adrenergic receptors have been identified throughout the brain employing receptor binding techniques that utilize [^{3}H]dihydroalprenolol (DHA) as the ligand. The stereospecific labeling of the β-adrenergic receptor by [^{3}H]DHA is saturable. Once β-adrenergic receptors are occupied, further increases in ligand concentration results in no further specific binding. The number of binding sites (β-adrenergic receptors) per milligram protein (B_{max}) corresponds to the maximal concentration of ligand ([^{3}H]DHA) specifically bound per milligram of tissue. The concentration of ligand at which half of the receptors are occupied (K_D) is a measure of the affinity of the receptor for a particular ligand (Cooper *et al.*, 1982).

Utilizing receptor binding techniques, one can therefore determine the density of a specific type of receptor (number of receptors per milligram of tissue) in various regions of the brain or in blood elements in patients. The number of receptors in a tissue such as leuko-

TABLE 8-1. Effects of Long-term Antidepressants upon NE- and Isoproterenol-stimulated cAMP

Antidepressant type	Drug	NE	Isoproterenol
Tricyclic	Imipramine	↓	
	Desipramine	↓	↓
	Clomipramine	↓	
	Amitriptyline	↓	
"Atypical"	Iprindole	↓	↓
	Mianserin	↓	0
	Zimelidine	↓	0
MAOI	Pargyline	↓	↓
ECT	—	↓	↓

Note. Table modified from Charney, Menkes, & Heninger (1981b).

cytes from patients with an affective disorder or from normal controls may be readily determined. Furthermore, the correlation between altered receptor number and clinical antidepressant response may be assessed. One can also determine if changes occur in the affinity of the receptor for its ligand (K_D) and, if such changes occur, whether they are associated with diagnosis or with the clinical effect of antidepressant drugs.

The finding that NE-stimulated cAMP generation was blunted by chronic antidepressant treatment (a functional effect) prompted the examination of the effects of drugs on adrenergic receptor number. Utilizing a ligand which specifically binds to β-adrenergic receptors ([^{3}H]DHA), Banerjee found that long-term antidepressant treatment reduced the density (B_{max}) of β-adrenergic receptors without changing receptor–ligand affinity (K_D) (Banerjee, Kung, Riggi, & Charida, 1977). This reduction in the number of β-adrenergic receptors (B_{max}) (as noted in Table 8-2) has been reported following chronic antidepressant drug treatment in multiple brain areas with various tricyclic antidepressants, atypical antidepressants (iprindole, trazodone, and buproprion), MAOIs, and courses of ECT. Only mianserin and zimelidine of the clinically effective antidepressants, fail to reduce β-adrenergic receptor binding (although both are effective in down-regulating the non-β component of NE-induced cAMP generation) (Table 8-1). The possi-

TABLE 8-2. Receptor Binding Changes following Long-term Antidepressant Treatment

Drug type	Drug	β-Adrenergic
Tricyclics	Imipramine	↓
	Amitriptyline	↓
	Chlomipramine	↓
	Doxepine	↓
	Nortriptyline	↓
	Desipramine	↓
"Atypical"	Mianserin	0
	Iprindole	↓
	Zimeladine	0
	Trazodone	↓
	Buproprion	↓
MAOIs	Phenelzine	↓
	Tranylcypromine	↓
	Clorgyline	↓
	Paragyline	↓
	Nialamide	↓
ECT	—	↓

Note. Table modified from Charney, Menkes, & Heninger (1981b).

bility that β-receptor binding decrements are related clinically to antidepressant effects is suggested by the finding that only long-term treatment and not acute treatment with antidepressant drugs is associated with both clinical antidepressant response and down-regulation of β-receptor number.

The mechanism by which antidepressant drugs down-regulate β-receptor number (decrease of B_{max}) and NE-stimulated cAMP production is not known. The initial hypothesis suggested that down-regulation of postsynaptic β-adrenergic systems occurs secondary to the antidepressant-induced increase in NE within the synaptic cleft. Since many receptor systems are known to homeostatically up-regulate or down-regulate both their receptor number and functional sensitivity in response to the quantity of synaptic neurotransmitter,[1] the prolonged increase of synaptic NE caused by reuptake inhibition, by blockade at presynaptic α_2-receptors (mianserin), or by inhibition of degradative enzymes (MAOIs), could conceivably result in a secondary down-regulation of postsynaptic β-receptor number and sensitivity. However, it is difficult to account for the down-regulation of NE-stimulated cAMP production and/or down-regulation of the number of β-receptors by drugs that have little or no effect on either NE reuptake or MAO inhibition, or even on presynaptic α_2-blockade, such as by drugs like amitriptyline, trazodone, iprindole, or buproprion.

Other speculations concerning the mechanism(s) by which antidepressant drugs down-regulate postsynaptic β-adrenergic or NE-stimulated systems concern more generalized, but as yet poorly defined membrane-related changes affecting receptors and receptor coupling processes. As we will further explore, not only the β-adrenergic/NE-stimulated cAMP system appears to show marked changes with chronic antidepressant drug treatment, but also chronic antidepressant drug treatment produces changes in pre- and postsynaptic α-adrenergic and serotonergic receptor systems. Even presynaptic dopamine systems may be affected.

The multiplicity of receptor or receptor-associated effects during chronic, but not acute antidepressant drug treatment suggests the possibility of major changes in membrane properties, including composition and fluidity/viscosity. Such generalized changes may affect not only the number of identifiable β-adrenergic recognition sites

1. Up-regulation of adrenergic receptor and function occurs following neurotransmitter depletion, such as by reserpine or presynaptic lesioning of adrenergic systems; down-regulation occurs in the presence of excess neurotransmitter, such as occurs following precursor loading or, presumably, with reuptake-inhibiting drugs.

(receptors) on the outer membrane bilayer, but also the movement of the bilayers that permit the linkage of receptors to transmembrane catalytic units, thus potentially affecting both receptor number and functional sensitivity of a variety of neuronal systems (Sulser & Mobley, 1981) (see Chapter 10 for a further discussion of membrane abnormalities in affective disorders).

The hypothesis that depression could be related to an excess of CNS β-adrenergic receptors and excess β-adrenergic function—a β-supersensitivity hypothesis of depression—and that antidepressant effects are achieved by down-regulating such β-adrenergic supersensitivity, has been difficult to test clinically owing to the lack of clear-cut behavioral or clinical markers of activity for central β-adrenergic systems.

The release of pineal melatonin appears to occur following activation of a β-adrenergic receptor and may eventually provide a means of comparing the β-adrenergic sensitivity in affective disordered patients to that of other control populations. Melatonin release could be used to study the effect of antidepressant upon β-adrenergic systems, at least from the viewpoint of the pineal β-adrenergic function (Lewy, 1982). Monitoring central β-adrenergic function by means of neuroendocrine response, such as the growth hormone response to insulin (which is known to be facilitated by a β-adrenergic receptor) is complicated by the significant contribution of α-adrenergic and 5-HT input into the regulation of such growth hormone responses as well.

Peripheral measures of β-adrenergic receptor function in the affective disorders have been limited to estimates of the numbers of β-adrenergic receptors and their function (in terms of cAMP) in leukocytes. Extein found that lymphocytes from patients with major depressive disorders had not increased, but *decreased* [^{3}H]DHA binding (41 $\pm$ 14 fmol/mg) as compared with both controls (52 $\pm$ 16) and to the same patients during a euthymic period (53 $\pm$ 18) (Extein, Tallman, Smith, & Goodwin, 1979). Moreover, both Extein *et al.* (1979) and Pandey, Dysken, Garver, and Davis (1979) have reported *decreased* isoproterenol-induced cAMP production from leukocytes from major depressive disordered patients.

Decreased β-receptor B_{max} and decreased isoproterenol-induced cAMP of leukocytes is the opposite of what would be expected if an abnormality of increased β-adrenergic sensitivity were not only present in the brain, but also generalized throughout other body tissues. Chronic drug treatment with desipramine or lithium also fails to have a significant effect on leukocyte [^{3}H]DHA binding or on isoproterenol-stimulated cAMP generation (Extein *et al.*, 1979). No evidence can yet be marshaled from peripheral studies in depressed patients to support a β-adrenergic hypersensitivity hypothesis of depression or to support the hypothesis that antidepressants down-regulate β-adrenergic systems in tissue devoid of adrenergic innervation (Schweitizer, Schwartz, & Friedhoff, 1979).

Noradrenergic Autoreceptor (α_2) Supersensitivity and Depression

The α_2 autoreceptor located on presynaptic adrenergic terminals and dendritic trees functions to slow the rate of firing of a noradrenergic neuron when α_2-receptors are activated by NE or by clonidine (Figure 8-2). The autoreceptor is a major component of a feedback loop that controls NE synthesis and impulse flow.

As noted above, there is strong evidence that chronic antidepressant drug treatment causes not only a down regulation of postsynaptic β-adrenergic systems, but also a functional α_2-adrenergic receptor subsensitivity.

Crews and Smith (1978) found that chronic treatment with desipramine was associated with marked increased sensitivity to NE released by electrical stimulation of (heart) atrial strips, suggesting that the inhibitory effects of α_2 stimulation on NE release was decreased by chronic desipramine. While the α_2-receptor agonist clonidine, ordinarily suppresses such electrically stimulated NE release, clonidine loses its ability to suppress such release in animals chronically treated with desipramine (Crews & Smith, 1978).

Other reports suggested that clonidine-induced suppression of MHPG (Tang, Helmesfe, & Stancer, 1978), as well as clonidine-induced suppression of nonadrenergic neuron-firing rate (Svensson & Usdin, 1978), were attenuated by chronic imipramine. These findings are consistent with the hypothesis that chronic antidepressant drug treatment functionally reduces the sensitivity of the presynaptic (α_2) autoreceptors on NE neurons. Subsequently, it has been demonstrated that specific binding of the α_2-receptor agonist [^{3}H]clonidine is reduced following 14 days of chronic imipramine administration (Smith, Garcia-Sevilla, & Hollingsworth, 1981) and following 21 days of clorgyline (a type A MAOI)[2] in animals (Charney *et al.*, 1981b).

2. It is not clear, however, that such reduction of clonidine binding represents *presynaptic* α_2 effects, since NE neuron destruction by 6-hydroxydopamine causes no significant change in total [^{3}H]clonidine binding (U'Prichard, Bechtel, Rouot, & Snyder, 1979).

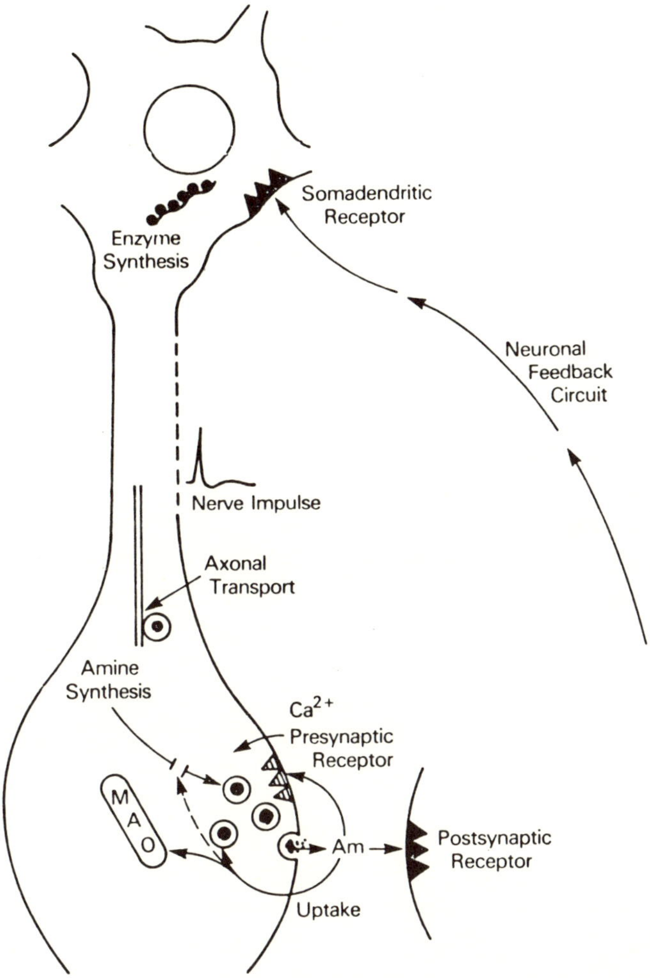

FIG. 8-2. Diagrammatic representation of an aminergic neuron. The presynaptic (auto) receptor inhibits the firing rate of the presynaptic neuron and the synthesis of its aminergic neurotransmitter (Am). From "Mode of Action of Antidepressants and Central Stimulants" by I. J. Kopin in H. M. van Praag, M. G. Lader, O. J. Rafaelsen, & E. J. Sachar (Eds.), *Handbook of Biological Psychiatry, Part IV: Brain Mechanisms and Abnormal Behavior*, New York: Marcel Dekker, 1981, p. 746. Reprinted by permission.

Only a few antidepressant agents have been studied with respect to down-regulation of α_2-receptor number and function during 10 of more days of chronic treatment (Charney *et al.*, 1981b). Yet, the hypothesis of supersensitivity of such autoreceptor effects in depression, and down-regulation of such effects by chronic antidepressant treatment is especially intriguing. Supersensitive NE-autoreceptors in depressed patients would be expected to down-regulate NE neuronal activity and cause a decrement in MHPG in depressed patients. Decreased urinary MHPG has been well documented in bipolar depressed patients (Garver & Davis, 1979).

Studies in depressed patients relevant to the α_2 hypersensitivity hypothesis of depression, and the effect of antidepressants on α_2-adrenergic systems, have included examination of the central effects of clonidine on plasma MHPG, blood pressure, and on platelet α_2-receptor binding peripherally.

Clonidine administered to depressed patients causes a decrement in plasma MHPG, which reaches its trough about 210 minutes following clonidine dosage. Following 4–6 weeks of desipramine, clonidine is no longer able to suppress plasma MHPG, suggesting that the α_2-receptor has functionally been down regulated by chronic antidepressant treatment (Charney *et al.*, 1981a) (Figure 8-3). The hypotensive effects of clonidine are believed to be modulated via α_2-adrenergic receptors (Starke & Altmann, 1973). Clonidine's hypotensive effects are attenuated by chronic treatment with desipramine (Charney *et al.*, 1981a) (Figure 8-4), imipramine, and with clorgyline (Siever, Cohen, & Murphy, 1981). These findings suggest that chronic antidepressant drug treatments reduces α_2-receptor sensitivity, perhaps releasing the adrenergic neuron from inhibitory α_2 control and causing increased synaptic NE.

The critical question is whether depressive disease itself, apart from drug treatment, could be a primary disorder of α_2-receptor supersensitivity. Here there have been provocative, yet not definitive findings.

As noted above, the finding of diminished urinary MHPG in some drug-free depressed patients (Garver & Davis, 1979) is consistent with α_2-adrenergic hypersensitivity, which slows the synthesis and turnover of NE. Clonidine's ability to suppress plasma MHPG has been studied by Charney in depressives and in controls. Clonidine reduced plasma MHPG only in depressed patients and not in controls, which suggested supersensitivity of the α_2-receptor in depression (Charney *et al.*, 1982) (Figure 8-5). However, as pointed out by Charney,

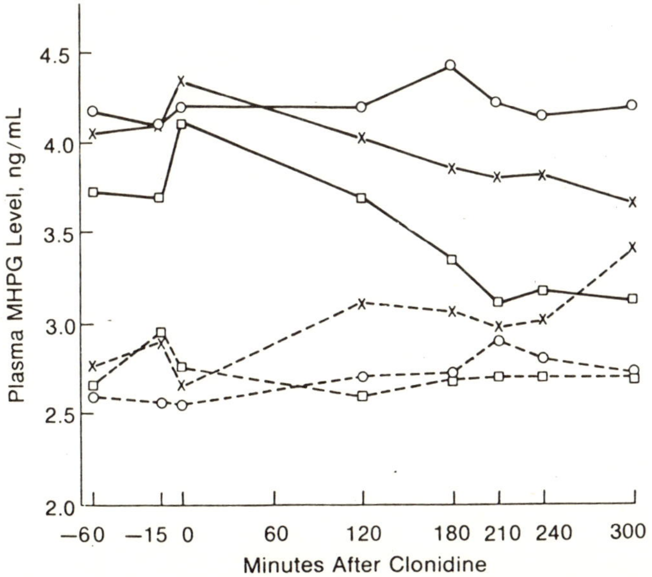

FIG. 8-3. Effect of long-term desipramine treatment on clonidine-induced decrease in mean plasma levels of MHPG. Solid line indicates placebo treatment; broken line, desipramine treatment; circles, no clonidine; X's, 1 μg clonidine/kg; squares, 5 μg clonidine/kg. From "Presynaptic Adrenergic Receptor Sensitivity in Depression: The Effect of Long-Term Desipramine Treatment" by D. S. Charney *et al.*, *Archives of General Psychiatry*, 1981a, *38*, 1336. Reprinted by permission.

control subjects appeared to have *increased* plasma MHPG 4 hours after placebo administration—perhaps related to diurnal variation—an increase absent following placebo injection in depressed subjects. The absence of increased MHPG in the placebo-treated depressed patients might be due to α_2 hypersensitivity suppressing the diurnal rise—or it might be due to an altered diurnal cycle in depressed patients. Such different plasma MHPG curves following placebo injections in depressed versus control groups make the changes in MHPG following clonidine (from each group's placebo MHPG level) *not* significantly different (Charney *et al.*, 1982).

Blood pressure effects of clonidine in depressed versus control groups have not shown significant differences, though in both Charney's report (Charney *et al.*, 1982), using 5μg/kg clonidine, and in Checkley's report (1979), using 2μg/kg clonidine, mean systolic blood pressure is lower at every point (including baseline) during the 2–6 hour period monitored in depressed patients compared with controls.

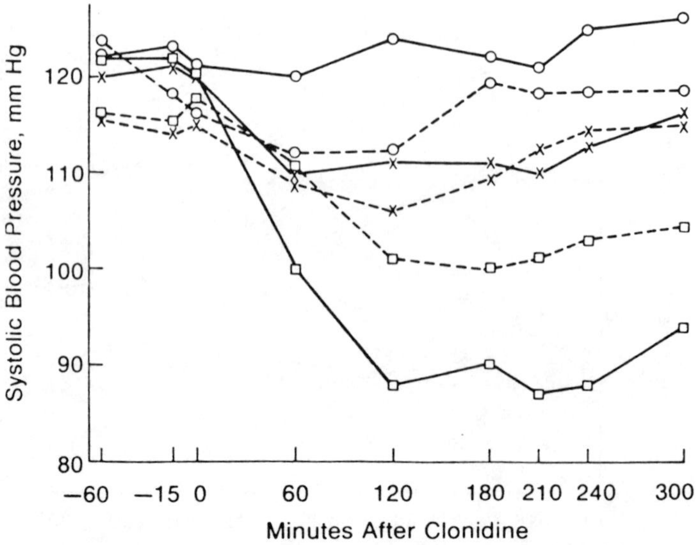

FIG. 8-4. Effect of long-term desipramine treatment on clonidine-induced decrease in mean sitting systolic blood pressure. Solid line indicates placebo treatment; broken line, desipramine treatment; circles, no clonidine; ×'s, 1 μg clonidine/kg; squares, 5 μg clonidine/kg. From "Presynaptic Adrenergic Receptor Sensitivity in Depression: The Effect of Long-Term Desipramine Treatment" by D. S. Charney *et al.*, *Archives of General Psychiatry*, 1981a, *38*, 1337. Reprinted by permission.

This suggests the possibility of an α_2-receptor supersensitivity in the depressed group throughout.

Moving from the CNS to the periphery for evidence of generalized supersensitivity of α_2-adrenergic receptors, several groups have examined the possibility that platelets might show increased numbers of α_2-adrenoreceptors or functional supersensitivity. Utilizing $[^3H]$clonidine as the ligand, Garcia-Sevilla reported that platelets from patients with major depressive disorders had a significantly greater number of identifiable α_2-receptors than did controls (45 ± 3 fmol/mg platelet protein vs. 34.2 ± 2.4 in controls) (Garcia Sevilla, Zis, Hollingsworth, Greden, & Smith, 1981). Moreover, this group reported that chronic treatment with either imipramine or amitriptyline resulted in decreased numbers of $[^3H]$clonidine-labeled α_2 platelet receptors in depressed patients. Following chronic antidepressant drug treatment, the receptor density of platelets from the depressed patients became indistinguishable from controls (Garcia-Sevilla *et al.*, 1981).

U'Pritchard has been unable to replicate this intriguing finding of differences in platelet α_2-receptor number in depressed patients. U'Pritchard used the α_2-antagonist ligand [^{3}H]yohimbine, with which he attempted to label the entire population of α_2-receptors, rather than only the high-affinity site identifiable most easily by [^{3}H]clonidine (U'Pritchard, Daiguji, Tang, Mitrius, & Meltzer, 1982).

The hypothesis of primary autoreceptor (α_2-adrenergic) supersensitivity underlying some forms of depressive disease is an intriguing one. The evidence favoring such a hypothesis is only fragmentary, consisting of controversial findings of exaggerated clonidine-induced reduction of MHPG and blood pressure in depressed patients and

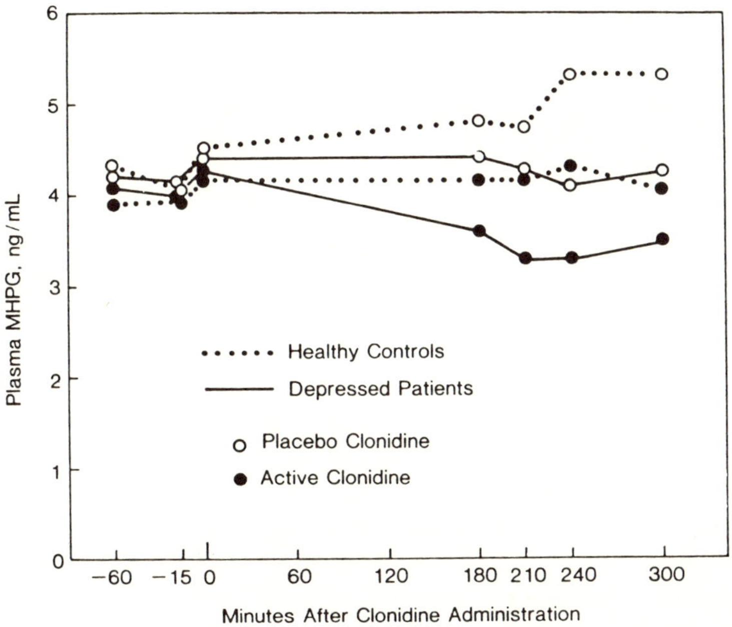

FIG. 8-5. Effect of placebo and clonidine, 5 μg/kg, on plasma MHPG in healthy controls ($n = 12$) and depressed patients ($n = 15$). Increase of plasma MHPG levels after placebo administration in controls was significantly greater than the small decrease seen in patients ($p < .05$). Decrease in plasma MHPG levels after clonidine in depressed patients was significantly greater than in controls ($p < .01$). Overall "net" effect of clonidine on plasma MHPG was not different between groups. From "Adrenergic Receptor Sensitivity in Depression: Effects of Clonidine in Depressed Patients and Healthy Subjects" by D. S. Charney *et al.*, *Archives of General Psychiatry*, 1982, *39*, 292. Reprinted by permission.

inconsistent evidence of increased α_2-adrenergic binding sites on platelets of depressed patients. The evidence concerning down-regulation of presynaptic α_2-autoreceptors by antidepressant drugs as being invariably associated with antidepressant effects is far from complete—and is undoubtedly a focus for future research.

Noradrenergic Postsynaptic (α_1) Subsensitivity and Depression

Antidepressants have both acute and chronic effects on postsynaptic central α-adrenergic systems. The acute effect of many antidepressants is to block α_1-receptors, which produces sedation and hypotension. A chronic effect of antidepressants is to sensitize postsynaptic α_1 (and perhaps some postsynaptic α_2) adrenergic systems, with a time-course that corresponds clinically to antidepressant effects.

α_1 *Acute Effects*

Clinically, many physicians have noted that some antidepressants are particularly effective in treating certain types of depression. Tertiary amine tricyclic antidepressants, such as amitriptyline and doxepin, acutely counteract psychomotor agitation and are associated with a high incidence of sedative and hypotensive side effects (U'Prichard, Greenberg, Sheehan, & Snyder, 1978; U'Prichard *et al.*, 1982). The sedating and hypotensive properties are seen immediately after administration of these drugs, rather than 2 or 3 weeks following chronic administration, which indicates that the sedative–hypotensive properties of antidepressants are an acute drug effect. Table 8-3 rank-orders antidepressants according to their affinity (K_D) for central α_1-receptors (Ventulani & Sulser, 1975), and indicates the sedative and orthostatic hypotensive potentials for each drug.

Tricyclic antidepressants such as doxepin and amitriptyline have a high affinity for the central α_1-receptor, as judged by their ability to displace [^{3}H]WB-4101 binding from postsynaptic α_1-receptors at low nanomolar concentrations. These two tricyclic antidepressants also display the highest incidence of sedation and hypotension among the tested compounds. Notably, neuroleptics, such as chlorpromazine and thioridazine, show an even higher affinity for central α_1-receptors (K_i = 5.2 and 5.4 nM respectively) than doxepin and amitriptyline

TABLE 8-3. Comparison of Drug Affinity for Central α_1-Receptors and Sedative–Hypotensive Properties

Drug	Sedation and hypotension	α_1 binding K_i (nM) [^{3}H]WB-4101
Neuroleptics		
Chlorpromazine	+++	5
Thioridazine	+++	5
Antidepressants		
Doxepin	++	23
Amitriptyline	++	24
Chlorimipramine	+	55
Imipramine	+	58
Trazodone	+	68
Nortryptamine	+	71
Mianserin	+	86
Desipramine	−	148
Protriptyline	−	277

(Peroutka, U'Prichard, Greenberg, & Snyder, 1977). These two neuroleptics are clinically well known for a high incidence of sedative and hypotensive side effects. At the other extreme are antidepressants that show little or no affinity for central α_1-adrenoceptors at clinically effective doses. These compounds, for example, desipramine and protriptyline, are much freer of sedative and hypotensive side effects. These compounds are well known for their ability to cause psychomotor agitation.

α_1 *Chronic Effects*

Chronic administration of antidepressants (iprindole, imipramine, desipramine, and amitriptyline, but not chlorpromazine) increases the sensitivity of postsynaptic α-adrenoreceptors to iontophoretically applied NE (Menkes & Aghajanian, 1981; Menkes, Aghajanian, & McCall, 1980). This enhanced responsiveness appears to represent an altered sensitivity of the postsynaptic α-adrenoreceptor complex, since the enhanced NE response is blocked by α-adrenoreceptor blocking agents. Postsynaptic supersensitivity as opposed to inhibition of NE uptake appeared responsible for the enhanced sensitivity to NE because: (1) the tested antidepressants varied considerably in their ability to block reuptake, yet they were uniformly effective in enhancing postsynaptic NE effects following chronic administration; (2) iprindole, which has almost no reuptake blocking ability (Fann *et al.*, 1974), enhanced the response to NE after chronic drug treatment; and (3) a similar enhanced responsiveness of postsynaptic cells to phenylephrine, an α_1-agonist with little or no affinity for the NE reuptake site, was observed after chronic antidepressant treatment. These data suggest that the enhanced postsynaptic responsiveness to NE observed after chronic antidepressants was not due to blockade of NE reuptake but, rather, to a developing supersensitivity of the postsynaptic α_1-adrenoreceptor complex.

While inhibition of NE reuptake cannot explain the antidepressant induced functional α_1 supersensitivity, neither can the α_1 blocking properties shown by many but not all antidepressants account for the α_1 supersensitivity. Table 8-3 shows the differential affinity of many antidepressants for the α_1-receptor. Amitriptyline, which is very effective in blocking α_1-receptors, also blocks the response of iontophoretically applied NE. These electrophysiological and receptor binding data indicate that chronic amitriptyline treatment would block α_1-receptors. Chronic receptor blockade could be associated with a compensatory receptor proliferation that could theoretically explain the enhanced NE responsiveness. Yet, an α_1-receptor proliferation can not explain the enhanced NE responsiveness seen after chronic antidepressant treatment for two reasons. First, chronic treatment with antidepressants that have little (imipramine) or no (iprindole) affinity for the α_1-receptor also enhances the responsiveness of α_1-adrenoreceptors to NE (Menkes *et al.*, 1981). Second, chronic blockade of central α_1-receptors by some antidepressants does not appear to have any effect on the number or affinity of the postsynaptic adrenoreceptor.

In summary, chronic, but not acute, antidepressant treatment enhances the responsiveness of central postsynaptic α_1-adrenoreceptors to NE. The mechanism by which antidepressants induce adrenoreceptor supersensitivity appears to be neither an effect on NE reuptake nor receptor blockade of α_1-adrenoreceptors.

Several lines of behavioral evidence suggest that chronic antidepressant treatment or ECT enhances central adrenergic responsiveness. Doses of clonidine above 100 μg/kg stimulate postsynaptic α_1-adrenoceptors and locomotor activity in animals (Anden, Trombom, & Svensson, 1973; Maj, Mogilnicka, & Klimek, 1979). While acute antidepressant treatment produced no enhancement in locomotor activity, chronic antidepressant treatment significantly enhanced clonidine-induced locomotion. Interestingly, the enhanced locomotion was most consistently observed 48 and 72 hours after the final antidepressant treatment, suggesting the importance of antidepressant clearance from brain adrenoreceptors before subsequent administration of the experimental drug. These data suggest that chronic antidepressant treatment produces a supersensitive central noradrenergic system probably related to postsynaptic α_1-adrenoreceptors. Similarly, chronic ECT enhanced clonidine-induced locomotor activity, while acute ECT was without effect (Modigh, 1975).

A second behavioral model that assays central adrenergic activity is clonidine- or apomorphine-induced aggressive behavior in animals. Chronic, but not acute antidepressant treatment, enhanced both clonidine- and apomorphine-induced aggression (Maj, Mogilnicka, & Kordecka, 1979a, 1979b). These behavioral studies support the above electophysiological studies indicating a supersensitive α_1-adrenoreceptor response after chronic antidepressant treatment.

Clinical studies also implicate postsynaptic α-adrenoreceptor dysfunction in endogenous depression and in the action of antidepressants. Human growth hormone (GH) release appears to be partially modulated by central α-adrenoreceptors; α-agonists, such as clonidine and amphetamine, stimulate GH release (Lal, Tolis, Martin, Brown, & Guyda, 1975; Langer, Heinze, Reim, & Matussek, 1976), while α-receptor blockers inhibit GH release (Gold, Donabedian, & Redmond, 1978). Numerous studies have demonstrated that patients with endogenous depression show a blunted GH response to insulin-induced hypoglycemia (Carroll, 1972; Casper, Davis, Pandey, Garver, & Dekirmenjian, 1977; Checkley, 1979; Czernik, 1978; Garver, Pandey, Dekirmenjian, & DeLeon-Jones, 1975; Mueller, Heninger, & McConald, 1969; Sachar, Finkelstein, & Hellman, 1971). Although these studies suggest that endogenously depressed patients may have subsensitive α-adrenergic systems, more convincing support is provided by studies employing adrenoreceptor agonists. Amphetamine, which releases both NE and dopamine, stimulates GH secretion. In endogenously depressed patients the GH response to amphetamine is severely blunted (Checkley, 1979; Langer *et al.*, 1976). The GH response to amphetamine appeared NE-mediated, as prior blockade of DA receptors by pimozide did not block the amphetamine-induced GH response in monkeys (Sachar, Roffwarg, Gruen, Altman, & Sassin, 1976). Similarly, clonidine, which stimulates postsynaptic α-adrenoreceptors in higher concentration, also significantly increases GH release (Lal *et al.*, 1975). The clonidine-induced GH response is severely blunted in patients with an endogenous depression[3] (Checkley, Slade, & Shur, 1981; Matussek *et al.*, 1980). The blunted GH response seen in endog-

3. The type of adrenergic receptor that mediates the clonidine-induced GH response is controversial, and may be a postsynaptic α_2-receptor (Maany *et al.*, 1979).

enously depressed patients does not appear due to a GH deficiency, as such patients have a normal GH response to apomorphine (Casper *et al.*, 1977; Maany, Mendels, Frazer, & Brunswick, 1979) or L-dopa infusion (Sachar *et al.*, 1975).

In summary, stimulation of GH secretion employing several methods including direct α-adrenoreceptor agonists implicate a subsensitive postsynaptic α-adrenergic system in endogenous depression. It would be interesting to know if the blunted GH response to α-agonist administration is reversed by chronic antidepressant treatment, ECT, or symptom remission.

Several studies have observed no effect of chronic antidepressant treatment on the number of central α_1-adrenoreceptors labeled with [^{3}H]WB-4101 (Peroutka & Snyder, 1980; Rosenblatt, Pert, Tallman, Pert, & Bunney, 1979; Tang, Seeman, & Kwan, 1981). Rehavi, Ramot, Yavetz, and Sokolovsky (1980), however, have identified two binding sites labeled by [^{3}H]WB-4010. The number of superhigh affinity sites (0.22 nM) significantly increased following chronic amitriptyline administration, while no change in the high-affinity site (3.5 nM) was observed. As the increased number of superhigh affinity sites would correlate well with the enhanced NE sensitivity observed in both electrophysiological and behavioral studies, the result is intriguing. It will be interesting to see if other laboratories confirm this finding, and if the α_1-adrenoreceptor supersensitivity occurs after treatment with antidepressants such as iprindole and desipramine, which are devoid of α_1-blocking properties.

In summary, electrophysiological, behavioral, and clinical studies suggest that endogenously depressed patients have a *subsensitive* postsynaptic adrenoreceptor system. The effect of antidepressants and ECT is to enhance the sensitivity of postsynaptic central α_1 and perhaps some postsynaptic α_2-adrenoreceptors. Therefore, available data on the α_1-receptor system supports at least a modification of the classical theory of depression. Here depression is seen as a deficiency in noradrenergic function, but related to postsynaptic insensitivity, which is itself reversed by antidepressant administration and ECT.

5-HT Receptor Subsensitivity and Depression

Recent findings suggest that antidepressants, during chronic treatment, also induce marked changes in postsynaptic 5-HT receptor sensitivity and, according to some studies, changes in receptor number.

Antidepressant drugs administered chronically enhance the postsynaptic single unit response to iontophoretically applied 5-HT in several regions of the CNS. Chronic, but not acute antidepressant treatment sensitizes the postsynaptic 5-HT response in the ventral and dorsal lateral geniculate (DeMontigny & Aghajanian, 1978; Menkes & Aghajanian, 1981), hippocampus (DeMontigny & Aghajanian, 1978; DeMontigny, Blier, Caille, & Kouassi, 1981; Gallagher & Bunney, 1979), amygdala (Wang & Aghajanian, 1980), and the facial nucleus (Menkes *et al.*, 1980).

While it may be argued that the enhanced 5-HT response might be due to presynaptic enhancing of 5-HT release or 5-HT uptake blockade by some antidepressants, three facts argue in favor of postsynaptic sensitization: (1) Chronic treatment with iprindole, which has little or no ability to block reuptake (Hall & Ogren, 1981), also enhanced 5-HT sensitivity; (2) increased sensitivity to 5-methoxy-dimethyltryptamine (5-MeODMT) and LSD, which are not substrates for the high-affinity reuptake process (Horn, 1973; Ross & Renyi, 1969), is seen after chronic antidepressant treatment, (3) the reuptake blockade is typically seen after both acute and chronic antidepressant treatment, while the enhanced 5-HT response is only seen after chronic treatment. Therefore, the enhanced 5-HT response appears to reflect an effect of chronic antidepressant treatment on the postsynaptic 5-HT receptor complex.

The enhanced 5-HT response seems to be specific to long-term treatments which alleviate depression. Acute or chronic treatment with the antipsychotic chlorpromazine, or 5-HT reuptake inhibitors devoid of antidepressant efficacy do not enhance the response to 5-HT (Menkes *et al.*, 1980; Menkes & Aghajanian, 1981; DeMontigny & Aghajanian, 1978; Wang & Aghajanian, 1980). Conversely, the relationship between enhanced 5-HT sensitivity and clinical antidepressant response is strengthened by the finding that repeated ECT enhances the sensitivity of iontophoretically applied 5-HT or 5-MeODMT (DeMontigny, 1980).

In summary, antidepressants share a common ability to enhance the sensitivity of the postsynaptic 5-HT receptor complex after chronic administration, as does repeated ECT. Further, this increased sensitivity appears specific to antidepressant drugs. The mechanism by which the enhanced responsiveness is accomplished is not related to 5-HT reuptake blockade.

The enhanced 5-HT sensitivity to chronic antidepressant treatment seen in the electrophysiological studies is clearly reflected in behavioral studies. Various behaviors including head twitches, sleep, wet dog shakes, and locomotor activity, which are regulated by 5-HT, can be reliably elicited by 5-HT agonist administration (Friedman & Dallob, 1979; Mogilnicka & Klimek, 1979). These studies indicate that the behavioral responses elicited by 5-HT agonist treatment are uniformly enhanced by chronic imipramine, amitripyline, desipramine, or mianserin treatment. Additionally, repeated ECT enhanced the 5-HT syndrome elicited by 5-HT agonists (Grahame-Smith, Green, & Costain, 1978; Green & Deakin, 1980; Green, Heal, & Grahame-Smith, 1977).

Clinical studies of central 5-HT transmitter systems have been hampered by the lack of a well-developed model in man. Initial studies have focused on prolactin release as a model. Prolactin release appears partially 5-HT dependent, as systemic administration of 5-HT (Lawson & Gala, 1975) or 5-hydroxytryptophan (Chen & Meites, 1975) induces prolactin release, as does injection of 5-HT into the third ventricle (Kamberi, Blake, Terkel, & Sawyer, 1973). Conversely, inhibition of 5-HT synthesis reduces plasma prolactin levels (Chen & Meites, 1975). Depressed patients were found to have decreased prolactin, compared with normal controls (Sachar *et al.*, 1980), suggesting a subsensitive central 5-HT system in depressed patients. In a recent study examining prolactin release elicited by thyrotropin-releasing hormone (TRH), the prolactin response was increased after ECT, with the increase in prolactin response being correlated with clinical outcome (Coppen, Rao Rama, Bishop, Abou-Saleh, & Wood, 1980). Although these data suggest that antidepressant response may be correlated with an increase in postsynaptic 5-HT sensitivity, additional studies will be required before firm conclusions can be drawn.

Both behavioral and clinical studies suggest that antidepressant treatment and clinical response may be correlated with an enhanced postsynaptic 5-HT receptor sensitivity. These studies support the electrophysiological studies that uniformly demonstrate an enhanced postsynaptic 5-HT receptor sensitivity following chronic antidepressant administration.

Numerous studies examining changes in 5-HT receptor number associated with chronic antidepressant treatment have been reported. No effect of chronic antidepressant administration on 5-HT_1 receptors labeled with [^{3}H]5-HT has been consistently observed (Bergstrom & Kellar, 1979; Peroutka & Snyder, 1980; Savage, Frazer, & Mendels, 1979). In spite of an increase in functional postsynaptic sensitivity, there is no documentation of an increase in the number of postsynaptic 5-HT_1 receptors. Like with the increase functional sensitivity of the postsynaptic α_1-receptor, chronic antidepressant treatment appears to up regulate the functional linkage between 5-HT_1 receptors and their transmembrane functional receptor complex.

Of particular interest are the reports that chronic antidepressant treatment decreases the number of 5-HT_2 receptors in cerebral cortex (Blackshear, Sternaka, & Sanders-Bush, 1980; Enna & Kendall, 1981; Kellar, Cascio, Butler, & Kurtzke, 1981; Mann & Enna, 1980; Peroutka & Snyder, 1980; Tang, Seeman, & Kwan, 1980) (see Table 8-4). These 5-HT_2 receptors, labeled preferentially by [^{3}H]spiroperidol, are found to be consistently reduced in number by antidepressants, including atypical antidepressants and MAOIs (Table 8-4). Although intriguing, many questions remain regarding the importance of down regulation of 5-HT_2 receptors by antidepressants. First, it is in the opposite direction from what would be expected from the electrophysiological, behavioral, and clinical studies reported above.[4] Second, ECT up regulated 5-HT_2 receptors (Kellar *et al.*, 1981) which draws into question the clinical importance of the 5-HT_2 down regulation. Third, there is some question as to the significance of the 5-HT_2 receptor. For

TABLE 8-4. Effect of Chronic Antidepressant Treatment on Numbers of 5-HT_1 and 5-HT_2 Receptors

Antidepressant	5-HT_2	5-HT_1
Tricyclics		
Amitriptyline	↓	0
Imipramine	↓	
Desipramine	↓	0
Iprindole	↓	0
Mianserin	↓	—
Trazadone	↓	—
MAOIs		
Pargyline	↓	
Tranylcypramine	↓	—
Neuroleptics		
Chlorpromazine	0	0
Haloperidol	0	0
ECT	↑	0

4. However, if some 5-HT_2 receptors were also autoreceptors, supressing 5-HT turnover, down-regulation (as with α_2 down-regulation) could further facilitate 5-HT neurotransmission during chronic antidepressant treatment. Currently, there is little direct evidence for a presynaptic role of 5-HT_2 systems; destruction of 5-HT neurons does not produce a net decrease in 5-HT_2 ([^{3}H]spiroperidol binding) in cortex, suggesting that such receptors may be on 5-HT neurons (Enna & Kendall, 1981).

example, 5-HT has a relative poor affinity for the 5-HT_2 receptor (K_D = 2770 nM), which makes one wonder whether some as yet undiscovered transmitter that shows a more expected affinity for the purported 5-HT_2 receptor will be found. In comparison the K_D of 5-HT for the 5-HT_1 receptor is 3.8 nM, a nearly 1000-fold higher affinity. Further, 5-HT_2 receptor displays very limited structural specificity to analogues of 5-HT (Middlemiss, Carroll, Fisher, & Mounsey, 1980). This suggests that [^{3}H]spiroperidol binding may not be specific for 5-HT receptors and the claim that spiroperidol labels a 5-HT receptor may be erroneous.

Clinical, behavioral, and electrophysiological studies then can be marshaled to support a 5-HT deficiency theory of depression. The data suggest that depression is related to a functional postsynaptic 5-HT receptor-complex deficiency condition, which is reversed at the postsynaptic receptor complex by antidepressant treatment or ECT. The receptor binding studies fail to document an antidepressant drug-induced increase in the number of 5-HT receptors. As with the postsynaptic α_1-adrenoreceptor, the 5-HT_1 binding studies are at odds with the results employing functional techniques. This makes a very important point. Changes in postsynaptic receptor function, at least in systems related to depression and antidepressant drugs, may be relatively independent of changes in receptor number or affinity. The implication for our clinical understanding of antidepressant action is that receptor *function* is the most important parameter to keep in mind. Receptor binding studies, for all their technical elegance, have several limitations in explaining how antidepressant therapies produce their clinical response.

Dopamine Presynaptic Supersensitivity and Depression

The discussion of depression, antidepressants, and receptors would be incomplete without at least a postscript concerning antidepressant drug-induced changes in central dopaminergic receptors.

In 1980, Chiodo reported delayed functional changes in presynaptic dopamine autoreceptor sensitivity following chronic treatment with imipramine, amitriptyline, or iprindole. He found that the ability of the presynaptic dopamine agonist apomorphine to reduce the firing rate of nigrostriatal dopamine neurons was significantly and progressively attenuated up to 7–10 days after initiation of antidepressant drug treatment (Chiodo & Antelman, 1980a, 1980b).

Behaviorally, chronic treatment with the above noted antidepressants resulted in an enhanced response to environmental stimuli, such as tail pinch (a behavioral paradigm for increased dopamine function) (Chiodo & Antelman, 1980a). Following 21 days of treatment with desipramine, Lee found a significant decrease in the B_{max} for [^{3}H] dopamine binding, presumably reflecting a change in presynaptic autoreceptor binding. There was no change in postsynaptic (α_2) receptors as indicated by [^{3}H]spiroperidol binding. Presynaptic [^{3}H]dopamine binding was reduced by 30% at day 28 of chronic desipramine treatment. Nomifensine also reduced the B_{max} for [^{3}H] dopamine binding by 21% following 28 days of treatment (Lee & Tang, 1982).

Such findings of reduced dopamine-autoreceptor function following treatment with antidepressants and the consequent increase in synaptic dopamine could support the suggestion of a supersensitive presynaptic dopamine receptor and consequent hypodopaminergic hypothesis of affective disorders (Randrup, Munkvad, & Fog, 1981), with normalization of dopamine systems by antidepressants through presynaptic down regulation.

The major difficulty with such a hypodopaminergic hypothesis (because of supersensitive dopamine autoreceptors) is the finding that *repeated* administration of antidepressants or ECT are *not* necessary to effect functional down-regulation of dopamine autoreceptors. Following 2 days of drug treatment or ECT, autoreceptor systems appear to progressively down-regulate over the next 7–50 days without further treatment (Chiodo & Antelman, 1980a, 1980b). If down-regulation of dopamine autoreceptors were critical clinically in antidepressant drug or ECT response, no more than 2–3 days of drug or ECT treatment would be necessary. Certainly, repeated dose readjustments of antidepressant drugs into therapeutic plasma ranges would be unnecessary—since the process of dopamine autoreceptor down-regulation, once triggered, proceeds at its own pace oblivious to the presence or absence of further drug treatment.

REFERENCES

Anden, N. E., Trombom, U., & Svensson, T. H. (1973). Dopamine and noradrenaline receptor stimulation: Reversal of reserpine-induced suppression of motor activity. *Psychopharmacologia, 29,* 289–298.

Banerjee, S. P., Kung, L. S., Riggi, S. J., & Charida, S. K. (1977). Development of β-adrenergic receptor subsensitivity by antidepressants. *Nature, 268,* 455–456.

Bergstrom, D. A., & Kellar, K. J. (1979). Adrenergic and serotonergic receptor binding in rat brain after chronic desmethylimipramine. *Journal of Pharmacology and Experimental Therapeutics, 209,* 256–261.

Blackshear, M. A., Steranka, R., & Sanders-Bush, E. (1980). Serotonin receptor subtypes after chronic treatment with tricyclic antidepressant drugs. *Neuroscience Abstracts, 6,* 860.

Carroll, B. J. (1972). Studies with hypothalamic-pituitary-adrenal stimulation tests in depression. In B. Davies, B. J. Carroll, & R. M. Mobray (Eds.), *Depressive illness: Some research studies* (pp. 149–201). Springfield, IL: Charles C Thomas.

Casper, R. C., Davis, J. M., Pandey, G. N., Garver, D. L., & Dekirmenjian, H. (1977). Neuroendocrine and amine studies in affective disorders. *Psychoneuroendocrinology, 2,* 105–114.

Charney, D. S., Heninger, G. R., Sternberg, D. E., Hafstad, K. M., Giddings, S., & Landis, D. H. (1982). Adrenergic receptor sensitivity in depression: Effects of clonidine in depressed patients and healthy subjects. *Archives of General Psychiatry, 39,* 290–294.

Charney, D. S., Heninger, G. R., Sternberg, D. E., Redmond, D. E., Leckmann, J. F., Mass, J. W., & Roth, R. H. (1981). Presynaptic adrenergic receptor sensitivity in depression: The effect of long-term desipramine treatment. *Archives of General Psychiatry, 38,* 1334–1340.

Charney, D. S., Menkes, D. B., & Heninger, G. R. (1981b). Receptor sensitivity and the mechanism of action of antidepressant drugs. *Archives of General Psychiatry, 38,* 1160–1180.

Checkley, S. A. (1979). Corticosteroid and growth hormone responses to methylaphetamine in depressive illness. *Psychological Medicine, 9,* 107–115.

Checkley, S. A., Slade, A. P., & Shur, E. (1981). Growth hormone and other responses to clonidine in patients with endogenous depression. *British Journal of Psychiatry, 138,* 51–55.

Chen, H. J., & Meites, J. (1975). Effects of biogenic amines and TRH on release of prolactin and TSH in the rat. *Endocrinology, 96,* 10–14.

Chiodo, L. A., & Antelman, S. M. (1980a). Repeated tricyclics induce a progressive dopamine autoreceptor subsensitivity independent of daily drug treatment. *Nature, 287,* 451–545.

Chiodo, L. A., & Antelman, S. M. (1980b). Electroconvulsive shock: Progressive dopamine autoreceptor subsensitivity of repeated treatment. *Science, 210,* 799–801.

Cooper, J. R., Bloom, F. E., & Roth, R. H. (1982). *The biochemical basis of neuropharmacology* (pp. 61–76, 335–346). New York: Oxford University Press.

Coppen, A., Rao Rama, V. A., Bishop, M., Abou-Saleh, M. T., & Wood, K. (1980). Neuroendocrine studies in affective disorders: I. Plasma prolactin response to thyrotropin-releasing hormone in affective disorders: Effects of ECT. *Journal of Affective Disorders, 2,* 311–315.

Crews, F. T., & Smith, C. B. (1978). Presynaptic α-receptor subsensitivity after long term antidepressant treatment. *Science, 202,* 322–324.

DeMontigny, C. (1980). Electroconvulsive shock treatment increases responsiveness of forebrain neurons to serotonin: A microiontophoretic study in the rat. *Neuroscience Abstracts, 6,* 453.

DeMontigny, C., & Aghajanian, G. K. (1978). Tricyclic antidepressants: Long term treatment increases responsivity of rat forebrain neurons to serotonin. *Science, 202,* 1303–1306.

DeMontigny, C., Blier, P., Caille, G., & Kouassi, E. (1981). Pre- and postsynaptic effects of zimelidine and norzimelidine on the serotoninergic system: Single cell studies in the rat. *Acta Psychiatrica Scandinavica, Supplementum, 63,* 79–90.

Enna, S. J., & Kendall, D. A. (1981). Interaction of antidepressants with brain neurotransmitter receptors. *Journal of Clinical Psychopharmacology, 1,* 125–165.

Extein, I., Tallman, J., Smith, C. C., & Goodwin, F. K. (1979). Changes in lymphocyte beta-adrenergic receptors in depression and mania. *Psychiatry Research, 1,* 191–197.

Fann, W. E., Davis, J. M., Janowsky, D. S., Kaufmann, J. S., Cavanaugh, J. H., & Oates, J. A. (1974). Effect of antidepressant and antimanic drugs on amine uptake in man. *Journal of Nervous and Mental Disease, 158,* 361–368.

Friedman, E., & Dallob, A. (1979). Enhanced serotonin receptor activity after chronic treatment with imipramine or amitriptyline. *Communications in Psychopharmacology, 3,* 89–92.

Gallagher, D. W., & Bunney, W. E., Jr. (1979). Failure of chronic lithium treatment to block tricyclic antidepressant-included 5-HT supersensitivity. *Naunyn-Schmiedebergs Archives of Pharmacology, 307,* 129–133.

Garcia-Sevilla, J. A., Zis, A. P., Hollingsworth, P. J., Greden, J. F., & Smith, C. B. (1981). α_2-adrenergic receptors in major depressive disorder. *Archives of General Psychiatry, 38,* 1327–1333.

Garver, D. L., & Davis, J. M. (1979). Biogenic amine hypothesis of affective disorders: Minireview. *Life Sciences, 24,* 383–394.

Garver, D. L., Pandey, N. G., Dekirmenjian, H., & DeLeon-Jones, F. (1975). Growth hormone and catecholamine in affective disorders. *American Journal of Psychiatry, 132,* 1149–1154.

Gold, M. S., Donabedian, R. K., & Redmond, D. E. (1978). Clonidine-induced increase in serum growth hormone: Possible role of epinephrine-mediated synapses. *Psychoneuroendocrinology, 3,* 187–194.

Grahame-Smith, D. G., Green, A. P., & Costain, D. W. (1978). Mechanism of the antidepressant action of electroconvulsive therapy. *Lancet, 1,* 254–257.

Green, A. R., & Deakin, J. F. W. (1980). Brain noradrenaline depletion prevents ECS-induced enhancement of serotonin- and dopamine-mediated behavior. *Nature, 285,* 232–233.

Green, A. R., Heal, D., J., & Grahame-Smith, D. G. (1977). Further observations on the effect of repeated electroconvulsive shock on the behavioral responses of rats produced by increases in the functional activity of brain 5-hydroxytryptamine and dopamine. *Psychopharmacology, 52,* 195–200.

Hall, H., & Ogren, S. O. (1981). Effects of antidepressant drugs on different receptors in the brain. *European Journal of Pharmacology, 70,* 393–407.

Hamburg, M. A., Gallager, D. W., Campbell, I. C., & Tallman, J. F. (1979). Alterations in ^{3}H-clonidine binding due to 6-hydroxydopamine and MAO inhibitors. *Abstracts of the Society for Neuroscience, 9th Annual Meeting,* p. 336. (Abstract No. 1110)

Horn, A. S. (1973). Structure activity relations for the inhibition of 5-HT uptake into rat hypothalamic homogenates by serotonin and tryptamine analogues. *Journal of Neurochemistry, 21,* 883–888.

Kamberi, I. A., Blake, C. A., Terkel, J., & Sawyer, C. H. (1973). Participation of serotonin-containing neurons in the suckling-induced rise in plasma prolactin levels in lactating rats. *Neuroendocrinology, 13,* 213–223.

Kellar, K. J., Cascio, C. S., Butler, J. A., & Kurtzke, R. N. (1981). Differential effects of electroconvulsive shock and antidepressant drugs on serotonin-2 receptors in rat brain. *European Journal of Pharmacology, 69,* 515–518.

Lal, S., Tolis, G., Martin, J. B., Brown, B. M., & Guyda, H. (1975). Effect of clonidine on growth hormone, prolactin, lutenizing hormone, follicle-stimulating hormone and thyroid-stimulating hormone in the serum of normal men. *Journal of Clinical Endocrinology and Metabolism, 41,* 827–832.

Langer, G., Heinze, G., Reim, B., & Matussek, N. (1976). Reduced growth hormone response to amphetamine in endogenous depressive patients. *Archives of General Psychiatry, 33,* 1471.

Lawson, D. M., & Gala, R. R. (1975). The influence of adrenergic, dopaminergic, cholinergic and serotonergic drugs on plasma prolactin levels in ovariectomized, estrogen-treated rats. *Endocrinology, 96,* 313–318.

Lee, T., & Tang, S. W. (1982). Reduced presynaptic dopamine receptor density after chronic antidepressant treatment in rats. *Psychiatry Research, 7,* 111–119.

Lewy, A. J. (1982). Human plasma malatonin: A marker for adrenergic function, circadian rhythms, and responsivity to environmental light. In E. Usdin & I. Hanin (Eds.), *Biological markers in psychiatry and neurology* (pp. 61–65). New York: Pergamon Press.

Maany, I., Mendels, J., Frazer, A., & Brunswick, D. (1979). A study of growth hormone release in depression. *Neuropsychobiology, 5,* 282–289.

Maj, J., Mogillnicka, E., & Klimek, V. (1979). The effect of repeated administration of antidepressant drugs on the responsiveness of rats to catecholamine agonists. *Journal of Neural Transmission, 44,* 221–235.

Maj, J., Mogilnicka, E., & Kordecka, A. (1979a). Effects of chronic administration of antidepressant drugs on aggressive behavior induced by clonidine in mice. *Pharmacology, Biochemistry and Behavior, 13,* 153–154.

Maj, J., Mogilnicka, E., & Kordecka, A. (1979b). Chronic treatment with antidepressant drugs: Potentiation of apomorphine-induced aggressive behavior in rats. *Neuroscience Letters, 13,* 337–341.

Mann, E., & Enna, S. J. (1980). Neurochemical and behavioral correlates of antidepressant drug action. *Neuroscience Abstracts, 6,* 800.

Matussek, N., Ackenheil, M., Hippius, H., Muller, F., Schroeder, H., Schultes, H., & Wasilewski, B. (1980). Effect of clonidine on growth hormone release in psychiatric patients and controls. *Psychiatry Research, 2,* 25–36.

Menkes, D. B., & Aghajanian, G. K. (1981). α-Adrenoceptor-mediated responses in the lateral geniculate nucleus enhanced by chronic antidepressant treatment. *European Journal of Pharmacology, 74,* 27–35.

Menkes, D. B., Aghajanian, G. K., & McCall, R. B. (1980). Chronic antidepressant treatment enhances α-adrenergic and serotonergic responses in the facial nucleus. *Life Sciences, 27,* 45–55.

Middlemiss, J. A., Carroll, J. A., Fisher, R. W., & Mounsey, I. J. (1980). Does ^{3}H-serotonin-spiroperidol label a 5-HT receptor in the frontal cortex of the rat? *European Journal of Pharmacology, 66,* 149–154.

Mishra, R., Janowsky, A., & Sulser, F. (1980). Action of mianserin and zimelidine on the norepinephrine receptor coupled adenylate cyclase system in brain: Subsensitivity without reduction in β-adrenergic receptor binding. *Neuropharmacology, 19,* 982–987.

Modigh, K. (1975). Electroconvulsive shock and postsynaptic catecholamine effects: Increased psychomotor stimulant action of apomorphine and clonidine in reserpine pretreated mice by repeated ECS. *Journal of Neural Transmission, 36,* 19–32.

Mogilnicka, E., & Klimek, V. (1979). Mianserin, danitracen and amitriptyline withdrawal increases the behavioral responses of rats to L-5-HTP. *Journal of Pharmacy and Pharmacology, 31,* 704–705.

Mueller, P. S., Heninger, G. R., & McConald, R. K. (1969). Insulin tolerance test in depression. *Archives of General Psychiatry, 21,* 587–594.

Pandey, G. N., Dysken, M. W., Garver, D. L., & Davis, J. M. (1979). Beta-adrenergic receptor function in affective illness. *American Journal of Psychiatry, 136,* 675–678.

Peroutka, S. J., & Snyder, S. H. (1980). Chronic antidepressant treatment decreases spiroperidol-labeled serotonin receptor binding. *Science, 210,* 88–90.

Peroutka, S. J., U'Prichard, D. C., Greenberg, D. J., & Snyder, S. H. (1977). Neuroleptic drug interactions with norephinephrine alpha-receptor binding sites in rat brain. *Neuropharmacology, 16,* 549.

Randrup, A., Munkvad, I., & Fog, R. (1981). Formulations of the dopamine hypothesis for affective disorders following the accumulation of new evidence. In C. Perris,

G. Struwe, & B. Jansson (Eds.), *Biological psychiatry* (pp. 732–737). Amsterdam: Elsevier.

Rehavi, M., Ramot, O., Yavetz, B., & Sokolovsky, M. (1980). Amitriptyline: Long-term treatment elevates α-adrenergic and muscarinic receptor binding in mouse brain. *Brain Research, 194,* 443–453.

Rosenblatt, J. E., Pert, C. B., Tallman, J. F., Pert, A., & Bunney, W. E. (1979). The effect of imipramine and lithium on α- and β-receptor binding in rat brain. *Brain Research, 160,* 186–191.

Ross, S. B., & Renyi, A. L. (1969). Inhibition of the uptake of tritiated 5-HT in brain tissue. *European Journal of Pharmacology, 4,* 270–277.

Sachar, E. J., Altman, N., Gruen, P. J., Glassman, A., Halpern, F. S., & Sassin, J. (1975). Human growth hormone response to L-DOPA in relation to menopause depression and plasma level of L-DOPA. *Archives of General Psychiatry, 32,* 502–503.

Sachar, E. J., Finkelstein, J., & Hellman, L. (1971). Growth hormone responses in depressive illness: I. Response to insulin tolerance test. *Archives of General Psychiatry, 32,* 263–269.

Sachar, E. J., Nathan, R. S., Asnis, G., Halbreich, U., Tabrizi, M. A., & Halpern, F. (1980). Neuroendocrine studies of major depressive disorder. *Acta Psychiatrica Scandinavica, Supplementum, 61,* 201–210.

Sachar, E. J., Roffwarg, H. P., Gruen, P. H., Altman, N., & Sassin, J. (1976). Neuroendocrine studies of depressive illness. *Pharmakopsychiatrie, 9,* 11–17.

Savage, D. D., Frazer, A., & Mendels, J. (1979). Differential effects of monoamine oxidase inhibitors and serotonin reuptake inhibitors on ^{3}H-serotonin receptor binding in rat brain. *European Journal of Pharmacology, 58,* 87–88.

Schweitizer, J. W., Schwartz, R., & Friedhoff, A. J. (1979). Intact presynaptic terminals required for β-adrenergic receptor regulation desipramine. *Journal of Neurochemistry, 33,* 377–379.

Siever, L. J., Cohen, R. M., & Murphy, D. L. (1981). Antidepressants and L_2-Adrenergic autoreceptor desensitization. *American Journal of Psychiatry, 138,* 681–682.

Smith, C. B., Garcia-Sevilla, J. A., & Hollingsworth, P. J. (1981). α_2-Adrenoceptors in rat brain are decreased after long term tricyclic antidepressant drug treatment. *Brain Research, 210,* 413–418.

Starke, K., & Altmann, K. P. (1973). Inhibition of adrenergic neurotransmission by clonidine: An action on prejunctional α-receptors. *Neuropharmacology, 12,* 339–347.

Sulser, F., and Mobley, P. L. (1981). Regulation of central noradrenergic receptor function: New vistas on the mode of action of antidepressant treatments. In E. Usdin, W. E. Bunney, Jr., & J. M. Davis (Eds.), *Neuroreceptor—Basic and clinical aspects.* (pp. 55–83). New York: Wiley.

Svensson, T. H., & Usin, T. (1978). Feedback inhibition of brain noradrenaline neurons by tricyclic antidepressants: α-Receptor mediation. *Science, 202,* 1084–1091.

Tang, S. W., Helmesfe, D. M., & Stancer, H. C. (1978). The effect of acute and chronic desipramine and amitriptyline treatment on rat brain total 3-methoxy-4-hydroxyphenylglycol. *Naunyn-Schmiedebergs Archives of Pharmacology, 305,* 207.

Tang, S. W., Seeman, P., & Kwan, S. (1980). Effect of chronic tricyclic antidepressant treatment on serotonergic and histaminergic receptors. *Neuroscience Abstracts, 6,* 861.

Tang, S. W., Seeman, P., & Kwan, S. (1981). Differential effect of chronic desipramine and amitriptyline on rat brain adrenergic and serotonergic receptors. *Psychiatry Research, 4,* 129–138.

U'Prichard, D. C., Bechtel, W. D., Rouot, B. M., & Snyder, S. H. (1979). Multiple apparent alpha-noradrenergic receptor binding sites in rat brain: Effect of 6-hydroxydopamine. *Molecular Pharmacology, 16,* 47–60.

U'Prichard, D. C., Daiguji, M., Tang, C., Mitrius, J. C., & Meltzer, H. Y. (1982). α_2-Adrenergic receptors: Comparative biochemistry of neural and non-neural receptors, and in vitro analysis in psychiatric patients. In E. Usdin & I. Hanin (Eds.), *Biological markers in psychiatry and neurology* (pp. 205–217). New York: Pergamon Press.

U'Prichard, D. C., Greenberg, D. A., Sheehan, P. P., & Snyder, S. H. (1978). Tricyclic antidepressants: Therapeutic properties and affinity for α-noradrenergic receptor binding sites in the brain. *Science, 199,* 197–198.

Ventulani, J., & Sulser, F. (1975). Action of various antidepressant treatments reduce reactivity or noradrenergic cyclic AMP-generating system in limbic forebrain. *Nature, 275,* 495–496.

Wang, R. Y., & Aghajanian, G. K. (1980). Enhanced sensitivity of amygdaloid neurons to serotonin and norephinephrine after chronic antidepressant treatment. *Communications in Psychopharmacology, 4,* 83–90.

9

Genetic Marker Studies of HLA Antigens and Affective Disorders: A Review and Report of a New Pedigree

RAYMOND R. CROWE
JANICE CAMPBELL
BRUCE PFOHL
NANCY GOEKEN
DAVID PAULS

Introduction

Since Amiel's report of an association between an HLA (human leukocyte antigen) antigen (4C) and Hodgkin's disease 19 years ago (Amiel, 1967), the literature has been filled with reports of HLA-disease associations, many of which are now well documented (Bach & Van Rood, 1976). In view of these intriguing findings in a variety of diseases, it is not surprising that similar associations have been sought with psychiatric disease states. This chapter will review the association and linkage literature with respect to affective disorder focusing on the major hypotheses and findings.

The major histocompatibility complex (where the HLA loci are located) occupies a small region on the short arm of chromosome 6. Four loci within this region code for cell surface antigens, which play

RAYMOND R. CROWE and BRUCE PFOHL. Department of Psychiatry, University of Iowa College of Medicine, Iowa City, Iowa.

JANICE CAMPBELL. Department of Psychiatry, University of Kansas College of Medicine, Kansas City, Kansas.

NANCY GOEKEN. Departments of Medicine and Pathology, University of Iowa College of Medicine, Iowa City, Iowa.

DAVID PAULS. Department of Human Genetics, Yale University College of Medicine, New Haven, Connecticut.

a major role in transplant compatibility and have shown strong associations with a number of diseases. These loci are labeled A, B, C, and D.

The first three are detected by serum antibodies and are referred to as serologically determined (SD). The D locus is detected by stimulation in the mixed lymphocyte culture test and for this reason is referred to as lymphocytically determined (LD). The A and B loci were the discovered first, and for this reason more antigenic specificities have been determined at these loci and they are more frequently the subject of HLA-disease association reports. All four loci are highly polymorphic; a large number of genes at each locus code for many antigenic specificities. Since each person has two sets of chromosomes, each individual has two sets of HLA antigenic specificities or haplotypes (e.g., A10/B16 and A8/B27). The haplotype concept is useful because the loci are so close to one another that crossing over between them rarely occurs, and the entire haplotype is transmitted as a single gene.

Before turning to the HLA studies on affective disorder, it would be instructive to consider some of the characteristics of the better documented HLA-disease associations (Bach & Van Rood, 1976). First, the diseases that have shown strong associations tend to fall into four disease categories. These are: (1) lymphomas and leukemias, (2) other malignancies, (3) immunopathic diseases, and (4) infectious diseases. Second, the associations are characterized by a relative risk greater than 4.0. This statistic expresses the ratio of the risk in persons with the antigen to that in those lacking it. A third characteristic is that the studies are homogeneous in indicating an association. Finally, the chi-square values for the association are quite large and therefore associated with a high level of statistical significance. For example, the strongest association yet reported is that between ankylosing spondylitis and B27, with good homogeneity among studies, a relative risk of 141, and a pooled chi-square of 290 (Bach & Van Rood, 1976).

Association Studies

Returning to affective disorder, a promising report of an association between bipolar illness and Bw16 appeared in 1976 (Shapiro, Bock, Rafaelsen, Ryder, & Svejgaard, 1976). Eight of 20 bipolar patients were found to have Bw16 (40%) compared with only 5.4% of 1967 controls. Although the etiology of affective disorder is unknown, it does not fall into any of the groups of diseases that are characterized by frequent

HLA associations. Thus it would not appear to be a logical candidate for an HLA association, but the relative risk was 11.7 and the chi-square value was 37.7. The same investigators studied an additional 87 bipolar patients and found only 7 with Bw16 (8.1%), still higher than the control rate but not significantly so (Shapiro, Ryder, Svejgaard, & Rafaelsen, 1977.

Since these two reports (which will be considered as one study here), an additional eight have appeared on the proposed association (Table 9-1) (Govaerts, Mendlewicz, & Verbanck, 1977; James, Smouse, Carroll, & Haines, 1980; Johnson, 1978; Propert, Tait, & Davies, 1981; Smeraldi *et al.*, 1978; Targum, Gershon, Van Eeredefwegh, & Rogentine, 1979 [two studies]; Wentzel, Roberts, & Whalley, 1982). Seven of the nine studies are associated with relative risks greater than 1.0, indicating an association in the expected direction, but only two achieved statistical significance. The degree of homogeneity among the nine studies can be expressed as a chi-square ($\chi = 6.66$, $df = 8$, $p = .57$), demonstrating excellent consistency and indicating that the data may be pooled. The degree of association in the pooled data can be expressed by a Mantel–Haenszel chi-square ($\chi^2 = 16.44$, $df = 1$, $p = .001$), indicating a highly significant association between Bw16 and bipolar illness. However, the relative risk is only 1.90, indicating

TABLE 9-1. HLA Bw16 and Bipolar Illness

Study	Bipolars		Controls		Relative risk
	n	% Bw16	*n*	% Bw16	
Shaprio, Ryder, Svejgaard, & Rafaelsen (1977)[a]	107	14.0	1967	5.4	2.9
Govaerts, Mendlewlcz, & Verbanck (1977)	50	6.0	113	4.4	1.4
Johnson (1978)	36	11.1	780	3.1	3.9
Smeraldi *et al.* (1978b)	50	10.0	676	7.0	1.5
Targum, Gershon, Van Eerdewegh, & Rogentine (1979)	92	14.1	210	8.1	1.9
Targum, Gershon, Van Eerdewegh, & Rogentine (1979)	21	38.1	552	25.0	1.8
James, Smouse, Carroll, & Haines (1980)	49	8.2	439	3.2	2.7
Propert, Tait, & Davies (1981)	47	2.1	586	2.2	1.0
Wentzel, Roberts, & Whalley (1982)	94	6.4	365	6.6	1.0

Note. Homogeneity $\chi = 6.66$, $p = 0.57$. Mantel–Haenszel $\chi^2 = 16.44$, $p = .001$.
[a]Includes data from Shapiro, Bock, Rafaelsen, Ryder, & Svejgaard (1976).

that the HLA–disease association is a weak one, consistent with most of the criteria set out above.

Proposed HLA–disease associations have been divided into three categories; those in which the association is well established, those in which the data indicate no association, and those for which the evidence is suggestive but the association remains unproven (Bach & Van Rood, 1976). Currently, the bipolar–Bw16 association appears to fall into the last category.

A number of explanations for HLA–disease associations have been proposed (Rosenberg & Kidd, 1977). First, they may represent a sampling artifact due to a disease occurring in an ethnic group with a high frequency of the antigen in question. An example of the degree to which antigen frequencies can vary between ethnic groups can be seen in the control population of the second Targum *et al.* sample, which consists of Ashkenazi Jews (Table 9-1). Twenty-five percent were found to have Bw16 compared with the remaining studies, which ranged from 2.2 to 8.1%. In fact, Targum *et al.* suggest that reports of a bipolar–Bw16 association may be due to precisely this kind of sampling bias. Secondly, the disease may be the result of an HLA tissue antigen leading to susceptiblity to certain diseases. This could occur either through lack of immunity or through the antigen acting as a cell surface receptor site for a virus. A third possibility is that linkage may exist between the HLA locus and a disease susceptibility gene.

Linkage Studies

Linkage differs from association, although the two are sometimes confused. Linkage refers to a trait (e.g., a disease) and a marker that are located sufficiently close to one another on the chromosome that crossing over between them occurs with a frequency of less than 1/2. This leads to two consequences that can be used to test for linkage. The first is that if a parent has both the trait and the marker, the two will not assort independently in the children. Thus if the trait and marker are on the same chromosome, children will tend to have both or neither, not one without the other. Of course, if the trait is on the other chromosome just the opposite will occur; offspring will tend to have either the trait or the marker but not both (or neither). This forms the basis of the LOD-score method of detecting linkage. The LOD score is a statistical test for linkage with which linkage can be excluded if the LOD score is less than −2.0 and accepted if the LOD score exceeds 3.0 (Morton, 1956).

The second consequence of linkage is the following. A pair of siblings may share in common at any locus two alleles, one allele or no alleles, and in the expected ratio of 1 : 2 : 1. However, if the locus is linked to a trait, and both sibs have the trait, the 1 : 2 : 1 ratio will be distorted in the direction of more sib pairs sharing one or two alleles. If an HLA haplotype can be thought of as an "allele," then the method is readily applied to studies of HLA–disease linkage. This method is termed the "Identity by Descent" (IBD) sib-pair method (Suarez, 1978).

A positive linkage finding was recently reported between the HLA locus and a disease susceptibility gene for depression (unipolar and bipolar) (Weitkamp, Pardue, & Huntzinger, 1980; Weitkamp, Stancer, Persad, Flood, & Guttormsen, 1981). The hypothesis tested was the following: (1) Multiple susceptibility genes for affective disorder exist. (2) The more susceptibility genes a person carries, the more likely that he or she will develop depression. (3) One of the susceptibility genes is linked to the major histocompatibility complex. (4) In families segregating for multiple susceptiblity genes (high genetic load families), the HLA–disease linkage will be obscured by susceptibility genes from other parts of the genome. (5) Linkage will therefore be detectable only in families with a low genetic load.

The investigators tested their hypothesis in sibships by separating them into high-load (more than two affected siblings) and low-load (only two affected siblings) sibships. The report pooled data from four published investigations in order to obtain 34 high-load and 7 low-load sibships. An IBD sib-pair analysis revealed the expected 1 : 2 : 1 distribution of shared haplotypes in the high-load sibships. However, the low-load sibships demonstrated departure from the 1 : 2 : 1 expectation in the direction of increased haplotype sharing. An LOD-score analysis of parent–offspring groups was also carried out. Low-load parents were defined as those who were unaffected and had unaffected parents and siblings. High-load parents were either affected or had an affected sibling. The LOD score obtained for the high-load parents was 0.15, but by contrast, that for the low-load parents was 3.6, again consistent with the hypothesis of linkage.

At the time these findings were published, we discovered a family in Iowa in which bipolar illness appeared over five generations. Such families are especially valuable for linkage studies because the illness is likely to be due to a single gene, thus eliminating the problem of genetic heterogeneity. This family consisted of 37 relatives over five generations identified through the mother of an 18-year-old boy in generation V who had committed suicide.

Twenty-two of the 37 relatives were interviewed using the Schedule for Affective Disorders and Schizophrenia, Lifetime Version (SADS-L) (Endicott & Spitzer, 1978). The mean age of the interviewd relatives was 41 ± 20 years and 13 were female. Ten were deceased and the remaining five refused. The interview schedules were reviewed blindly by a psychiatrist who made diagnoses according to the Research Diagnostic Criteria (RDC) (Spitzer, Endicott, & Robins, 1978) for interviewed relatives and the Family History–Research Diagnostic Criteria (FH-RDC) (Andreasen *et al.*, 1977) for the remainder, on whom information was collected from the interviewed ones. Typing for HLA antigens was performed by the University of Iowa Hospitals tissue-typing laboratory. Twenty samples were typed for 17 A and 31 B locus antigens by the modified Amos lymphocytotoxicity method using local and NIH antisera (Ray, Hare, & Kayhoe, 1976). The linkage analysis was performed by the LOD-score method of Ott (Ott, 1976).

The pedigree is shown in Figure 9-1. Thirteen individuals within the family and one spouse were positive for affective disorder. The diagnoses included four cases of major depressive disorder, two of bipolar disorder, two mania, two hypomania, one schizoaffective, and one minor depressive disorder. There are two instances of father–son transmission; in one the father, an obligate carrier, had two affected sons, and in the other an affected father had a son who is an obligate carrier by virtue of having an affected child. Therefore this kindred is not compatible with a sex-linkage hypothesis. Bw16 has subsequently turned out to comprise two antigenic specificities, Bw38 and Bw39. None of the individuals in our pedigree were positive for either of these antigenic specificities, so the proposed association with Bw16 could not be tested. Moreover, visual inspection of the pedigree reveals no association between affective disorder and any HLA haplotype.

Since only one pair of affected sibs could be typed for HLA antigens, we analyzed the family by the LOD-score method. The linkage analysis was run using published gene frequencies for the HLA alleles, and the gene frequency for bipolar illness was varied from 0.01 to 0.10 in increments of 0.01. The analyses were run assuming both a dominant and a recessive disease susceptibility gene. In none of these analyses did the LOD score exceed 0; thus there was no evidence for linkage between the MHC and affective disorder in this pedigree.

Table 9-2 presents our results in light of other published HLA linkage studies. Targum *et al.* examined nine pedigrees of bipolar and unipolar illness using the LOD-score method and finding no evidence

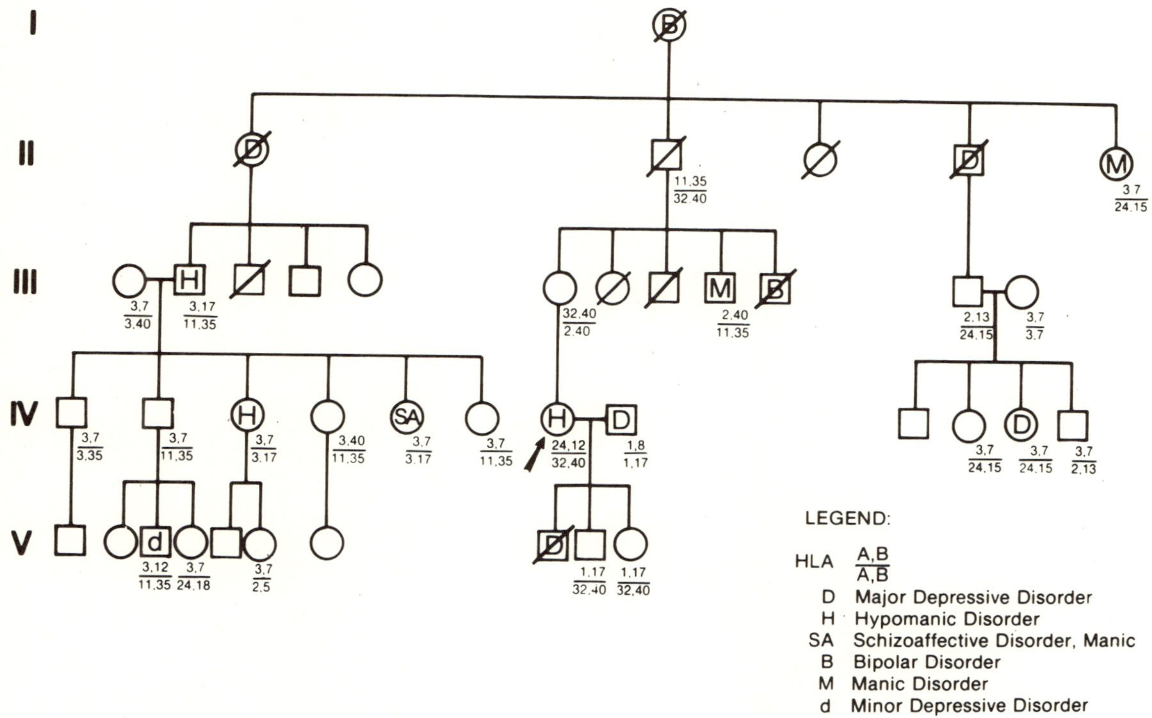

FIG. 9-1. The "P" kindred.

TABLE 9-2. Summary of Linkage Studies of HLA and Affective Disorder

Study	Data	Analysis	Findings
Targum, Gershon, Van Eerdewegh, & Rogentine (1979)	9 families	LOD	No linkage
Weitkamp, Stancer, Persad, Flood, & Guttormsen (1981)[a]	41 sibships	IBD	Linkage in low-load sibships only
Smeraldi & Bellodi (1981)	30 sibships	IBD	Linkage
Turner & King (1981)	7 families	LOD	Linkage in father–son families only
Johnson, Hunt, Robertson, & Doran (1981)	4 families	LOD	No linkage
Goldin, Clerget-Darpoux, & Gershon (1982)[b]	27 families	LOD/IBD	No linkage
Suarez & Croughan (1982)	10 sibships	LBD	No linkage
Present study (1982)	1 kindred	LOD	No linkage

[a]Includes data from Smeraldi *et al.* (1978a), Targum *et al.* (1979), and Weitkamp, Pardue, & Huntzinger (1980).

[b]Includes the nine families from Targum *et al.* (1979).

of linkage (Targum *et al.*, 1979). The Weitkamp *et al.* (1980, 1981) report has already been discussed in detail. Smeraldi *et al.* reported a positive linkage finding in 30 sibships of affective disorder (unipolar and bipolar) using the IBD sib-pair method (Smeraldi & Bellodi, 1981; Smeraldi *et al.*, 1978a). It should be noted that the families Smeraldi *et al.* reported overlapped to some extent with those reported by Weitkamp *et al.* (1981). Turner and King (1981) reported seven bipolar families analyzed by the LOD-score method with a positive linkage finding in the two families with father–son transmission but no evidence of linkage in the remaining five families. Four bipolar families reported by Johnson *et al.* were analyzed by the LOD-score method and no evidence of linkage was obtained (Johnson, Hunt, Robertson, & Doran, 1981). Visual inspection of their two families with father–son transmission indicates that the HLA haplotypes from the affected parent assort independently of affective disorder in the offspring. Goldin *et al.* examined 27 bipolar and unipolar families in a report that overlapped with the nine reported by Targum *et al.* (Goldin, Clerget-Darpout, & Gershon, 1982). They divided the families into high-load and low-load sibships in the same manner as Weitkamp *et al.* and analyzed the data by the IBD sib-pair method. The results yielded no evidence of linkage. Finally, Suarez and Croughan (1982) reported ten bipolar and unipolar sibships analyzed by the IBD sib-pair method and no evidence of linkage was found.

Discussion

The problem of a false-positive finding (Type I error) is very real in association studies because of the number of associations tested. This problem has been commented on by other investigators and methods of correcting for it have been proposed (James *et al.*, 1980; Svejgaard, Jersild, Nielsen, & Bodmer, 1974). The most reliable method for dealing with this problem, however, is replication of the finding. The first study can be thought of as proposing a hypothesis which the remaining studies test. If the studies are consistent (homogeneous) and the overall results support the association, then the probability of a Type I error is small. This has proved to be the case with the association between bipolar illness and HLA Bw16.

The false-negative finding (Type II error) is equally problematic in association studies and has been less widely discussed. This problem is likely to occur in studies employing small sample sizes when an association is one of low relative risk. In the case of the bipolar–Bw16 association, the relative risk was estimated at 1.9 and many of the studies employed relatively small samples. However, seven of the nine studies show a trend in the predicted direction, and analysis of the pooled data indicates a statistically significant association. Thus the data are consistent with a real but relatively weak association between bipolar affective disorder and HLA Bw16.

In contrast to the association studies, the linkage findings are notable for their inconsistency. Comparing the studies is difficult because of differences in methodology. First, different types of depression have been included, with some studies limited to unipolar depression; others, bipolar illness; and still others include a mixture of the two. The only one that focused on unipolar depression was an analysis of a large unipolar kindred in which increased haplotype sharing among affected sibs was found (Weitkamp *et al.*, 1980). Three studies have examined bipolar families; one found evidence for linkage in families with father–son transmission (Turner & King, 1981), and the other two found no evidence of linkage (Targum *et al.*, 1979; Johnson *et al.*, 1981). The first two were analyzed by the LOD-score method, and the third by both the LOD-score and the IBD sib-pair method. Turning to studies which have included mixed bipolar-unipolar samples, two found evidence of linkage using the IBD sib-pair method, and another two found no evidence of linkage using the same method (Smeraldi & Bellodi, 1981; Goldin *et al.*, 1982; Suarez & Croughan, 1982; Weitkamp *et al.*, 1981). However, only one of the last two subdivided the families into high-load and low-load sibships (Goldin *et al.*, 1982).

A second difference between studies lies in whether all individuals or a subsample of them were analyzed. HLA haplotype sharing among affected individuals was initially suggested by a large kindred of unipolar depression, but the result could only be replicated when low-load sibships were analyzed separately (Weitkamp *et al.*, 1980, 1981). An independent study found evidence of increased haplotype sharing without subdividing the sibships (Smeraldi & Bellodi, 1981), but an attempt to replicate this finding in low-load sibships failed (Goldin *et al.*, 1982). The second positive linkage finding was obtained by analyzing families with father–son transmission using the LOD-score method (Turner & King, 1981). However, large families of both unipolar (Weitkamp *et al.*, 1980) and bipolar illness (present investigation), both with father–son transmission, have shown no evidence of HLA linkage by the LOD-score method.

The third methodological difference between studies is the type of linkage analysis employed. As Weitkamp *et al.* (1980) have pointed out, affective disorder could be produced by a single autosomoal dominant gene, and the HLA-linked gene may be a secondary disease susceptibility gene producing the illness in individuals who have the affective disorder gene. In this case the LOD-score method would not be sensitive to linkage, but the sib-pair method would show increased haplotype sharing. Three of the studies which have suggested linkage have employed the sib-pair method, although one negative study employed the same methodl (Goldin *et al.*, 1982; Smeraldi & Bellodi, 1981; Weitkamp *et al.*, 1980, 1981).

Perhaps these differences can be resolved in future linkage investigations confined to probands with a homogenous form of affective disorder (i.e., either unipolar or bipolar illness) and employing the same methodology. Until this is accomplished, it would be premature to conclude that linkage between affective disorder and the major histocompatibility complex has either been demonstrated or ruled out.

REFERENCES

Amiel, J. L. (1967). Study of the leucocyte phenotypes in Hodgkin's disease. E. S. Curtoni, P. L. Mattiuz, & R. M. Tosi (Eds.), *Histocompatibility testing 1967* (pp. 79–81). Copenhagen: Munksgaard.

Andreasen, N. C., Endicott, J., Spitzer, R. L., & Winokur, G. (1977). The family history method using diagnostic criteria: Reliability and validity. *Archives of General Psychiatry, 34,* 1229–1235.

Bach, F.H., & Van Rood, J. J. (1976). The major histocompatibility complex: Genetics and biology. *New England Journal of Medicine, 295,* 927–936.

Endicott, J., & Spitzer, R. L. (1978). A diagnostic interview: The schedule for affective disorders and schizophrenia. *Archives of General Psychiatry, 35,* 837–844.

Goldin, L. R., Clerget-Darpoux, F., & Gershon, E. S. (1982). Relationship of HLA to major affective disorder not supported. *Psychiatry Research 7*, 29–45.

Govaerts, A., Mendlewicz, J., & Verbanck, P (1977). Manic-depressive illness and HLA. *Tissue Antigens, 10,* 60–62.

James, N. M., Smouse, P. E., Carroll, B. J., & Haines, R. F. (1980). Affective illness and HLA frequencies: No compelling association. *Neuropsychobiology, 6,* 208–216.

Johnson, G. F. S. (1978). HLA antigens and manic-depressive disorders. *Biological Psychiatry, 13,* 409–412.

Johnson, G. F. S. (1978). HLA antigens and manic-depressive disorders. *Biological Psychiatry, 13,* 409–412.

Johnson, G. F. S., Hunt, G. E., Robertson, S., & Doran, T. J. (1981). Linkage study of manic-depressive disorder with HLA antigens, blood groups, serum proteins and red cell enzymes. *Journal of Affective Disorder, 31,* 43–58.

Morton, N. E. (1966). Sequential tests for the detection of linkage. *American Journal of Human Genetics, 7,* 277–318.

Ott, J. (1976) Estimation of the recombination fraction in human pedigrees: Efficient computation of the likelihood for human linkage studies. *American Journal of Human Genetics, 26,* 588–597.

Propert, D. N., Tait, B. D., & Davies, B (1981). HLA antigens and affective illness. *Tissue Antigens, 18,* 335–340.

Ray, J. G., Hare, D. B., & Kayhoe, D. E. (1976). *Manual of tissue typing techniques* (Publication 76-545). Bethesda, MD: U.S. Department of Health, Education and Welfare.

Rosenberg, L. E., & Kidd, K. K. (1977). HLA and disease susceptibility: A primer. *New England Journal of Medicine, 297,* 1060–1062.

Shapiro, R. W., Bock, E., Rafaelsen, O. J., Ryder, L. P., & Svejgaard, A. (1976). Histocompatibility antigens and manic-depressive disorders. *Archives of General Psychiatry, 33,* 823–825.

Shapiro, R. W., Ryder, L. P., Svejgaard, A., & Rafaelsen, O. J. (1977) HLA antigens and manic-depressive disorders: Further evidence of an association. *Psychological Medicine 7,* 387–396.

Smeraldi, E., & Bellodi, L. (1981). Possible linkage between primary affective disorder susceptibility locus and HLA haplotypes. *American Journal of Psychiatry, 138,* 1231–1234.

Smeraldi, E., Negri, F., Melica, A. M., & Scorza-Smeraldi, R. (1978a). HLA system and affective disorders: a sibship genetic study. *Tissue Antigens, 12,* 270–274.

Smeraldi, E., Negri, F., Melica A. M., Scorza-Smeraldi, A. M., Fabio, R., Bonara, G., Bellodi, L., Sachetti, E., Sabbadini-Villa, M. G., Cazzullo, C. L., & Zanussi, C. (1978b). HLA typing and affective disorders: A study in the Italian population. *Neuropsychobiology, 4,* 344–352.

Spitzer, R. L., Endicott, J., & Robins, E. (1978). Research diagnostic criteria. *Archives of General Psychiatry, 35,* 773–782.

Suarez, B. K. (1978). The affected sib-pair IBD distribution for HLA linked disease susceptibility loci. *Tissue Antigens, 12,* 87–93.

Suarez, B. K., & Croughan, J. (1982). Is the major histocompatibility complex linked to genes that increase susceptibility to affective disorder? A critical Appraisal. *Psychiatry Research, 7,* 19–27.

Svejgaard, A., Jersild, C., Nielsen, L. S., & Bodmer, W. F. (1974). HLA antigens and disease: Statistical and genetic considerations. *Tissue Antigens, 4,* 95–105.

Targum, S. D., Gershon, E. S., Van Eerdewegh, M. V., & Rogentine, N. (1979). Human leukocyte antigen system not closely linked to or associated with bipolar manic-depressive illness. *Biological Psychiatry, 14,* 615–636.

Turner, W. J., & King, S. (1981). Two genetically distinct forms of bipolar affective disorder? *Biological Psychiatry, 16,* 417–439.

Weitkamp, L. R., Pardue, L. H., & Huntzinger, R. S. (1980). Genetic marker studies in a family with unipolar depression. *Archives of General Psychiatry, 37*, 1187–1192.
Weitkamp, L. R., Stancer, H. C., Persad, E., Flood, C., & Guttormsen, S. (1981). Depressive disorders and HLA: A gene on chromosome 6 that can affect behavior. *New England Journal of Medicine, 305*, 1301–1306.
Wentzel, J., Roberts, D. F., & Whalley, L. J. (1982). HLA in manic–depressive psychosis. *Psychological Medicine, 12*, 275–278.

10

Toward a Molecular Basis for Affective Disorders

JAY W. PETTEGREW

Introduction

Advances in neuroscience have been closely linked with advances in scientific technology. However, technological advances in and of themselves are of less importance than the innovative applications of these technologies to neuroscience research. One of the goals of neuroscience research is to understand the molecular basis of normal and abnormal human behavior. To more fully understand the molecular basis of behavior, it is becoming increasingly apparent that noninvasive methods of investigating intact living systems (cells, tissues, organs, intact animals and humans) must be sought so the experimental procedure itself does not alter the very molecular events that are being studied. Such technologies are being developed and two of these technologies (fluorescence and nuclear magnetic resonance spectroscopy) will be discussed.

To understand the basis for abnormal behavior researchers initially examined the brain grossly to determine if there was an anatomical basis for normal and abnormal behavior. Even today there are anatomical studies that try to correlate hemispheric lateralization with behavioral phenotypes (Flor-Henry, 1979; Flor-Henry & Koles, 1980; Heilman, Scholes, & Watson, 1975; Hommes & Panhuysen, 1971; Ross, 1981; Ross, Harney, deLacoste-Utamsing, & Purdy, 1981; Ross & Mesulam, 1979; Ross & Rush, 1981). A comprehensive review of this area has appeared. This review raises important questions that must be considered in evaluating the validity of this approach (Marin & Tucker, 1981).

One might also ask if alterations in brain cytoarchitectonics, especially in the limbic system, might correlate with behavioral phenotype. I am unaware of any studies in this area. One should also

JAY W. PETTEGREW. Department of Psychiatry, University of Pittsburgh School of Medicine and Western Psychiatric Institute and Clinic, Pittsburgh, Pennsylvania.

remember that the brain is composed of glia, as well as neurons, and as more is learned about brain metabolism it is realized that glia play very important roles in supporting and complementing neuronal metabolism (Stewart & Rosenberg, 1979). Could primary alterations in glial metabolism/function give rise to secondary alterations in neuronal metabolism/function, with resultant alterations in behavioral phenotype?

An enormous amount of investigative effort has gone into studying neurotransmitters and their receptors in manic–depressive illness (MDI) (Charney, Menkes, & Heninger, 1981; Garver & Davis, 1979; Garver & Zemlan, Chapter 8, this volume; Sulser & Mobley, 1981). These studies have not only contributed to understanding MDI, but also brain function in general. A popular concept has been that different classes of neurotransmitters may be either functionally increased or decreased in MDI accounting for mania or depression. This could be due to changes in the levels of the various neurotransmitters or changes in their receptors. The receptors themselves may be either increased or decreased in number, or perhaps because of altered neurotransmitter–receptor interaction, the receptors may have either increased or decreased function.

We now know that many neurotransmitters are present throughout the central nervous system, and there is even evidence that a given neuron may contain two or more different neurotransmitters (Chan-Palay *et al.*, 1981; Chan-Palay, Engel, Palay, & Wu, 1982; Chan-Palay, Ito, Tongroach, Sakurai, & Palay, 1982; Chan-Palay, Lin, Palay, Yamamoto, & Wu, 1982). Neurons have also been shown to contain presynaptic receptors for the neurotransmitters released, and activation of the presynaptic receptors may in general modulate the biosynthesis, degradation, release, and perhaps even physiological function of various neurotransmitters (see Chapter 8, this volume).

Use of Peripheral Tissues to Study a Genetic Disease

At this time the preponderance of available evidence strongly suggests that MDI is a genetically predisposed disorder. The exact mode of genetic transmission is still unknown, but most workers would agree on its genetic predisposition (Crowe, Campbell, Pfohl, Goeken, & Pauls, Chapter 9, this volume). If MDI is a genetic disorder, then every cell in the body must carry the abnormal gene, but every cell does not necessarily have to express that abnormal gene.

Peripheral tissues have been successfully studied in a large number of genetic neurological disorders, and the study of peripheral tissues has provided significant insight into the molecular defect in these diseases. Perhaps the same will be true for MDI. Perhaps investigators can study peripheral tissues and gain insight into possible molecular defects within the affected neurons and/or glia in the central nervous system.

Possible Membrane Alteration in Affective Illness

Over the past 15 years evidence has accumulated in support of a membrane defect in MDI. Several studies have focused on lithium distribution as a reflection of altered membrane function (Albrecht & Muller-Oerlinghausen, 1976; Carroll, 1979; Cazzullo, Smeraldi, Sacchetti, & Bottinelli, 1975; Demisch & Bochnik, 1976; Elizur, Shopsin, Gershon, & Ehlenberger, 1972; Frazer, Mendels, & Brunswick, 1978; Glen, Ongley, & Robinson, 1968; Mendels & Grazer, 1973; Rybakowski, Chlopoctia, & Kapelski, 1974; Soucek, Zvolsky, & Kurlitz, 1974). Other investigators have demonstrated lower Na^{+}–K^{+} ATPase activity and lower ouabain-sensitive K^{+} influx (both membrane-associated phenomena) in the symptomatic versus the asymptomatic patient with MDI (Naylor, Dick, Dick, Le Poidevin, & Whyte, 1973; Naylor, Glutz, & Dick, 1976; Sen *et al.*, 1976). Finally, the effect of lithium on membrane activities such as choline accumulation (Jope, Jenden, Ehrlich, & Diamond, 1978) and modulation of cyclic AMP-dependent events (Gelfand, Dosch, Hastings, & Shore, 1979) has been cited as indirect evidence of a membrane defect in MDI. In all of these studies, the abnormalities were demonstrated in peripheral tissue (i.e., erythrocytes and lymphocytes) from MDI patients. However, none of these studies addressed the question of whether there might be a genetically determined alteration in the membrane molecular dynamics in peripheral cells obtained from MDI patients that might account for the above cited neurochemical alterations.

Possible Effect of Membrane Dynamics on Membrane Function

With the foregoing in mind, one might ask the following question: Could it be that the molecular alteration in MDI is not in the neurotransmitters themselves or their receptors but in the molecular milieu surrounding the receptors (i.e., the neuronal membrane itself)? An alteration in the molecular dynamics of the membrane milieu could secondarily lead to alterations in membrane-bound receptor function, which could then give rise to alterations in behavioral phenotype. If the critical unknown membrane constituent(s) that controls membrane molecular dynamics is under a regulatory gene control, then this could possibly explain the periodic alterations in behavioral phenotype typical of MDI.

How could alterations in membrane molecular dynamics give rise to altered membrane function, such as neurotransmitters–receptor interaction or ionophore function? This can perhaps be illustrated by a simple analogy: Suppose four men are each in a rowboat, and all four men are constrained (by whatever reason) to row at a given constant rate, no faster, no slower. Suppose that three of the rowboats form a semicircle, and the other rowboat points at the entrance of the semicircle. Suppose also that the waves of the water are such that the man rowing the boat situated at the entrance of the semicircle can just enter the semicircle with one rowing stroke, and the men in the two rowboats at the ends of the semicircle with one rowing stroke can then transiently close the semicircle before the next series of waves come and open the semicircle and push the one rowboat back outside. If the waves are relatively steady and the rowing by the men is also relatively steady, this process will be repeated over and over. Now suppose the waveforms decrease (in amplitude and periodicity), but the men's rowing does not change. Then the one rowboat will enter the semicircle, the ends will close, and the boats will collide against each other. Alternately, if the waveforms increase, the one rowboat will not be able to enter the semicircle, which will also not be able to close.

Therefore, if an important function were initiated by the one rowboat (such as a neurotransmitter, or the like) being able to go in and out of the semicircle (e.g., a receptor) in a regular fashion, then that function could be altered (increased or decreased) by an alteration in the waveforms (membrane milieu) without any alteration in the constituents (the men and the rowboats) or the rate of rowing by the men. If one were then to isolate the constituents (the men and the rowboats) and study them, one would conclude there was nothing wrong, although the overall function was obviously altered because the waves (milieu) were altered.

This same conceptual principle must apply to membrane receptors and ionophores. The receptors or ionophores may be entirely normal, but their function may be drastically altered by alterations in the membrane (milieu) molecular dynamics. The next question then is how one might study membrane molecular dynamics in intact living cells? To achieve this, we chose to use fluorescence spectroscopy, an experimental approach uniquely capable of investigating membrane molecular dynamics. The theoretical aspects of fluorescence are given in Appendix I.

Fluorescence Spectroscopy of Living Cells

Fluorescence spectroscopy is a powerful method for studying cellular membrane dynamics, and a great deal of work has been done on model membranes and isolated cellular membranes (Radda 1971; Radda & Vanderkooi, 1972). However, caution must be used in attempting to extrapolate findings on isolated membranes to the plasma membrane of intact living cells. For this reason, studies on intact living cells are needed. In order to perform intact living cell studies, one must choose fluorophore labeling conditions that minimally perturb the cell and maximally label the plasma membrane to the exclusion of other cellular membranes and compartments. We have performed such studies on intact human erythrocytes and lymphocytes using fluorescamine as a plasma membrane surface label and 12(9) anthroyl stearate (12(9)AS) as a plasma membrane hydrocarbon core label (Pettegrew, Nichols, & Stewart, 1979, 1980, 1981a, 1981b).

It has been demonstrated by independent experimental approaches that 12(9)AS preferentially reports on molecular motion in the hydrocarbon core of membranes (Podo & Blasie, 1977; Thulborn & Sawyer, 1978; Yguarabide & Stryer, 1971). In a separate study we demonstrated that under our fluorophore labeling conditions, both fluorescamine and 12(9)AS are highly localized to the plasma membrane of intact human erythrocytes and lymphocytes. Furthermore, by phosphorus-31 nuclear magnetic resonance (^{31}P NMR) analysis, fluorophore labeling did not alter cellular high energy phosphate metabolism or cellular permeability to Mn^{2+}. Therefore, these fluorophores are potentially powerful probes of human erythrocyte and lymphocyte plasma membrane dynamics in inherited and acquired disease states (Pettegrew, Minshew, & Nichols, 1982a). Because one fluorophore (fluorescamine) monitors molecular motion at the plasma membrane surface and the other (12(9)AS) monitors molecular motion at the hydrocarbon core of the plasma membrane, a cross-sectional analysis of molecular motion is obtained for each studied cell type (see Figure 10-1).

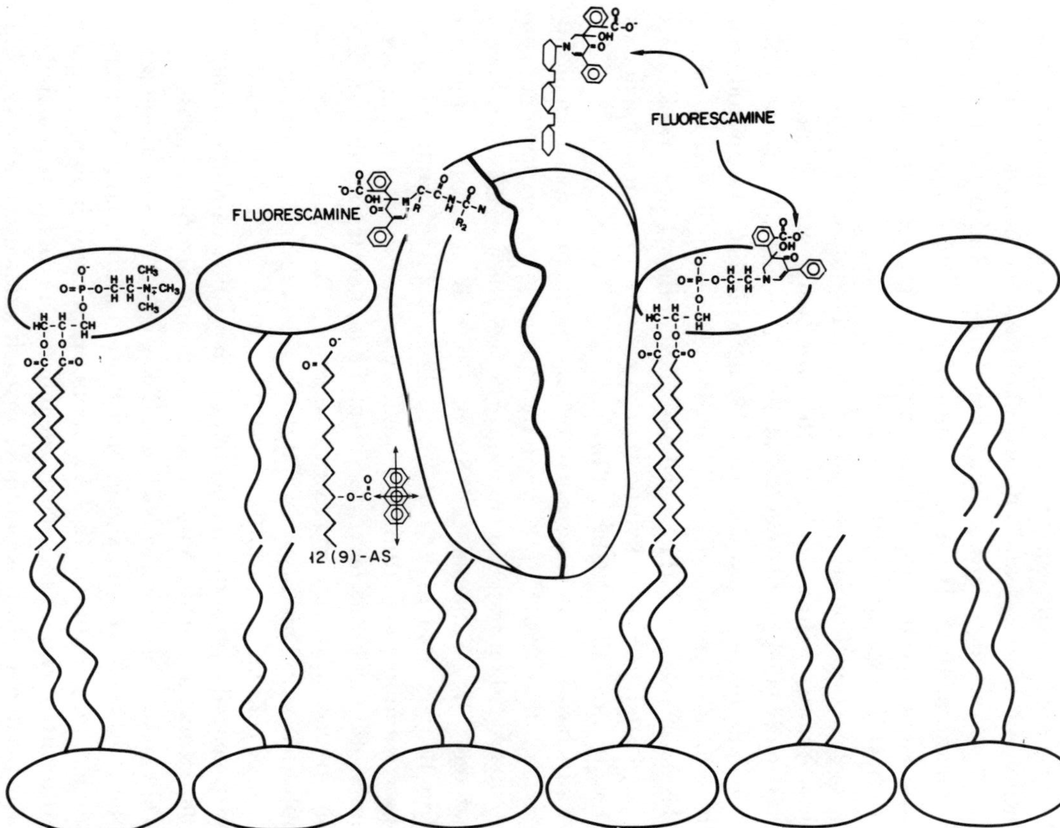

FIG. 10-1. Schematic diagram of a plasma membrane showing the possible membrane locations for fluorescamine and 12(9)AS. The arrows drawn on the anthroyl moiety of 12(9)AS depict the 255-nm (directed along the anthroyl long axis) and 346-, 365-, 385-nm (directed along the anthroyl short axis) excitation transitions.

Monitoring Changes in Microenvironment

Another characteristic of membrane probes, besides their site specificity, is their excitation and emission energies. These spectral characteristics may change, however, if the probe microenvironment changes—for example, if the probe should insert deeper into the cell membrane than normal. This change in probe microenvironment can be recognized by a change in emission energy. For probes with polar excited states (which is true of the probes included in this study), a shift to a shorter wavelength (a blue shift or higher energy state) would accompany a change to a more apolar environment (see Appendix I). Therefore, the emission spectral characteristics provide information on a probe's microenvironment or changes in that microenvironment.

Monitoring Changes in Rotational Mobility

Besides spectral energy changes (red-blue shifts), the rotational mobility of a probe in a specific membrane area can be monitored. Rotational mobility of a probe refers to its ability to move within the membrane. The probe rotational mobility is inversely related to the frictional drag imposed on the probe by the membrane microenvironment. The probe rotation within a membrane can be described as occurring in three planes: *xy*, *yz*, and *xz* (with *x*, *y*, and *z* referring to the membrane axes). Furthermore, the rotational mobility of a probe cannot be assumed to be equal in all three planes (i.e., the rotational movement is not isotropic). If a molecule is constrained so no movement can occur during its excited state, then the molecule's fluorescence polarization is given by the von Jablonski equation (von Jablonski, 1935):

$$P_0 = \frac{3\cos^2\theta - 1}{\cos^2\theta + 3}$$

where θ is the angle between μ_{ex} and μ_{em}. If $\theta = 0$, $P_0 = 0.5$ and if $\theta = 90°$, $P_0 = -0.33$. Changes in a probe's rotational mobility are monitored by the probe's excitation fluorescence polarization. These changes are quantified by the Perrin equation (Perrin, 1926):

$$\frac{1}{P} - \frac{1}{3} = \left(\frac{1}{P_0} - \frac{1}{3}\right)\left(1 + \frac{3\tau}{\rho}\right)$$

where P is the experimentally observed polarization, P_0 is the limiting fluorophore polarization in the absence of molecular motion, τ is the fluorophore excited state lifetime, and ρ is the harmonic mean of the in-plane and out-of-plane rotational relaxation times. The rotational relaxation time is defined as the time it takes the fluorophore to rotate through an angle θ such that $\cos \theta = e^{-1}$.

Studies to Date

In a preliminary study we demonstrated distinct abnormalities in the plasma membrane molecular dynamics of MDI erythrocytes and lymphocytes when compared with normal controls matched for age, sex, and race. There were no dietary differences between the two groups. The reported abnormalities did not appear to be affected by medication or phase of the illness, and therefore may be a molecular trait marker for the MDI gene (Pettegrew *et al.*, 1981b; Pettegrew, Nicholas, Minshew, Rush, & Stewart, 1982b) (Figures 10-2 and 10-3).

With the finding of an alteration in the plasma membrane hydrocarbon core of MDI intact erythrocytes, we decided to determine if this alteration adversely affected erythrocyte physiology. In our preliminary studies we chose to examine erythrocyte metabolism by ^{31}P NMR (see Appendix II for a brief summary of NMR theory). The readily identifiable phosphatic compounds include 2,3-diphosphoglycerate (2,3-DPG), inorganic orthophosphate (Pi), serum phospholipids (SPL),

FIG. 10-2. Excitation polarization values for fluorescamine and 12(9)AS labeled control and manic-depressive erythrocytes; p values calculated by the Mann–Whitney U test.

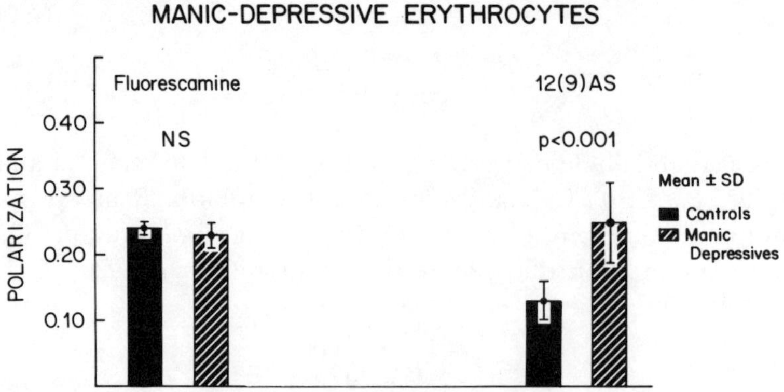

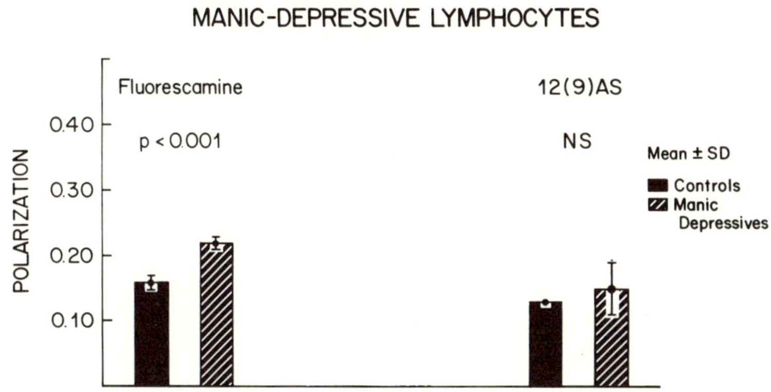

FIG. 10-3. Excitation polarization values for fluorescamine and 12(9)AS labeled control and manic-depressive lymphocytes; *p* values calculated by the Mann-Whitney U test.

and adenosine triphosphate (ATP) (Figure 10-4). These preliminary studies revealed no alteration in the phosphatic profile of physiologically intact MDI erythrocytes.

We next chose to determine if there were any alterations in the permeability of MDI erythrocyte membranes to the divalent cation manganese (Mn^{2+}). If Mn^{2+} enters the erythrocyte, the strong paramagnetic properties of Mn^{2+} will cause a quenching of the phosphorus NMR signals coming from the intracellular phosphorus metabolites. Therefore, when Mn^{2+} is added to plasma surrounding erythrocytes, the extracellular serum phospholipid signal is immediately quenched, followed by a time-dependent penetration of the erythrocyte plasma membrane by Mn^{2+}. This is reflected in an initial increase followed by a decrease in the 2,3-DPG signal. The initial increase and subsequent decrease in the 2,3-DPG signal is not due to altered 2,3-DPG metabolism, since perchloric acid extraction reveals no changes in the amount of 2,3-DPG over the course of the experiment. Therefore, the alterations in the 2,3-DPG signal probably reflect alterations in the 2,3-DPG cationic milieu as influenced by the presence of Mn^{2+}.

Whatever the mechanism, the changes in the 2,3-DPG NMR signal do reflect the penetration of the erythrocyte membrane by Mn^{2+}. If one analyzes the data by utilizing a least-squares linear regression fit of the experimental data points for 2,3-DPG and then expresses the data as the slopes of the two resulting straight lines, one obtains the data given in Figure 10-5.

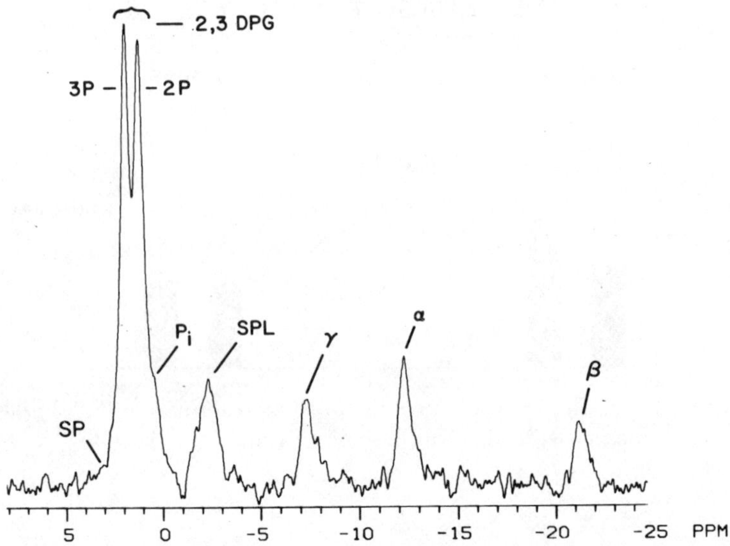

FIG. 10-4. Phosphorus NMR spectra (80.92 MHz) of freshly obtained human venous blood. SP = sugar phosphates, 2,3-DPG = 2,3 diphosphoglycerate, P_i = inorganic orthophosphate, SPL = serum phospholipids. The γ, α, β peaks refer to the corresponding phosphates in ATP. The γ and α peaks also contain contributions from ADP.

From the data shown in Figure 10-5, there does not appear to be any alteration in the permeability of MDI erythrocytes to Mn^{2+}. A further refinement of this approach is to determine the time-dependent alterations in the 2,3-DPG spin–spin (T_2) relaxation time as determined by a Carr–Purcell–Meiboom–Gill sequence. Such studies are now underway, and the T_2 time course for a normal control is shown in Figure 10-6. Note that the rate of Mn^{2+} entry equals the reciprocal of the slope of this logarithmic function. Therefore one can more directly study the rate of Mn^{2+} entry into living erythrocytes and determine if there is any alteration in the MDI erythrocyte. If such an alteration should be found, this may reflect a more generalized alteration in the permeability to other divalent cations (such as Ca^{2+} and Mg^{2+}).

Finally, one would like to be able to study the state of sodium and sodium transmembrane fluxes in MDI erythrocytes. The reason for studying sodium is predicated on the findings of altered lithium cellular distribution in MDI cells (Dorus *et al.*, 1979; Dorus, Pandey, Frazer, & Mendels, 1974; Dorus, Pandey, Shaughnessy, & Davis, 1980; Duhm, 1982; Johnston, Naylor, Dick, Hopwood, & Dick, 1980; Naylor, Dick,

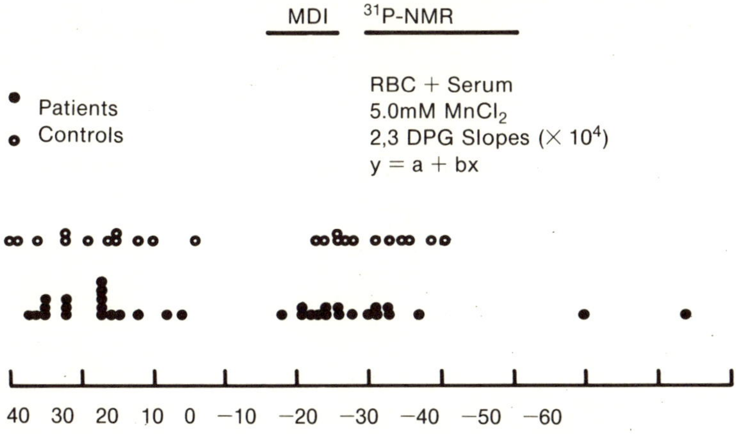

FIG. 10-5. The data points plotted represent the slopes obtained from the time course (3.18 hours) rise and fall of erythrocyte 2,3-DPG intensity in the presence of 5.0 mM $MnCl_2$ as measured by phosphorus NMR. The data demonstrate no difference in the rate of Mn^{2+} entry (monitored by the effect on intracellular 2,3-DPG) between manic-depressive and control erythrocytes.

FIG. 10-6. The time-course change in erythrocyte 2,3-DPG T_2 relaxation times as determined by the Carr-Purcell-Meiboom-Gill sequence for control blood incubated with 5.0 mM $MnCl_2$.

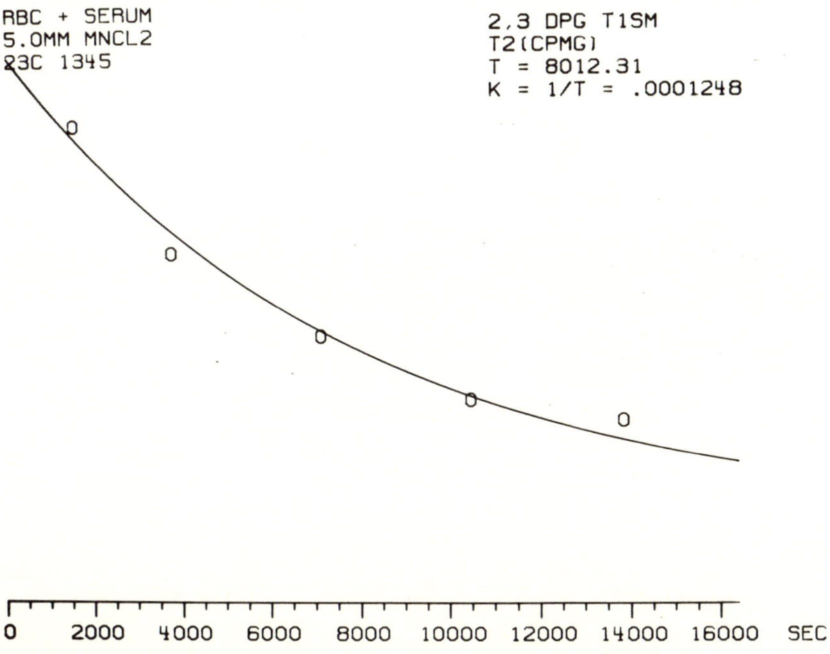

& Dick, 1976; Naylor, Reid, Dick, & Dick, 1976; Pandey *et al.*, 1977, 1978) and the therapeutic benefit of lithium treatment in MDI. It may well be that a genetic alteration in MDI alters the intracellular state of sodium and/or sodium fluxes and that lithium treatment modulates this alteration back to normal.

Recently developed NMR shift reagents (Gupta & Gupta, 1982) now enable one to distinguish intracellular and extracellular sodium signals in intact living cells. We have extended this work using the dysprosium:tripolyphosphate complex (Dy:TPP) shift reagent and developed a procedure using Dy:TPP which does not alter cellular metabolism as monitored by ^{31}P NMR, does not alter cellular morphology as monitored by phase microscopy, and in which there is no entry of Dy:TPP into the cells monitored over a 5-hour time period. We can now quantitate intracellular sodium concentration, determine the physical state of the intracellular sodium, and monitor transmembrane sodium flux all in intact living cells (Figure 10-7). These studies are now being extended to MDI patients.

FIG. 10-7. Sodium NMR on freshly obtained human venous blood to which was added 5.0 mM Dy:TPP. The resonance at ca. 0.8 ppm represents the intracellular sodium and the resonance at ca. −5 ppm represents the extracellular sodium.

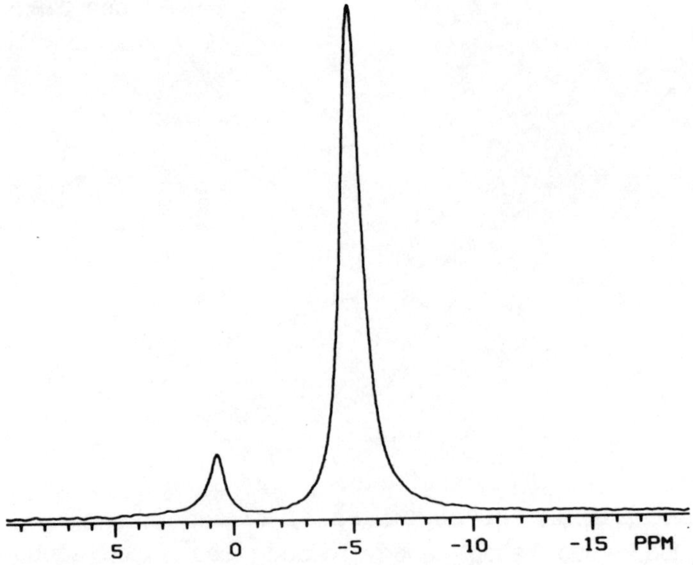

Summary

The molecular basis of human behavior is still unknown. We have demonstrated alterations in the molecular dynamics of the hydrocarbon core of MDI erythrocytes. Such alterations, if they also occur in CNS cells (neurons and/or glia), may give rise to altered neurotransmitter receptor function and produce the behavioral phenotype seen in MDI. We are also investigating other membrane-associated functions (such as divalent cation permeability, sodium flux, and sodium intracellular chemical state), which might be altered in MDI. In so doing we hope to gain a more complete understanding of the molecular dynamics and chemical functioning of intact cellular membranes in general and MDI membranes in particular.

Appendix I: Theory of Fluorescence

A molecule will absorb a photon of energy from impinging electromagnetic radiation if there exists in the molecule a ground state (Ψ_g) and an excited state (Ψ_e) whose energy difference ($\Delta E = E_e - E_g$) is the same as the energy of the electromagnetic radiation E_R. If this condition is fulfilled, then the probability of the transition occurring is given by

$$P = \left| \int_{\infty}^{\infty} \Psi_e \mid O \mid \Psi_g \, d\tau \right|^2$$

where Ψ_g and Ψ_e are the ground and excited state eigenfunctions, O is the electric moment operator (an odd function), $d\tau$ implies integration over all coordinate space, and | | means the absolute value. From symmetry considerations, it is seen that only transitions between eigenstates of differing symmetry will be formally allowed.

Assuming that the transition is formally allowed, the absorption of a photon occurs in 10^{-15} seconds. During this time the molecule undergoes rearrangement of its electron cloud in going from the solvent-relaxed ground state (SRGS) to the Franck–Condon excited state (FCES). Next, the more sluggish moving atomic nuclei readjust themselves to the new electron cloud distribution and the molecule progresses to an equilibrium excited state (EES) and this occurs over 10^{-12} seconds. Finally, the solvent molecules that surround the excited state molecule readjust to the new molecular geometry of the excited molecule. This occurs over 10^{-11} seconds, giving rise to the solvent-relaxed excited state (SRES). If the molecule in the excited state is more polar than it is in the ground state, the SRES will be raised in energy by nonpolar solvents and lowered in energy by polar solvents.

Once in the SRES, the molecule can further lose its remaining energy of excitation in one of three ways. The first is by collisional deactivation (referred to as internal conversion), which occurs over 10^{-9} to 10^{-7} seconds. The second is by a change in the electron spin multiplicity, which is usually a singlet state going to a triplet state. This is referred to as intersystem crossover and occurs over 10^{-8} to 10^{-7} seconds. A photon may then be emitted by the triplet state and this is called phosphorescence. The third way of losing the excitation energy is by emitting a photon and proceeding from the SRES to a Franck-Condon ground state (FCGS) with accompaning redistribution of the electron cloud. This process occurs over a 10^{-9}-second time interval and is termed fluorescence. From the FCGS the atomic nuclei again readjust to the change in electron cloud distribution to form the equilibrium ground state (EGS), and this occurs over 10^{-12} seconds. Once again the solvent molecules readjust to the new molecular coordinates to form the SRGS, and this occurs over 10^{-11} seconds (Figure 10-8).

The process of photon absorption during which the molecule goes from the SRGS to the FCES can be described by a transition

FIG. 10-8. A time versus energy diagram for the absorption and emission of a photon by a hypothetical fluorophore.

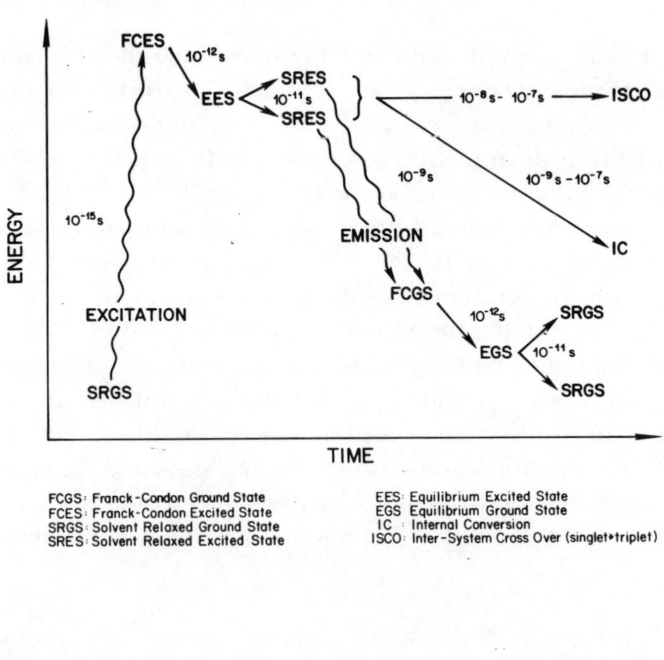

excitation moment (μ_{ex}) which has both magnitude and direction with respect to the molecule's atomic frame work. Likewise re-emission of the photon (fluorescence) during which the molecule goes from the SRES to the FCGS can be described by a transition emission moment (μ_{em}). The transition excitation moment (μ_{ex}) and the transition emission moment (μ_{em}) may be colinear, but usually are not, and always will have different magnitudes (i.e., the energy of the emitted photon is always less than the energy of the absorbed photon).

Appendix II: Theory of Nuclear Magnetic Resonance

Atomic nuclei are composed of protons and neutrons, both of which have intrinsic spin and a spin quantum number of 1/2. Another important nuclear property is the nuclear distribution of positive charge. This charge distribution is determined by the nuclear quadrupple, eQ, where e is the unit of electrostatic charge and Q is a measure of the deviation of the charge distribution from spherical symmetry. If all the nuclear particle spins are paired, there will be no net spin and the nuclear spin quantum number, I, will be zero. This will be the case for atomic nuclei with even numbers of protons and neutrons. The distribution of positive charge will be spherical and the nuclear quadrupole movement, eQ, will also be zero. A spherical nonspinning nucleus is an example of a nucleus in which $I = 0$ and $eQ = 0$. A nucleus may have $I = 1/2$ (presence of an unpaired spin) and $eQ = 0$, in which case the nucleus will be spherical and spinning. The presence of an unpaired spin also gives rise to a nuclear magnetic moment μ_m.

Nuclei that have $I > 1$ will not only have a nuclear spin, but will also have a nonspherical distribution of positive charge. The charge distribution will in this case be ellipsoidal. A positive value for Q indicates that the ellipsoid major axis will be oriented along the direction of an applied magnetic field H_0. Atomic nuclei, which have negative values for Q, will orient themselves in an applied magnetic field such that the ellipsoid long axis is perpendicualr to the applied magnetic field (Figure 10-9).

Atomic nuclei also have nuclear spin angular momentum quantum numbers, m_ℓ, which indicate the allowed orientations of the nuclear magnetic moment μ_m with respect to an applied magnetic field (H_0). The quantum number m_ℓ has values: I, $(I - 1)$, . . . $-(I - 1)$, $-$I. For $I = 1/2$, m_ℓ has the values of $+1/2$ or $-1/2$. For $I = 1$,

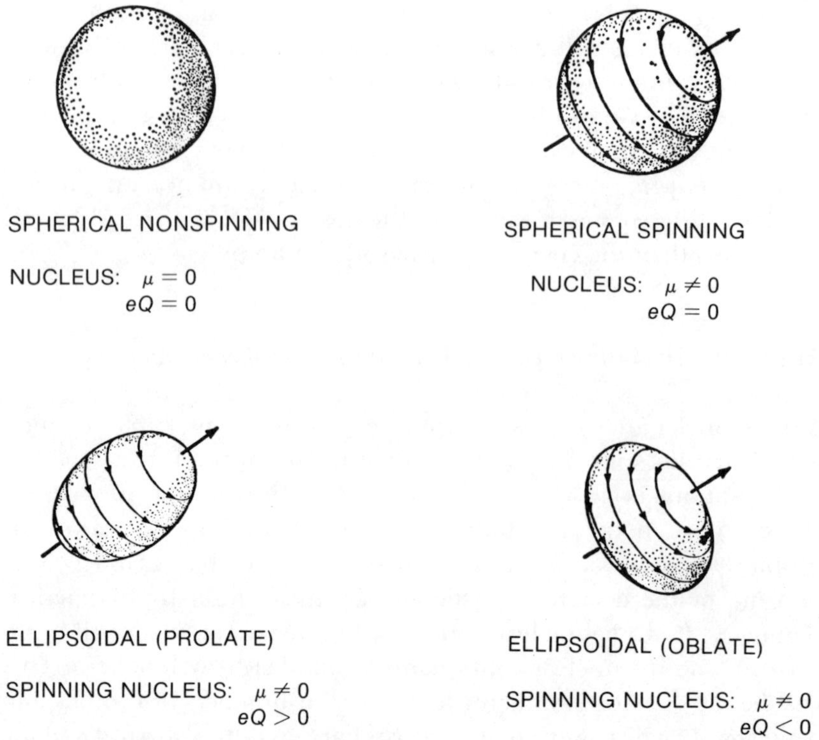

FIG. 10-9. Schematic diagram showing atomic nuclei with various nuclear properties.

m_ℓ has values of +1, 0, and −1. For $I = 3/2$, m_ℓ has values of 3/2, 1/2, −1/2, −3/2.

In the absence of a magnetic field, all orientations of the nuclear magnetic moment are degenerate. In the presence of an applied magnetic field, the degeneracy is removed. For nuclei with spin quantum number $I = 1/2$ in the presence of an applied field, $m_\ell = +1/2$ corresponds to the nuclear magnetic moment aligned with the applied moment and $m_\ell = -1/2$ corresponds to the nuclear magnetic moment aligned opposed to the applied magnetic field.

One possible transition exists between the $m_\ell = +1/2$ and $m_\ell = -1/2$ quantum states. For nuclei with $I = 1$, the presence of an applied magnetic field gives rise to m_ℓ values of +1, 0, and −1 corresponding, respectively, to alignments of the ellipsoid major axis with, perpendicular, and opposed to the applied magnetic field. Two possible transitions now exist: one between the $m_\ell = +1$ and $m_\ell = 0$ quantum states and another between the $m_\ell = 0$ and $m_\ell = -1$ quantum states. For nuclei with $I = 3/2$, the presence of an applied magnetic field gives use to four possible orientations of the nuclear magnetic moment with respect to the applied field. This in turn gives rise to three possible transitions: $m_\ell = 3/2$ to $m_\ell = 1/2$, $m_\ell = 1/2$ to $m_\ell = -1/2$ and $m_\ell = -1/2$ to $m_\ell = -3/2$ (Figure 10-10). Examples of atomic nuclei with $I = 1/2$ are ^{1}H, ^{13}C, ^{19}F, and ^{31}P; with $I = 1$, ^{2}H and ^{14}N; and with $I = 3/2$, ^{7}Li, ^{23}Na, ^{35}Cl, and ^{39}K.

In the presence of an applied magnetic field H_0, a nuclear magnetic moment will precess (rotate) around H_0. The precessional frequency is referred to as the Larmor frequency (ω_0) and is given by

$$\omega_0 = \gamma H_0$$

where γ is the gyromagnetic ratio of the atomic nucleus. Therefore ω_0 is linearly dependent on H_0. The values of ω_0 are in the radio frequency range (Figure 10-11.)

In order to induce transitions between different quantum states (m_ℓ) one needs to apply a magnetic field (H_1) which has the same frequency as the Larmor frequency ω_0. This is accomplished by pulsing a radiofrequency field (H_1) along an axis orthogonal to H_0. The

FIG. 10-10. Schematic representation of the effect of an applied magnetic field on angular momentum quantum levels.

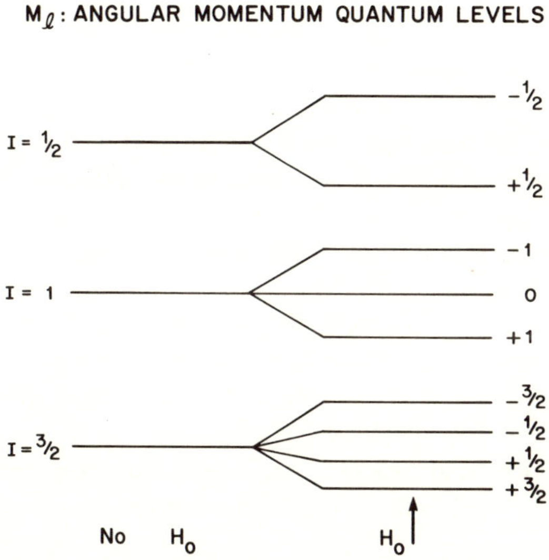

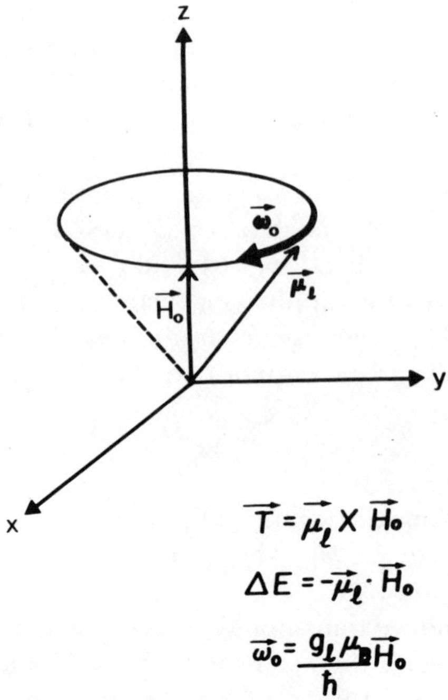

FIG. 10-11. Schematic representation of the effect of an applied magnetic field (H_0) on a nuclear magnetic moment (μ_ℓ). T = the torque, ΔE = the energy change, ω_0 = the Larmor frequency, g_ℓ = the nuclear proportionality constant (5.58855 for a free proton), μ_B = the nuclear magneton, $\hbar$ = Planck's constant (h) divided by 2π.

atomic nucleus will then absorb energy and go from one spin angular momentum quantum state (m_ℓ) to another.

When atomic nuclei are covalently bonded together, the electron distribution surrounding a given nuclide will be different for different types of chemical moieties. For example, the electron cloud surrounding a phosphorus atom will be different for the phosphorus in sugar phosphates (such as glucose-6-phosphate), inorganic orthophosphate, the γ, α, β phosphates of ATP, and so on. In the presence of an applied magnetic field H_0, there will be an induced motion in the electron cloud such that the moving electrons will generate a magnetic field opposed to the applied field H_0. This is referred to as diamagnetic shielding. The magnitude of the shielding will depend on the nature of the electron cloud surrounding the nucleus in question. Therefore, the magnitude of the effective field experienced by a nucleus is given by

$$H_{\text{eff}} = H_0 - H_0\sigma = H_0(1-\sigma)$$

where σ is a nondimensional shielding constant. The resonance frequency will therefore be decreased by the shielding. It is because of this diamagnetic shielding contribution, that atoms in different chemical moieties come into resonance at different frequencies of the pulsed H_1 field (see Figure 10-4). Because of this phenomenon, NMR can be used as an analytical tool. Under appropriate instrumental conditions, the integrated area under a NMR signal peak corresponds to the number of atoms of that particular chemical moiety in the sample.

Once a particular nucleus has been excited to a higher quantum state by an applied radiofrequency field H_1, the nucleus can lose its excitation potential energy by two different relaxation processes. The first is called spin–lattice relaxation (T_1) and is produced by rapidly fluctuating magnetic fields directed along the X and Y axes of a coordinate system rotating about the Z axis at the Larmor frequency (rotating frame). The other relaxation mechanism is called spin–spin relaxation (T_2) and is produced by both rapidly and slowly fluctuating magnetic fields directed along the X, Y, and Z axes of the rotating frame.

The interaction mechanisms involved in relaxation processes include: dipole–dipole, quadrupole, chemical shift anisotropy, scalar coupling, and spin–rotation. Space does not permit a full discussion of these mechanisms (see Farrar & Becker, 1971). In all of these relaxation mechanisms, however, two molecular parameters determine the rate of the relaxation. The first is the magnitude of the particular type of interaction and the other is the correlation time, τ_c, which can be defined as the "average" time between molecular collisions for a molecule in some state of motion. More specifically is the importance of the magnitude of τ_c in relation to ω_0. From these considerations one can define ranges of molecular motion as fast (extreme narrowing limit, $\omega_0^2\ \tau_c^2 << 1$), intermediate ($\omega_0^2\ \tau_c \simeq 1$), or slow (high-field limit, $\omega_0^2\ \tau_c^2 >> 1$). It is also apparent that the range of molecular motions available for study will depend on the strength of the applied field H_0 since $\omega_0 = \gamma H_0$.

REFERENCES

Albrecht, V. J., & Muller-Oerlinghausen, B. (1976). Zur klinischen bedeutung der intraerythrozytären Lithium-Konzentration:Ergebnisse einer katamnestischen Studie. *Arzneimittel-Forschung, 26,* 1145–1145.

Carroll, B. J. (1979). Prediction of treatment outcome with lithium. *Archives of General Psychiatry, 36,* 870–878.

Cazzullo, C. L., Smeraldi, E., Sacchetti, E., & Bottinelli, S. (1975). Intracellular lithium concentration and clinical response. *British Journal of Psychiatry, 126,* 198–300.

Chan-Palay, V., Engel, A. G., Palay, S. L., & Wu, J.-Y. (1982). Synthesizing enzymes for four neuroactive substances in motor neurons and neuromuscular junctions: Light and electron microscopic immunocytochemistry. *Proceedings of the National Academy of Sciences of the United States of America, 79,* 6717-6721.

Chan-Palay, V., Ito, M., Tongroach, P., Sakurai, M., & Palay, S. (1982). Inhibitory effects of motilin, somatostatin, (leu) enkephalin, (met)enkephalin, and taurine on neurons of the lateral vestibular nucleus: Interactions with γ-aminobutyric acid. *Proceedings of the National Academy of Sciences of the United States of America, 79,* 3355–3359.

Chan-Palay, V., Lin, C-T, Palay, S., Yamamoto, M., & Wu, J.-Y. (1982). Taurine in the mammalian cerebellum: Demonstration by autoradiography with (^{3}H) taurine and immunocytochemistry with antibodies against the taurine-synthesizing enzyme, cysteine-sulfinic acid decarboxylase. *Proceedings of the National Academy of Sciences of the United States of America, 79,* 2695–2699.

Chan-Palay, V:, Nilaver, G., Palay, S. L., Beinfeld, M. C., Zimmerman, E. A., Wu, J.-Y. & O'Donohue, T. L. (1981). Chemical heterogeneity in cerebellar Purkinje cells: Existence and coexistence of glutamic acid decarboxylase-like and motilin-like immunoreactivities. *Proceedings of the National Academy of Sciences of the United States of America, 78.* 7787–7791.

Charney, D. S., Menkes, D. B., & Heninger, G. R. (1981). Receptor sensitivity and the mechanism of action of antidepressant drugs. *Archives of General Psychiatry, 38,* 1160–1180.

Demisch, V. L., & Bochnik, H. J. (1976). Zur verbesserung der Lithium-Prophylaxe endogener phasischer psychosen: Aspekte der parallelen Lithiumbestimmung in serum und in erythrozyten. *Arzneimittel-Forschung, 26,* 1149–1151.

Dorus, E., Pandey, G. N., Frazer, A, & Mendels,J. (1974). Genetic determinant of lithium on distribution: I. An in vitro monozygotic–dizygotic twin study. *Archives of General Psychiatry, 31,* 463–465.

Dorus, E., Pandey, G. N., Shaughnessey, R., Gaviria, M., Val, E., Ericksen, S., & Davis, J. M. (1979). Lithium transport across red cell membrane: A cell membrane abnormality in manic–depressive illness. *Science, 205,* 932–934.

Dorus, E., Pandey, G. N., Shaughnessy, R., & Davis, J. M. (1980). Lithium transport across the RBC membrane: A study of genetic factors. *Archives of General Psychiatry, 37,* 80–81.

Duhm, J. (1982). Lithium transport pathways in erythrocytes. In H. M. Emrich, J. B. Aldenhoff, & H. D. Lux (Eds.), *Basic mechanisms of the action of lithium* (pp. 1–20). Amsterdam: Excerpta Medica.

Elizur, A., Shopsin, B., Gershon, S., & Ehlenberger, A. (1972). Intra/extracellular lithium ratios and clinical course in affective states. *Clinical Pharmacology and Therapeutics, 13,* 947-952.

Farrar, T. C., & Becker, E. D. (1971). *Pulse and fourier transform NMR: Introduction to theory and methods* (pp. 46–65). New York: Academic Press.

Flor-Henry, P. (1979). On certain aspects of the localization of the cerebral systems regulating and determining emotions. *Biological Psychiatry, 14,* 677–698.

Flor-Henry, P., & Koles, Z. J. (1980). EEG studies in depression, mania and normals: Evidence for partial shifts of laterality in the affective psychoses. *Advances in Biological Psychiatry, 4,* 21–43.

Frazer, A., Mendels, J., & Brunswick, D. (1978). Erythrocyte concentration of the lithium ion: Clinical correlates and mechanisms of accumulation. *Psychopharmacology Bulletin, 14,* 14–16.

Garver, D. L., & Davis, J. M. (1979). Biogenic amine hypothesis of affective disorders: Minireview. *Life Sciences, 24,* 383–394.

Gelfand, E. W., Dosch, H. M., Hastings, D., & Shore, A. (1979). Lithium: A modulator of cyclic AMP-dependent events in lymphocytes. *Science, 203,* 365–367.

Glen, A. I. M., Ongley, G. C., & Robinson, K. (1968). Diminished membrane transport in manic-depressive psychosis and recurrent depression. *Lancet, 2,* 241–243.

Gupta, R. K., Gupta, P. (1982). Direct observation of resolved resonances from intra- and extracellular sodium-23 ions in NMR studies of intact cells and tissues using dysprosium(III)tripolyphosphate as paramagnetic shift reagent. *Journal of Magnetic Resonance, 47,* 344–350.

Heilman, K. M., Scholes, R., & Watson, R. T. (1975). Auditory affective agnosia. *Journal of Neurology, Neurosurgery and Psychiatry, 38,* 69–72.

Hommes, O. R., & Panhuysen, L. H. (1971). Depression and cerebral dominance: A study of bilateral intracarotid Amytal in 11 depressed patients. *Psychiatria, Neurologia, Neurochirurgia, 74,* 259–270.

Johnston, B. B., Naylor, G. J., Dick, E. G., Hopwood, S. E., & Dick, D. A. T. (1980). Predictions of clinical course of bipolar manic-depressive illness treated with lithium. *Psychological Medicine, 10,* 329.

Jope, R. S., Jenden, D. J., Ehrlich, B. E., & Diamond, J.M. (1978). Choline accumulates in erythrocytes during lithium therapy. *New England Journal of Medicine, 299,* 833–834.

Marin, R. S., & Tucker, G. J. (1981). Psychopathology and hemispheric dysfunction: A review. *Journal of Nervous and Mental Disease, 169,* 546–557.

Mendels, J., & Grazer, A. (1973). Intracellular lithium concentration and clinical response: Towards a membrance theory of depression. *Journal of Psychiatric Research, 10,* 9–18.

Naylor, G. J., Dick, D.A.T., Dick, E. G., Le Poidevin, D., & Whyte, S. F. (1973). Erythrocyte membrane cation carrier in depressive illness. *Psychological Medicine, 3,* 502–508.

Naylor, G. J., Dick, D. A. T., & Dick, E. G. (1976). Erythrocyte membrance cation carrier, relapse rate of manic-depressive illness and response to lithium. *Psychological Medicine, 6,* 257.

Naylor, G. J., Glutz, D. A. T., & Dick, E. D. (1976). Erythrocyte membrance cation carrier, relapse rate of manic depressive illness and response to lithium. *Psychological Medicine, 6,* 257–263.

Naylor, G. J., Reid, A. H., Dick, D. A. T., Dick, E. G. (1976). A biochemical study of short-cycle manic-depressive psychosis in mental defectives. *British Journal of Psychiatry, 128,* 169.

Pandey, G. N., Ostrow, D. G., Haas, M., Dorus, E., Casper, R. C., Davis, J. M., & Tosteson, D. C. (1977). Abnormal lithium and sodium transport in erythrocytes of a manic patient and some members of his family. *Proceedings of the National Academy of Sciences of the United States of America, 74,* 3607–3611.

Pandey, G. N., Sarkadi, B., Haas, M., Gunn, R. B., Davis, J. M., & Tosteson, D. C. (1978). Lithium transport pathways in human red blood cells. *Journal of General Physiology, 72,* 233–247.

Perrin, M. F., Polarisation de la lumière de fluorescence: Vie moyenne des molécules dans l'état excité. *Journal du Physique Radium (Series G), 7,* 390–401.

Pettegrew, J. W., Minshew, N. J. & Nichols, J. S. (1982a). Fluorescence probes specific for the plasma membrane of intact human erythrocytes and lymphoctyes. *Life Sciences, 30,* 1101–1105.

Pettegrew, J. W., Nichols, J. S., & Stewart, R. M. (1979). Fluorescent studies of fibroblasts, lymphocytes, and erythrocytes in Huntington's disease. *Transactions of the American Neurological Association, 104,* 61–66.

Pettegrew, J. W., Nichols, J. S., & Stewart, R. M., (1980). Membrane studies in Huntington's disease: Steady state fluorescence of intact erythrocytes. *Annals of Neurology, 8,* 381–386.

Pettegrew, J. W., Nichols, J. S., & Stewart, R. M. (1981a). Membrane studies in neuropsychiatry: Fluorescence spectroscopy of intact human fibroblasts, lymphocytes and erythrocytes in genetic disease. In S. H. Gershon (Ed.), *Genetic strategies in psychobiology and psychiatry* (pp. 171-185). Pacific Groves, CA: Boxwood Press.

Pettegrew, J. W., Nichols, J. S., & Stewart, R. M. (1981b). Membrane studies in Huntington's disease: Steady state and time dependent fluorescence spectroscopy of intact lymphocytes. *Journal of Neurochemistry, 36,* 1966-1976.

Pettegrew, J. W., Nichols, J. S., Minshew, N. J., Rush, A. J., & Stewart, R. M. (1982b). Membrane biophysical studies of lymphocytes and erythrocytes in manic-depressive illness. *Journal of Affective Disorders, 4,* 237-247.

Podo, F., & Blasie, J. D. (1977). Nuclear magnetic resonance of lecithin biomolecular leaflets with incorporated fluorescent probes. *Proceedings of the National Academy of Sciences of the United States of America, 74,* 1032-1036.

Radda, G. D. (1971). The design and use of fluorescent probes for membrane studies. *Current Topics in Bioengineering, 4,* 81-126.

Radda, G. D., & Vanderkooi, J. (1972). Can fluorescent probes tell us anything about membranes? *Biochimica et Biophysica Acta, 265,* 509-549.

Ross, E. D. (1981). The aprosodias: Functional-anatomical organization of the affective components of language in the right hemisphere. *Archives of Neurology, 38,* 561-569.

Ross, E. D., Harney, J. H., deLacoste-Utamsing, C., & Purdy, P. D. (1981). How the brain integrates affective and propositional language into a unified brain function: Hypothesis based on clinicopathological correlations. *Archives of Neurology, 38,* 745-748.

Ross, E. D., & Mesulam, M.-M (1979). Dominant language functions of the right hemisphere? Prosody and emotional gesturing. *Archives of Neurology, 36,* 144-148.

Ross, E. D., & Rush, A. J. (1981). Diagnosis and neuroanatomical correlates of depression in brain-damaged patients: Implications for a neurology of depression. *Archives of General Psychiatry, 38,* 1344-1354.

Rybakowski, J., Chlopoctia, M., & Kapelski, A. (1974). Red blood cell lithium index in patients with affective disorders in the course of lithium prophylaxis. *Internal Pharmacopsychiatry, 9,* 166-171.

Sen, A. K., Murthy, R., Stancer, H. D., Awad, A. G., Godse, D. D., & Grof, P. (1976). The mechanism of action of lithium ion in affective disorders: A new hypothesis. In L. Bolis, J. F. Hoffman, & A. Leah (Eds.), *Membranes and disease* (pp. 109-122). New York: Raven Press.

Soucek, K., Zvolsky, P., & Kurlitz, R. (1974). The levels of lithium in serum and in red blood cells and its ratios in manic depressive patients. *Activitas Nervosa Superior (Praha),* 16, 193-194.

Stewart, R. M., & Rosenberg, R. N. (1979). Physiology of glia: Glial-neuronal interactions. In J. R. Symthies & R. J. Bradley (Eds.), *International review of neurobiology,* (Vol. 21, pp. 275-309). New York: Academic Press.

Sulser, F., & Mobley, P.. L. (1981). Regulation of central noradrenergic receptor function: New vistas on the mode of action of antidepressant treatments. In E. Usdin, W. E. Bunney, Jr. & J. M. Davis (Eds.), *Neuroreceptor—basic and clinical aspects* (pp. 55-83). New York: Wiley.

Thulborn, K. R., & Sawyer, W. H. (1978). Properties and the locations of a set of fluorescent probes sensitive to the fluidity gradient of the lipid bilayer. *Biochimica et Biophysica Acta, 511,* 125-140.

von Jablonski, A. (1935). Zur Theorie der Polarisation der Photolumineszenz von Farbstofflosungen. *Zeitshcrift fuer Physik, 96,* 236-246.

Yguarabide, J., & Stryer, L. (1971). Fluorescent spectroscopy of an oriented model membrane. *Proceedings of the National Academy of Sciences of the United States of America, 68,* 1217-1221.

11

The New Generation of Antidepressants

JOHN P. FEIGHNER

Current chemotherapy of major depressive disorders, although generally successful in 85% to 90% of patients, is problematic in that the commonly used tricyclic antidepressants and the monoamine oxidase inhibitors have a slow onset of action, numerous untoward side effects, and can be lethal when used in suicide attempts. During the past decade, new classes of antidepressants have been developed with evidence for increased biologic specificity, efficacy, and safety (Feighner, 1981).

This chapter will review a number of the newer compounds our Research Institute has been investigating over the last few years and which either have already been released or should be clinically available within 1 to 5 years. Theoretical issues will be considered in the course of the discussion on specific drugs, and summary Tables 11-1 and 11-2 provide an overview of these new compounds.

The New Tricyclic Drugs

Trimipramine (Surmontil) is one of the earliest tricyclic antidepressive drugs in the new group. It is an iminodibenzyl that has proven to be effective in more than 21 years of use (Settle & Ayd, 1980). Unlike imipramine, it has a relatively short half-life that ranges from 3 to 8 hours, depending on which metabolites are examined. It is a tertiary amine with serotonergic activity, but its sedative effects are related to central nervous system (CNS) H_1 receptor blockade, and like other tricyclic antidepressants, it has moderate atropinelike effect. Additional evidence indicates that trimipramine has considerable H_2 recep-

JOHN P. FEIGHNER. Department of Psychiatry, University of California, San Diego, La Jolla, California, and Feighner Research Institute, La Mesa, California.

TABLE 11-1. Pharmacological Profile in Therapeutic Dosage

Drug	Serotonergic	Noradrenergic	Dopaminergic	Anticholinergic effect	Antihistamine effect	Cardiovascular toxicity	Other effects
Trimipramine	4+	1+	0	4+	4+	4+	
Amoxapine	1+	3+	0	2+	2+	3+	7-Hydroxymetabolite is a dopamine antagonist with potential for extrapyramidal side effects and possible tardive dyskinesia.
Maprotiline	0	4+	0	2+	2+	2+	
Oxaprotiline	0	4+	0	1+	2+	2+	
Mianserin	0	2+	0	0	4+	0	
Trazodone	3+	0	0	0	0	1+	α-Adrenergic blocker with potential for sedation and reduced blood pressure.
Zimelidine	4+	0	0	0	0	0	
Fluoxetine	4+	0	0	0	0	0	
Fluvoxamine	4+	0	0	0	0	0	
Nomifensine	0	3+	2+	0	0	1+	
Bupropion	0	0	1+	0	0	0	Mechanism of CNS action essentially unknown.
Alprazolam	0	0	0	0	0	0	GABA-ergic; has an effect on REM sleep similar to that of tricyclic antidepressants—mechanism of action unknown.

Note. 0 = no significant clinical effect; 4+ = marked clinical effect; GABA = γ-aminobutyric acid.

tor blockade, and early clinical trials indicate significant clinical effect in acid-peptic disease (Nitter, Haraldsson, & Holck, 1976). Its spectrum of clinical application for depression is similar to imipramine and amitriptyline, and it appears to have a somewhat lower side effect profile (Rifkin, Saraf, Kane, Ross, & Klein, 1980).

Amoxapine (Ascendin) is a more recent tricyclic compound of the dibenzoxazepine family with noradrenergic and mild dopaminolytic effect. It is a demethylated derivative of loxapine succinate, and, like other demethylated derivatives of some of the neuroleptics, such as the thioxanthines and the piperazine phenothiazines, it has antidepressive effects (Greenblatt, Hardy, & Kelly, 1979). Its action has been examined in 108 studies utilizing over 2000 patients in the United States.

According to its manufacturers, Lederle and Company, its onset is more rapid, and its antidepressant effect greater than standard tricyclics such as amitriptyline (Elavil) or imipramine (Tofranil). Maximum improvement on the Hamilton Rating Scale for Depression (HRS-D) was greater at the end of the first week for patients on amoxapine than those on imipramine or amitriptyline, but at endpoint[1] the treatment groups were equal (Lederle Laboratories, 1982). The dosage range is generally from 200 to 400 mg but it may at times be necessary to raise this to as high as 600 mg, particularly if the patient is in a hospital setting. Amoxapine has moderate atropine effect and antihistaminic activity.

The major active antidepressant metabolite is 8-hydroxyamoxapine, and it is a potent noradrenaline reuptake inhibitor with a 30-hour half-life. Thus, the drug can be given in divided doses or as a single bedtime dose. The 7-hydroxyamoxapine metabolite, which is a dopamine antagonist, accounts for a small percentage (Greenblatt *et al.*, 1979; Lederle Laboratories, 1982; Riess *et al.*, 1975) of the activity of the compound and has a short 3–4 hour half-life. However, the presence of this antipsychotic metabolite raises the possibility of extrapyramidal side effects and potentially tardive dyskinesia.

Another claim made for amoxapine by the manufacturers is that it has low cardiovascular toxicity, even in cases of overdose. Both this and the earlier mentioned claim concerning the rapidity of onset of effectiveness in treatment of depression must be substantiated by further study.

Because of dopamine antagonist effect, the possibility of extrapy-

1. Endpoint analysis refers to the last evaluable visit for each patient regardless of when this occurs during the study and includes all patients evaluated.

TABLE 11-2. Clinical Profile

Drug	Chemical class	Efficacy	Common side effects	Dosage
Trimipramine	Tricyclic tertiary amine	Similar to standard (std) tricyclic antidepressant (TCA).	Atropinelike, weight gain, sedation	50–300 mg; single dose at bedtime or divided dose with major portion at bedtime.
Amoxapine	Tricyclic dibenzoxazepine	Similar to std TCA.	Atropinelike, sedation	100–400 mg; single dose at bedtime or divided dose with major portion at bedtime.
Maprotiline	Tetracyclic (bridged tricyclic)	Similar to std TCA.	Atropinelike	50–300 mg; single dose at bedtime or divided dose with major portion at bedtime.
Oxaprotiline	Tetracyclic (bridged tricyclic)	Similar to std TCA.	Atropinelike	25–200 mg; single dose at bedtime or divided dose with major portion at bedtime.
Mianserin	Tetracyclic	Similar to std TCA.	Sedation, weight gain	30–150 mg; single dose at bedtime.
Trazodone	Triazolopyridine	Similar to std TCA. Low propensity to induce mania or exacerbate psychotic symptoms. Useful in depressed schizophrenics and bipolar affective disorders.	Sedation, lethargy, headaches, gastric distress	50–600 mg; single dose at bedtime or divided dose with major portion at bedtime.

Zimelidine	Pyridylallylamine	Similar to std TCA.	Restlessness, tremulousness, nausea, diarrhea	150–300 mg; single or divided daytime dose.
Fluoxetine	Phenylpropylamine	Similar to std TCA.	Restlessness, tremulousness, nausea, diarrhea, weight loss	20–80 mg; single or divided daytime dose.
Fluvoxamine	Aralkylketone oxime ether	Similar to std TCA.	Restlessness, tremulousness, nausea, diarrhea	150–300 mg; single or divided daytime dose.
Nomifensine	Tetrahydroisoquinolone	Greatest effect in psychomotor retarded depression. Significant propensity to exacerbate mania and psychotic symptoms. Anticonvulsant effect and useful in depressed epileptics.	Restlessness, tremulousness, insomnia, dry mouth	50–200 mg; single or divided daytime dose.
Bupropion	Chlorpropiophenone	Similar to std TCA. Low propensity to exacerbate mania. Useful in bipolar affective disorders.	Restlessness, insomnia, diaphoresis	200–600 mg; divided daytime dose.
Alprazolam	Triazolobenzodiazepine	Effective in unipolar anxious depressives—not effective in psychomotor retarded depressives.	Sedation, other common benzodiazepine side effects	0.5–4.0 mg; divided dose with major portion at bedtime.

ramidal side effects and tardive dyskinesia exists. However, because of the dopaminolytic action, amoxapine may be most effective in treatment of the agitated or psychotic subtypes of depression. More systematic study of the effects of amoxapine on patients with psychotic depressions is, therefore, indicated.

Tetracyclic Compounds

Maprotiline (Ludiomil) is the first available tetracyclic compound in the United States, and it has been in use for several years as a prescription drug on a worldwide basis. It is a tetracyclic compound with potent noradrenergic and antihistaminic effect. The dosage range is from 50 to 300 mg and may be given in divided doses or as a single bedtime dose. The compound has a relatively long half-life (40–50 hours) and is suitable for single-dose maintenance therapy (Riess *et al.,* 1975). Results from our own research clinic show it to be at least as effective in its antidepressive action as imipramine, with a moderately better therapeutic index due to reduced atropine effect (Loque, Sachais, & Feighner, 1979). Because of the somewhat lower atropine effect, the compound may be more useful in geriatric depression and in patients with cardiovascular disease (Selvini, Rossi, Belli, Corallo, & Lucchelli, 1976). However, further clinical studies in these areas are warranted.

Oxaprotiline, which is a hydroxyanalogue of maprotiline, is a more potent norepinepherine reuptake inhibitor than its parent compound and has considerably less atropine effect (Ciba-Geigy, 1982). Animal studies indicate its potency to be 5–50 times greater than that of maprotiline; however, our own clinical studies using both open-label and double-blind trials on both inpatients and outpatients indicate a dosage range of 50–150 mg, usually given at bedtime (Feighner & Roffman, 1981).

Results from a large double-blind multicenter study comparing oxaprotiline with amitriptyline and placebo in 278 outpatients with major depressive disorder indicate equal efficacy for both drugs, and both drugs are statistically superior to placebo (Roffman *et al.,* 1982). Oxaprotiline had a superior side effect profile with much lower sedative and anticholinergic effects. Fewer patients dropped out because of adverse effects and, overall, oxaprotiline was much better tolerated than amitriptyline. This is especially important for patient compliance and long-term maintenance therapy.

Mianserin is a tetracyclic compound that has been used extensively in Europe and most industrialized countries. It has been administered to over 100,000 patients and is considered a safe and effective antidepressant (Brogdon, Heel, Speight, & Avery, 1978). The results of double-bind and open-label studies carried out on over 10,000 patients have shown it to be as effective as imipramine and amitriptyline, but with no atropine side effects, minimal cardiovascular toxicity even with overdose, and little adverse drug interaction with other psychotropic and cardiovascular drugs (Conti, Cassano, & Sarteschi, 1979). Its dosage range is 30–150 mg, given as a single dose at bedtime; common side effects include weight gain, drowsiness, and lethargy.

Mianserin is theoretically interesting because it functions as an α_2 presynaptic blocker, thus, enhancing the production and release of norepinephrine. On the other hand, its sedative properties appear to be related to its potent antihistaminic affect. It has no monoamine oxidase inhibition and no effect on dopamine or serotonin (Coppen & Kopera, 1978).

We recently completed a 6-week double-blind, parallel, random assignment, comparison with mianserin and amitriptyline on 81 outpatients who fulfilled the Feighner critieria for primary depression and Research Diagnostic Criteria for major depressive disorder, and who had a minimum baseline score of 19 on the 21-item HRS-D (Feighner, Jacobs, Jackson, Hendrickson, Merideth, & O'Meara, 1983).

Patients were evaluated weekly with standard clinical and side effect scales. The demographic characteristics were comparable for both groups and consistent with depressed outpatient populations. The mean daily dose for mianserin was 105 mg at bedtime, and for amitriptyline was 154 mg at bedtime. Both groups showed statistically significant improvement from baseline on all parameters, and both drugs were similar on all efficacy parameters. At end of treatment, 57% of mianserin patients and 54% of amitriptyline patients achieved a 50% or greater reduction on the HRS-D.

The greatest difference between the drugs was on the side effect profile, as 26 of the 41 mianserin patients reported drug-related side effects and 39 of the 40 amitriptyline patients reported drug-related side effects. The efficacy index demonstrated clear superiority of mianserin over amitriptyline. The most common side effects for amitriptyline were anticholinergic, whereas the most common side effect for mianserin was drowsiness. These findings support the results of international studies (Peet, 1977).

Because of its efficacy and low side effect profile, mianserin should be particularly suited for geriatric depression and in patients who cannot tolerate the anticholinergic side effects. Lack of placebo-controlled data has delayed the appearance of this important compound as a prescription drug in the United States.

Triazolopyridine Derivatives

Trazodone is the first of the triazolopyridine derivatives to be used clinically. Its pharmacological profile is atypical of antidepressive drugs in use at present in that it has virtually no effect on dopamine or norepinephrine, no atropine effect, and no monoamine oxidase inhibitor effect (Riblet & Taylor, 1981). Its antidepressant action appears to be associated with its inhibition of serotonin reuptake and it potentiates 5-hydroxytryptophan. In addition, it has peripheral antiserotonin effect and is an α-adrenergic blocker (Brogdon, Heel, Speight, & Avery, 1982).

Trazodone has been extensively investigated in Europe over the last 13 years and in the United States for the past 6 years (Ayd, 1979). It has low cardiovascular toxicity and no atropine-like effect. The dosage range is 50–800 mg, and, because of its sedative effects, the main dose is usually administered at bedtime. The hypnotic effect is therapeutically useful. We have found the compound to be most effective in depressed patients with agitation, anxiety, and insomnia. Negative side effects are lethargy, headaches, nausea, and mild gastrointestinal distress (Feighner, 1980).

In addition to its use in major depressive disorders, trazodone has demonstrated usefulness in schizophrenics with secondary depression (Singh & Saxena, 1977). Trazodone does not appear to exacerbate psychotic symptoms and has no potentiating atropine effect to complicate neuroleptic therapy. In addition, trazodone has minimal effect on the dopamine system and theoretically should not exacerbate manic symptoms to the same extent as other antidepressants (Friedman, Fang, & Gershon, 1977; Larochelle, Hamet, & Enjalbert, 1979). A large multicenter trial with trazodone revealed no manic episodes, and there were no reports in the scientific literature of trazodone-induced mania (Gershon, Mann, Newton, & Gunther, 1981). Further study of trazodone and its role in bipolar major effective disorder, schizophrenia with secondary depression, and in schizoaffective disorder is warranted.

We have carried out two double-blind studies, one on severely ill hospitalized depressives and the other on outpatients (Feighner, 1980; Feighner, Merideth, & Hendrickson, 1981). The former compared the effects of trazodone with imipramine and placebo over a period of 28 days. The latter, which was a long-term study with 1-year follow-up, was carried out with trazodone and imipramine only. Results from the inpatient study showed trazodone to have a more rapid onset of action than imipramine and to be clearly superior to placebo. A 50% reduction of depression between pretreatment level and endpoint scores as measured by the HRS-D and the Clinical Global Impression Scale (CGIS) was used as an index of significant improvement. At endpoint analysis, 53% of the trazodone patients, 28% on imipramine, and none on placebo had significantly improved.

The outpatient double-blind study was carried out on 79 patients, of whom roughly twice as many were on trazodone as were on imipramine. Virtually all parameters favored trazodone over imipramine, and both drugs were effective over the year-long study. At endpoint, 56% of trazodone patients showed significant improvement compared with 36% on imipramine. Common side effects included atropinelike effects for imipramine, and drowsiness, lethargy, occasional headaches, and occasional nausea for trazodone. Fewer trazodone than imipramine patients dropped out due to side effects. This makes trazodone a useful drug for long-term treatment of depression to prevent relapse, especially during the first treatment year.

Because of its lack of anticholinergic effect, trazodone may be well suited for geriatric patients with major depressive disorders. Gerner *et al.* compared trazodone with imipramine in 60 geriatric depressed patients and found equal efficacy, but noted that trazodone had a lower side effect profile, with fewer dropouts and was better tolerated overall than imipramine (Gerner, Estabrook, Steuer, & Jarvick, 1980).

The above studies and others summarized by Brogdon, Heel, Speight, and Avery (1982) indicate a potential wide range of clinical application for this triazolopyridine derivative (Feighner, 1980).

Selective Serotonin Reuptake Inhibitors

Zimelidine is a bicyclic compound that is a potent serotonin reuptake inhibitor. It is void of atropine, dopamine, norepinephrine, and antihistaminic effects (Bertilsson, Tuck, & Siewers, 1980). Its cardiovascular toxicity is low. Its dosage range is from 100 to 300 mg per day, given in a single or divided daytime dose as it has minimal sedative effects.

Common side effects include hyperactivity, restlessness, tremulousness, nausea, diarrhea, and occasionally headaches (Burgess, Montgomery, Wadsworth, & Turner, 1979; Coppen, Rao, Swade, & Wood, 1979).

Results of both national and international studies indicate that zimelidine has equal efficacy to amitriptyline, imipramine, and newer antidepressants such as maprotiline, nomifensine, and mianserin (Georgotas, Mann, Bush, & Gershon, 1980; Montgomery, 1980; Swift, Haythorne, Clark, & Stevenson, 1981). Its major advantage is in a high therapeutic index with a low side effect profile; it is generally well tolerated by most patients.

Despite its lack of sedation, zimelidine demonstrates stablization of both anxiety symptoms and sleep disturbance that accompany the depressive syndrome (Coppen *et al.*, 1979). In addition, because of its lack of antihistaminic and anticholinergic effects, zimelidine is well suited for geriatric depression, obese patients, and other patients who cannot tolerate the atropinelike side effects (Montgomery, 1980).[2]

Fluoxetine is a highly selective serotonin reuptake inhibitor (Wong, Horng, Bymaster, Hauser, & Molloy, 1974). Its effect on dopamine and norepinephrine is not clinically significant, and, unlike the tricyclic antidepressants, it is void of anticholinergic and antihistaminic side effects.

In man, the inhibition of serotonin uptake by fluoxetine has been investigated by Lemberger (1976). They demonstrated that fluoxetine caused a diminution of endogenous serotonin in platelets and showed that fluoxetine had no effect on the noradrenergic response, as measured by the pressor effect to tyramine and noradrenaline. This demonstrated a highly specific serotonin effect for both fluoxetine and its primary desmethyl metabolite.

Results of initial open-label studies in patients with major depressive disorder were postitive, and suggested potent antidepressive effect with minimal side effects in a dosage range of 20–80 mg per day (Lemberger, 1976).

We recently completed a double-blind, random assignment comparison of fluoxetine and amitriptyline on 44 outpatients with primary major depressive disorder (Feighner, 1985). Study included 1 week of single-blind placebo washout to eliminate apparent placebo respond-

2. Because of neurotoxic effects, including Gullain-Barré syndrome, this compound has been removed from international use.

ers, and then was followed by 5 weeks of active medication. Standard rating scales for efficacy and safety were performed weekly and appropriate laboratory data including blood count, urinalysis, chemistry panel, ECG, and ophthalmological exams were obtained pre- and poststudy.

The demography of the patients was consistent for outpatient depressives and there were no significant differences between the two treatment groups. The baseline 21-item HRS-D score had to be at least 20, with a minimum Raskin Depression Scale score of 8.

Results from the study showed that both treatment groups demonstrated statistically significant improvement with overall fewer side effects than the amitriptyline patients. Only 3 of 22 fluoxetine patients discontinued the study because of adverse effects, whereas 9 of 22 amitriptyline patients discontinued the study because of adverse effects. The most common side effects for amitriptyline were related to sedation and anticholinergic effects. The most common side effects for fluoxetine were nausea, diarrhea, and restlessness. One drug-related minor arrhythmia was noted in the amitriptyline group. Of interest was the fact that there was a nonsignificant weight gain in the amitriptyline group, whereas in the fluoxetine group there was an average weight loss of 3 lbs. This was significant between the two groups and suggests that fluoxetine may be useful in obese depressed patients. In addition, because of its lack of anticholinergic and antihistaminic effects, fluoxetine may be well suited in geriatric depressed patients, patients with cardiovascular disease, and in patients who are intolerant of the atropinelike side effects.

Fluvoxamine is chemically different but pharmacologically similar to both zimelidine and fluoxetine. It is a highly selective serotonin reuptake inhibitor, with no anticholinergic, antihistaminic, noradrenergic, or dopaminergic effects (Claassen, Davies, Hertting, & Placheta, 1977). It has remarkably few active metabolites and the kidney is the sole excretory organ, with 95% of an oral dose recovered in the urine within 48 hours after a single dose.

Early clinical trials indicate antidepressant activity with a low side effect profile and a dosage range of 100–300 mg per day given in a single or divided dose (Doogan, 1980). Common side effects are similar to zimelidine and include nausea, diarrhea, and restlessness. Further study is in progress on a national and international basis with both fluvoxamine and a structurally similar compound, clovoxamine (Saletu, Grunberger, Rajna, & Karobath, 1980).

New Drugs of Other Classes

Nomifensine is an tetrahydroisoquinoline compound of particular interest because it is both a norepinephrine and a dopamine reuptake inhibitor (Brogdon *et al.,* 1979). In addition, nomifensine has essentially no anticholinergic or antihistaminic effects and in therapeutic doses may have anticonvulsant properties (Hoffman, 1977). In addition, Burrows *et al.* have demonstrated lower cardiovascular toxicity for nomifensine, as opposed to the tricyclic antidepressants (Burrows, Vohra, Dumovic, Scoggins, & Davies, 1978). Nomifensine is readily absorbed and is rapidly conjugated to the glucuronide metabolite with a plasma half-life of 2–4 hours and is excreted predominantly in urine (Brogdon *et al.*, 1979).

The dosage range is 50–200 mg per day given in divided daytime doses. Common side effects include dry mouth, tremulousness, restlessness, insomnia, and infrequently drug fever (Poldinger & Gammel, 1978). In addition, nomifensine, because of its dopaminergic activity, should be used cautiously in bipolar major affective disorders and in schizophrenic disorders (Singh & Saxena, 1977). Exacerbation of both manic episodes and psychotic symptoms has been noted clinically (Brogdon *et al.,* 1979).

Studies done in our clinic in primary depression indicate that nomifensine is an effective antidepressant with greatest effect noted in psychomotor retarded depressions (Feighner, Merideth, Nash, & Hendrickson, 1982). Also, a comparative trial with nomifensine and imipramine in geriatric depression done in our clinic indicates that nomifensine is well tolerated by geriatric patients with equal efficacy noted between treatment groups (Feighner *et al.,* 1982). This is consistent with international studies (Moizeszowicz & Subira, 1977).

Nomifensine has had extensive international utilization since 1977, and became available in the U.S. for clinical use in 1985. (Nomifensine was recently withdrawn worldwide because of untoward reactions.)

Alprazolam is a triazolobenzodiazepine and represents a unique class of benzodiazepines by incorporation of a triazole ring in the basic structure, resulting in a different metabolic pathway with rapid absorption and elimination (Gail, Kamdar, & Collins, 1978). According to Schatzberg and Cole (1978), who did an extensive literature review, the classic benzodiazepines are not effective in major depressive disorders. Benzodiazepines, however, have generally a low incidence of serious adverse affects with a lack of anticholinergic side effects, low cardiotoxicity, and minimal potential for lethality with overdose

(Feighner, 1982). Alprazolam was first studied as an anxiolytic by Fabre (1976) and was noted in early clinical trials to demonstrate antidepressant effect beyond that accounted for by its anxiolytic and hypnotic properties (Fabre & Mclendon, 1976). In addition, although alprazolam has a potent GABA-ergic effect similar to other benzodiazepines, it has an effect on REM sleep in depressed patients similar to the monoamine oxidase inhibitors and tricyclic antidepressants. Also, it has an effect similar to desipramine on the reserpine-induced model of depression in rats (Sethy & Hodges, 1982; Sulser, 1980).

Because of earlier findings suggesting antidepressant activity, we participated in a five-center double-blind, randomized, 6-week trial comparing alprazolam with imipramine and placebo in 906 outpatients with unipolar major depressive disorder of at least 1-month duration (Feighner, Aden, Fabre, Rickels, & Smith, 1983). All patients fulfilled the Feighner criteria for depression and in addition were required to have a minimum baseline score of 18 or more on the 21-item HRS-D, 8 or more on the Raskin Depression Scale, and a Covi Anxiety Scale score less than or equal to the Raskin score (Feighner, *et al.*, 1972).

Of the 906 outpatients enrolled in the study, 183 were not evaluable for a variety of administrative reasons; these patients were evenly distributed within the three treatment groups. Results from the remaining 723 patients revealed that both alprazolam and imipramine were superior to placebo in virtually all efficacy parameters. The effect of alprazolam was comparable to imipramine and alprazolam demonstrated a faster onset of action ($p < .001$). The efficacy parameters were highly concordant between physician and patient rating scales. These data strongly support antidepressant effect for alprazolam in this patient population.

The dosage range for alprazolam is 0.5–4.0 mg per day given in divided doses, with the majority of the dose given at bedtime. Common side effects include drowsiness and lethargy. Alprazolam is generally well tolerated by most patients. Further study is clearly indicated to support the antidepressant effects of alprazolam, and a reanalysis of current biochemical mechanisms in major depressive disorders is warranted.

Bupropion is a chlorpropiophenone and is the first of this unique monocyclic amino ketone class of drugs to be used clinically (Soroko, Mehta, Maxwell, Ferris, & Schroder, 1977). It is different from all other antidepressants in that it has no significant effect on norepinephrine or serotonin and has mild dopaminergic activity that is not thought to be clinically significant. Essentially its mechanism of action is unkown (Ferris, Cooper, & Maxwell, 1983). It has no monomine oxidase inhibition or direct stimulant effect, and no anticholinergic or antihistaminic effects. It is nonsedating and has no interaction with alcohol (Burroughs Wellcome Company, 1982, on file) (Table 11-3).

Animal studies predictive of antidepressant activity were postitive with bupropion only on the reversal of tetrabenazine sedation and the potentiation of L-dopa effects (Ferris *et al.*, 1983). In studies of animals and man, bupropion has essentially no adverse cardiac effects, as it has no effect on conduction time and no effect on blood pressure and pulse with no tendency for orthostatic hypotension. Bupropion produces a slight reduction of appetite, and there is a tendency for patients on maintenance therapy to lose weight (Harto-Truax, Stern, Miller, Sato, & Cato, 1983). Bupropion has anticonvulsant properties in mice, but like the tricyclic antidepressants it has slight epileptogenic properties in man (Peck, Stern, & Watkinson, 1983).

Extensive clinical studies, both inpatients and outpatients with major depressive disorders, reveal significant antidepressant activity. Placebo controlled, double-bind trials on 219 inpatients with marked-to-severe major depressive disorders in four different centers reveal an average significant response for bupropion of 60% to 70%, and only a 20% to 30% response for placebo when comparing endpoint clinical efficacy parameters (Schatzberg & Cole, 1978). (Table 11-4). Two double-blind comparisons of amitriptyline with bupropion in 166 depressed outpatients show comparable significant efficacy for both drugs with trends favoring bupropion (Table 11-5).

We have recently completed a 28-day double-blind, random assignment, bupropion versus placebo study on 67 inpatients with marked-to-severe primary major depressive disorders (Feighner, Meri-

TABLE 11-3. Pharmacology of Bupropion

- Reverses tetrabenazine-induced sedation in the mouse.
- Potentiates L-dopa effects in rats.
- Anticonvulsant in mice.
- No anticholinergic properties in oxotremorine behavioral test or on cholinergic receptor binding in rat brain.
- No antihistaminergic effects on guinea pig ileum.
- No effects on cardiac conduction, blood pressure, or heart rate in dogs.

Note. Adapted from Soroko, Mehta, Maxwell, Ferris, & Schroeder (1977).

Table 11-4. Double-Blind Placebo-Controlled Studies of Bupropion

Study	Number of centers	Number of patients	Patient status	Percentage responders at termination[a]	
				Bupropion	Control
06	3	75	Inpatient	61	28
08	3	59	Inpatient	60	23
14-01	1	49	Inpatient	76	7
09	2	82	Outpatient	64	45
14-02	1	36	Inpatient	62	50

[a]CGIS rating of much or very improved.

deth, Stern, Hendrickson, & Miller, 1984). Standard rating scales for efficacy and adverse effects were done at days 5, 8, 11, 14, 21, and 28. Endpoint data analysis revealed a highly significant ($p < .001$) effect for bupropion over placebo. At endpoint, 63% of bupropion and only 10% of placebo patients had a 50% or greater improvement in HRS-D scores. CGIS scores of moderate improvement or better were achieved by 76% of the bupropion patients and by only 5% of the placebo patients (Table 11-6). This study and other clinical studies offer substantial evidence that bupropion is an effective antidepressant.

The average dosage range for outpatients is 300–450 mg per day, and for inpatients 450–600 mg per day, usually given in divided doses (Table 11-7). Common side effects include restlessness, insomnia, tremor, dizziness, dry mouth, diaphoresis, and nausea. In general, the side effect profile is extremely low for this compound, and in the placebo-controlled trials, the placebo patients reported as many side

Table 11-5. Double-Blind Amitriptyline-Controlled Studies of Bupropion

Study	Number of centers	Number of patients	Patient status	Percentage responders at termination[a]	
				Bupropion	Control
15	6	101[b]	Outpatient	85	81
21	5	65[b]	Inpatient	79	74

[a]CGIS rating of much or very improved.
[b]Study in progress.

TABLE 11-6. Patients Showing 50% Improvement on Hamilton Scale and CGI (Score of 1 or 2)

	Bupropion	Placebo
HRS-D	26/41 (63%)	2/21 (10%)
CGI	31/41 (76%)	1/21 (5%)

effects as did those patients on bupropion (Burroughs Wellcome Company, 1982, on file) (Table 11-8). Also, during both the short-term acute studies and long-term maintenance studies, there were considerably less than expected hypomanic or manic episodes, and double-blind controlled trials with lithium and placebo are now underway in bipolar patients.

Because of its low side effect profile and nonsedating properties, bupropion is well suited for geriatric depression, maintenance antidepressant therapy, patients with cardiovascular disease, and those who are intolerant of anticholinergic side effects (Table 11-9). In addition, data from the double-blind trials indicate that 60% of patients who were previously poor responders to the tricyclic antidepressants demonstrate moderate improvement or better when treated with bupropion (Stern, Harto-Truax, & Bauer, 1983). This finding adds further evidence that bupropion has a broad spectrum of clinical application in major depressive disorders.

Conclusion

Each of the new compounds discussed in this chapter represents incremental improvement over existing chemotherapy of major depressive disorders. In general, these new compounds are safer, especially if

TABLE 11-7. Bupropion: Recommended Dosages (Three Times a Day)

Mild to moderate depression:	Start: 300 mg per day Max: 450 mg per day
Severe depression:	Start: 300 mg per day Max: 750 mg per day
Maintenance:	150–450 mg per day

Note. Dose increments not to exceed 150 mg per day every 3 days.

TABLE 11-8. Treatment-Related Adverse Events (Percent of Patients)

Adverse event	Bupropion	Placebo	Bupropion minus placebo
Allergic			
Dermatologic reaction (usually urticaria or pruritis)	3	0	3
Autonomic			
Blurred vision	5	1	4
Constipation	6	0	6
Diarrhea	1	0	1
Dry mouth	15	1	14
Nasal congestion	1	1	0
Nausea/vomiting	6	1	5
Sweating	1	1	0
Central nervous system			
Akathisia	0	0	0
Drowsiness	2	1	1
Dystonic symptoms	0	1	0
Excitement/agitation	4	1	3
Increased motor activity	4	1	3
Decreased motor activity	1	0	1
Insomnia	3	1	2
Rigidity	0	0	0
Tremor	4	0	4
Cardiovascular			
Dizziness	6	0	6
Hypotension	1	0	1
Palpitations	1	0	1
Other			
Decreased appetite	2	1	1
Headache	1	0	1
Weight gain	1	0	1
Weight loss	0	1	0

TABLE 11-9. Summary of Clinical Profile of Bupropion

Efficacy
Depression and accompanying anxiety
Onset of 5 days to 3 weeks
Tricyclic antidepressant nonresponders[a] (active)
Older patients
Maintenance
Manic episodes[a] (negative)

Safety
Cardiovascular[a] (negative)
Anticholinergic[a] (minimal/negative)
Mental sedation[a] (negative)
Alcohol potentiation[a] (negative)
Weight gain[a] (negative)
Seizure

[a]Disadvantages of current tricyclic/tetracyclic antidepressants not found with bupropion.

taken in overdose, more specific with fewer clinically significant side effects, and many have a more rapid onset of action than existing antidepressants. In addition, many intractable patients respond favorably to these new compounds, thus enlarging the spectrum of antidepressant activity. It is imperative that the clinician be aware of the optimum clinical usage of these new compounds as they become available over the next several years.

REFERENCES

Ayd, F. (1979). Trazodone: A unique new broad-spectrum antidepressant. *International Drug Therapy News Letter,* (1980). *14,* 33–40.

Bertilsson, L., Tuck, J. R. , & Siewers, B. (1980). Biochemical effects of zimelidine in man. *European Journal of Clinical Pharmacology, 18,* 483–487.

Brogdon, R. N., Heel, R. C., Speight, T. M., & Avery, G. S. (1978). Mianserin: A review of its pharmacologic properties and therapeutic efficacy in depressive illness. *Drugs, 16,* 273–301.

Brogdon, R. N., Heel, R. C., Speight, T. M., & Avery, G. S. (1979). Nomifensine: A review of its pharmacologic properties and therapeutic efficacy in depressive illness. *Drugs, 18,* 1–24.

Brogdon, R. N., Heel, R. C., Speight, T. M., & Avery, G. S. (1982). Trazodone: A review of its pharmacological properties and therapeutic use in depression and anxiety. *Drugs, 21,* 401–429.

Burgess, C. D., Montgomery, S., Wadsworth, J., & Turner, P. (1979). Cardiovascular effects of amitriptyline, mianserin, zimelidine, and nomifensine in depressed patients. *Postgraduate Medical Journal, 55,* 704–708.

Burroughs Wellcome Company. (1982). *Data on file,* Research Triangle Park, NC.

Burrows, G. D., Vohra, J., Dumovic, P., Scoggins, B. A., & Davies, B. (1978). Cardiological effects of nomifensine, a new antidepressant. *Medical Journal of Australia, 1,* 341–345.

Ciba-Geigy Pharmaceutical Research Division. (1982, January) *Summary for Investigation: Oxaprotiline,* Summit, NJ.

Claassen, V., Davies, J. E., Hertting, G., & Placheta, P. (1977). Fluvoxamine: A specific 5-hydroxytryptamine uptake inhibitor. *British Journal of Pharmacology, 60,* 505–516.

Conti, L., Cassano, G. B., & Sarteschi, P. (1979). Clinical experience with mianserin. In G. Drykonigen, W. L. Rees, & R. C. Ogara (Eds.), *Mianserin hydrochloride: Progress in the pharmacotherapy of depression.* Amsterdam: Excerpta Medica.

Coppen, A., & Kopera, H. (1978). Workshop on the clinical pharmacology and efficacy of mianserin. *British Journal of Clinical Pharmacology, 5,* 915–995.

Coppen, A., Rao, V., Swade, C., & Wood, K. (1979). Zimelidine: A therapeutic and pharmacokinetic study in depression. *Psychopharmacology, 63,* 199–202.

Doogan, D. P. (1980). Fluvoxamine as an antidepressant drug. *Neuropharmacology, 19,* 1215–1216.

Fabre, L. F., (1976). Pilot open-label study with alprazolam (U-31, 899) in outpatients with neurotic depression. *Current Therapeutic Research, 19,* 661–668.

Fabre, L. F., & McLendon, D. M. (1979). A double-blind study comparing the efficacy and safety of alprazolam with diazepam and placebo in anxious outpatients. *Current Therapeutic Research, 25,* 519–526.

Feighner, J. P. (1980). Trazodone, a triazolopyridine derivative in primary depression. *Journal of Clinical Psychiatry, 41,* 250–255.

Feighner, J. P. (1981). Clinical efficacy of the newer antidepressants. *Journal of Clinical Psychopharmacology, 6,* 235–265.

Feighner, J. P. (1982). Benzodiazepines as antidepressants: A triazolobenzodiazepine used to treat depression. In H. Lehmann (Ed.), *Modern problems in pharmacopsychiatry.* Basel: Karger.

Feighner, J. P., (1985). A comparative trial of fluoxetine and amitriptyline in outpatients with major depressive disorder. *Journal of Clinical Psychiatry, 46,* 369–372.

Feighner, J. P., Aden, G. C., Fabre, L. F., Rickels, K., & Smith, W. T. (1983). Comparison of alprazolam, imipramine, and placebo in the treatment of depression. *Journal of the American Medical Association, 249,* 3057–3064.

Feighner, J. P., Jacobs, R. S., Jackson, R. E., Hendrickson, G., Merideth, C. H., & O'Meara, P. D. (1983). A double-blind comparative trial with mianserin and amitrityline in outpatients with major depressive disorders. *British Journal of Clinical Pharmacology* (Supplement), *15,* 227–237.

Feighner, J. P., Merideth, C. H., & Hendrickson, G. (1981). Maintenance antidepressant therapy: A double-blind comparison of trazodone and imipramine. *Journal of Clinical Psychopharmacology, 6,* 45S–48S.

Feighner, J. P. Merideth, C. H., Nash, R. J., & Hendrickson, G. (1982). *A double-blind comparison of nomifensine vs. placebo in major depressive disorder.* Paper presented at CINP, Jerusalem.

Feighner, J. P., Merideth, C. H., Stern, W. C., Hendrickson, G., & Miller, L. L. (1984). A double-blind study of bupropion and placebo in depression. *American Journal of Psychiatry, 141,* 525–529.

Feighner, J. P., Robins, E., Guze, S. D., Woodruff, R. A., Winokur, G., & Muñoz, R. (1972). Diagnostic criteria for use in psychiatric research. *Archives of General Psychiatry, 26,* 57–62.

Feighner, J. P., & Roffman, M. (1981). An early clinical trial of oxaprotiline in hospitalized patients with primary depression. *Current Therapeutic Research, 29,* 363–369.

Ferris, R. M., Cooper, B. R., & Maxwell, R. A. (1983). Studies of bupropion's mechanism of antidepressant activity. *Journal of Clinical Psychiatry, 44,* 74–78.

Friedman, E., Fang, F., & Gershon, S. (1977). Antidepressant drugs and dopamine uptake in different brain regions. *European Journal of Pharmacology, 42,* 47–51.

Gail, M., Kamdar, G. V., & Collins, R. J. (1978). Pharmacology of some metabolites of triazolam, alprazolam, and diazepam prepared by a simple one-step oxidation of benzodiazepines. *Journal of Medicinal Chemistry, 21,* 1290–1294.

Georgotas, A., Mann, J., Bush, D. & Gershon, S. (1980). A clinical trial of zimelidine in depression. *Communications in Psychopharmacology, 4,* 71–77.

Gerner, R., Estabrook, W., Steuer, J. & Jarvik, L. (1980). Treatment of geriatric depression with trazodone, imipramine and placebo: A double-blind study. *Journal of Clinical Psychiatry, 41,* 216–220.

Gershon, S., Mann, J., Newton, R. & Gunther, B. J. (1981). Evaluation of trazodone in the treatment of endogenous depression: Results of a multi-center double-blind study. *Journal of Clinical Psychopharmacology, 1,* 39S–44S.

Greenblatt, E. N., Hardy, R. A., & Kelly, R. G. (1979). Amoxapine. In M. E. Goldberg, *Pharmacological and biochemical properties of drug substances* (Vol. II). Washington, D.C.: American Pharmaceutical Association.

Harto-Truax, N., Stern, W. C., Miller, L. L., Sato, T. L., & Cato, A. E. (1983). The effects of bupropion on body weight. *Journal of Clinical Psychiatry, 44,* 183–186.

Hoffman, I. (1977). A comparative review of the pharmacology of nomifensine. *British Journal of Clinical Pharmacology* (Supplement 2),*4,* 69–78.

Larochelle, P., Hamet, P., & Enjalbert, M. (1979). Responses to tyramine and norepinephrine after imipramine and trazodone. *Clinical Pharmacology and Therapeutics, 26,* 24–30.

Lederle Laboratories, (1982). *Data on file,* Wayne, NJ.

Lemberger, L. (1976). The effect of Lilly compound 94939, a potential antidepressant on biogenic amine uptake in man. *British Journal of Clinical Pharmacology, 3,* 215–218.

Loque, J., Sachais, B., & Feighner, J. P. (1979). Comparisons of maprotiline with imipramine in severe depression: A multicenter controlled trial. *Journal of Clinical Pharmacology, 19,* 64–74.

Moizeszowicz, J., & Subira, S. (1977). Controlled trial of nomifensine and viloxazine in the treatment of depression in the elderly. *Journal of Clinical Pharmacology, 17,* 81–84.

Montgomery, S. A. (1980). Maprotiline, nomifensine, mianserin, zimelidine: A review of antidepressant efficacy in inpatients. *Neuropharmacology, 19,* 1185–1190.

Nitter, L., Jr., Haraldsson, A., & Holck, P. (1976). The effect of trimipramine on the healing of peptic ulcer. A double-blind study. *Scandinavian Journal of Gastroenterology, 11,* 39–41.

Peck, A. W., Stern, W. C., & Watkinson, C. (1983). Incidence of seizures during treatment with tricyclic antidepressant drugs and bupropion. *Journal of Clinical Psychiatry, 44,* 197–201.

Peet, M. (1977). Recent clinical and pharmacological studies of the novel antidepressant Org GB94. *Drug Experimental Clinical Research, 1,* 363–367.

Poldinger, W., & Gammel G. (1978). Differences in effect between nomifensine and nortriptyline. *International Pharmacopsychiatry, 13,* 58–62.

Riblet, L. A. & Taylor, D. P. (1981). Pharmacology and neurochemistry of trazodone. *Journal of Clinical Psychopharmacology, 1,* 17S–22S.

Riess, W., Dubey, L., Funfgeld, E. W., Imhof, P., Hurzeler, H., Matussek, N., Rajogopalan, T. G., Raschdorf, F., & Schmid K. (1975). The pharmakinetic properties of maprotiline in man. *Journal of Internal Medical Research, 3,* 16–41.

Rifkin, A., Saraf, K., Kane, J., Ross, D., & Klein, D. F. (1980). A comparison of trimipramine and imipramine: A controlled study. *Journal of Clinical Psychiatry, 41,* 124–129.

Roffman, M., Gould, E. E., Brewer, S. J., *et al.* (1982). A double-blind comparative study of oxaprotiline with amitriptyline and placebo in moderate depression. *Current Therapeutic Research, 32,* 247–256.

Saletu, B., Grunberger, J., Rajna, P., & Karobath, M. (1980). Clovoxamine and fluvoxamine—two biogenic amine reuptake inhibiting antidepressants; quantative EEG, psychometric, and pharmacokinetic studies in man. *Journal of Neural Transmission, 49,* 63–86.

Schatzberg, A. F. & Cole, J. P. (1978). Benzodiazepines in depressive disorders. *Archives of General Psychiatry, 35,* 1359–1365.

Selvini, A., Rossi, C., Belli, C., Corallo, S., & Lucchelli, P. E. (1976). Antidepressant treatment with maprotiline in the management of emotional disturbances in patients with acute myocardial infarction: A controlled study. *Journal of Internal Medical Research, 4,* 42–46.

Sethy, V. H., & Hodges, D. H. (1982, April). *Role of* B-*adrenergic receptors in the antidepressant activity of alprazolam.* Paper presented at Benzodiazepine Symposium, National Institutes of Health.

Settle, E. C., Jr., & Ayd, F. J. (1980). Trimipramine: Twenty years' worldwide clinical experience. *Journal of Clinical Psychiatry, 41,* 266–274.

Singh, A. N., & Saxena, B. (1977). A controlled clinical study of trazodone in chronic schizophrenic patients with pronounced depressive symptomatology. In F. Antonelli (Ed.), *Therapy in psychosomatic medicine.* (Vol. III). Rome: Puzzi.

Soroko, F. E., Mehta, N. D., Maxwell, R. A., Ferris, R. M., & Schroder, D. H. (1977). Bupropion hydrochloride: A novel antidepressant agent. *Journal of Pharmacy and Pharmacology, 29,* 767–770.

Stern, W. C., Harto-Truax, N., & Bauer, N. (1983). Efficacy of buproprion in tricyclic-resistant or intolerant patients. *Journal of Clinical Psychiatry, 44,* 148–152.

Sulser, F. (1980). Pharmacology: Current antidepressants. *Psychiatric Annals* (Supplement), *10,* 381–387.

Swift, C. G., Haythorne, J. M., Clarke, P., & Stevenson, I. H. (1981). Cardiovascular, sedative and anticholinergic effects of amitriptyline and zimelidine in young and elderly volunteers. *Acta Psychiatrioa Scandiavica, 63,* 425–432.

Wong, D. T., Horng, J. S., Bymaster, F. P., Hauser, K. L., & Molloy, B. B. (1974). 3-(*p*-Trifluoromethylphenoxy)-*N*-methyl-3-phenylpropylamine. *Life Sciences, 15,* 471–479.

Author Index

Subject Index